THE END OF THE ASIAN CENTURY

THE END OF
THE ASIAN
CENTURY

War, Stagnation, and
the Risks to the
World's Most
Dynamic Region

Michael R. Auslin

Yale UNIVERSITY PRESS
New Haven & London

Published with assistance from the Kingsley Trust Association Publication Fund established by the Scroll and Key Society of Yale College.

Yale University Press books may be purchased in quantity for educational, business, or promotional use. For information, please e-mail sales.press@yale.edu (U.S. office) or sales@yaleup.co.uk (U.K. office).

Set in Galliard type by Westchester Publishing Services
Printed in the United States of America

Library of Congress Control Number: 2016942335

ISBN 978-0-300-21222-8 (hardcover : alk. paper)

A catalogue record for this book is available from the British Library.

This paper meets the requirements of ANSI/NISO Z39.48–1992 (Permanence of Paper).

10 9 8 7 6 5 4 3 2 1

IN MEMORY OF MY FATHER,
DONALD E. AUSLIN (1933–2016)

CONTENTS

PREFACE: THE ASIA NOBODY SEES

I am hunched over, almost on my hands and knees, nearly 250 feet below ground. Behind me is close to a mile of tunnel, hewn through solid rock. In front of me is a steel door set into a concrete barricade. Through its tiny window I can see another barricade and steel door, maybe another one hundred feet ahead. Beyond that lies North Korea.

I have crawled into one of the dozens of "tunnels of aggression" dug by the Pyongyang regime into South Korean territory. Discovered in 1978, it lies only twenty-seven miles from Seoul and was designed to bring waves of North Korean saboteurs and special forces under the heavily defended border to wreak havoc in case of war. It is the only tunnel open to the public, and the tour buses that bring visitors to this no-man's-land pass by hills that still contain hundreds of land mines aimed at stopping an invasion from the North.

Yet as much as Tunnel Number Three is a reminder that the Korean border, the ironically named "Demilitarized Zone," remains one of the most dangerous spots on earth, it also is a metaphor for all of Asia. While dynamic and peaceful on the surface, the continent is riddled with un-seen threats, from economic stagnation to political unrest and growing military tensions. These risks also threaten the rest of the world, thanks to the extraordinary economic, political, and military growth of Asia over the past decades.

To put it starkly, what we are seeing today may be the beginning of the end of the "Asian Century." For decades, prominent and knowledgeable observers, from bankers and industrialists to scholars and politicians, have predicted the rise of the Asia-Pacific and an era of unparalleled Asian power, prosperity, and peace. At the same time, many writers assure us that the East is replacing the West, in a great shift of global power that will permanently reshape our world.[1] All those predictions now are themselves at risk.

I did not travel to Asia looking for trouble. Just the contrary. After nearly a quarter-century studying and dealing with Asia, I initially planned on writing a book on how America's future would be tied to a resurgent Indo-Pacific, a variant of what then secretary of state Hillary Clinton called "America's Pacific Century."[2] To my surprise (and initial resistance), the more I traveled around the region, starting around 2010, the more I became aware of the risks we in the West were ignoring.

Such a view remains controversial. Only in recent months have the popular press and casual observers begun to worry about growing risk, from China's stock market collapse to the danger of armed conflict in the South China Sea. But in a world where headlines continue to focus on the bloody spread of the Islamic State or on Russia's invasion of Ukraine and intervention in the Syrian civil war, only cursory attention is being paid to Asia's dangers.

As this is being written, China's economy has dramatically slowed, North Korea claims that it has a hydrogen bomb and is widely believed to be able to put nuclear weapons on top of ballistic missiles, Thailand's military has launched its second coup in a decade, and Chinese newspapers warn that war with America is "inevitable" if Washington does not back down from opposing China's territorial claims in the South China Sea.[3] These are just some of the more visible dangers that perturb the Indo-Pacific. We are on the cusp of a change in the global zeitgeist, from celebrating a strong and growing Asia to worrying about a weak and dangerous Asia. For all its undeniable successes and strengths, the broader Indo-Pacific region faces significant, potentially insurmountable challenges.

The rest of us should worry because none of these problems threaten only Asia. Whether one cares about the Indo-Pacific or not, it is half of our world. Today, one out of every three persons on earth is of Chinese or Indian descent, and the countries of the Indo-Pacific already account for 60 percent of the world's population.[4] The International Monetary Fund estimates that the economies of Asia produce nearly 40 percent of total global output,[5] and they are central to everything from weaving textiles to crafting the most advanced electronic technology. The militaries of Asia's countries have grown dramatically, and China, India, and North Korea are nuclear powers. Democracies jostle with authoritarian states as neighbors in the world's most dynamic region.

But the globalization that we continue to celebrate has its dark side as well. If an economic or security crisis erupted in Asia, it would reverberate around our increasingly interconnected world. Those risks are festering, some visible, others still hidden. The number one priority for the countries of the Asia-Pacific, and the rest of the world, over the coming decade is managing and mitigating the risks that threaten the Asian Century.

Yet despite the threat to the larger global system from Asia's risks, no book or article has yet offered a comprehensive view of the various major dangers Asia faces, or how they are intertwined. Many predictions are thus misleadingly rosy, such as the assumption that China and Japan will not go to war over disputed island territory because their economic ties are too deep, or that North Korea will not launch a nuclear missile at Seoul or Tokyo because to do so would be a suicidal act. Similarly, investors and manufacturers simply assume that if one Asian country falters, another will take its place, as China replaced Japan in the 1990s.

Little attention has been paid to understanding the broader economic slowdown that could cause global growth to grind to a halt. Or how the combination of nationalism and miscalculation could result in armed conflict over territorial disputes. A succession of crises could in turn lead to political upheaval and revolution, plunging some societies into civil war and crushing democracy in others. For all these reasons, getting ahead of the risk curve in Asia is necessary if prosperity, freedom, and stability are to be protected and nurtured. That is what is at stake if the Asian Century ends.

No book can cover everything happening in this vibrant region, nor is this one meant to repeat the latest headlines. Instead, my goal is to explore the factors that threaten Asia's future and put at risk what we have imagined as the Asian Century. Some readers will be disappointed that I do not discuss certain countries or that I mention them only in passing, even though they are fascinating and important. For example, Mongolia is recapturing its native traditions and simultaneously globalizing its economy and playing a larger role in regional security, but I hardly cover it. The countries of the Mekong River region get far less attention here than their neighbors, whom I see as the more important drivers of risk. Russia, too, deserves more than the occasional remark. I have excluded these nations from this book because the numerous Asian business leaders, officials, and experts with whom I talked were focused on other matters.

I have also omitted some subjects that may rank high on popular lists of concerns. Prominent among these is the question of energy security and the future of civilian nuclear power. As important as these are, I don't consider them significant risk factors in the coming decades that could cause a crisis inside Asia with the potential to spill over onto the global stage. A book dealing fully with the political, economic, and social conditions of all the manifold countries of Asia would be literally thousands of pages long.

Instead, I have created a "risk map" of Asia. Unlike a traditional geographic map, this map is a conceptual tool for identifying the most important trends in the region and assessing their risk. Think of this book as you would an annotated geographical map: a user's guide to the dangers growing in the world's most dynamic region and an analysis of what they mean for Asia, the United States, and the rest of the world. The risk map, like any other analysis, is the product of judgment calls, such as discussing environmental pollution in a chapter on demographics, or postulating that the lack of regional political community is a danger.

Moreover, just like a real map, its components—what I call "risk regions"—vary in size. Those with a higher degree of risk are treated more extensively than those presenting fewer dangers. Nor are the borders always so clear; what happens in one risk region often has spillover effects in others. The regions are, at a minimum, contiguous risk areas, and often interconnected.

It is important to make clear that this is not a book of predictions. It does not forecast the imminent collapse of the Chinese Communist Party or war between North and South Korea. Instead, it is a diagnostic tool.

Prudent investors, managers, diplomats, policymakers, and scholars should be just as aware of risk in the Indo-Pacific region as they are of its many opportunities. Indeed, from a business or policy perspective, understanding risk by itself creates numerous opportunities, either to take advantage of potentially negative outcomes or to try to alter current trends.

This book, therefore, attempts several things. For business leaders, it provides the political and security context in which to understand what may threaten economic growth, trade, and development. For policymakers, it highlights potential causes of war and political disruption, and offers a roadmap to greater Western engagement in Asia. For journalists, students, and scholars, it is a comprehensive look at threats to democratic development or multilateral cooperation. Readers interested in only one area can of course skip to that chapter, but they should note that the chapters are designed as a coherent whole and an integrated argument.

For those already knowledgeable about Asia, a book such as this might well make sense even if they disagree with many or all of its conclusions. Yet I believe that "bearish" books like this should play a larger role than they now do in business planning, government policymaking, and academic scholarship.

For at least the last quarter-century, since 1989, the Western world has regularly been taken by surprise and sometimes shocked by events: the fall of the Iron Curtain, the collapse of the Soviet Union, the dot-com bubble, the new age of Islamist terrorism, 9/11, the mistakes of the Iraq and Afghanistan Wars, the 2008 financial crisis, the Eurozone crisis, Russia's invasion of Ukraine, the Ebola epidemic, the rise of the Islamic State, and on and on. In each case, there has been a rushed and imperfect response or a refusal to deal with the problem. The whiplash of repeated shocks has caused economic instability, political paralysis, and domestic dissension.[6]

If we wish to avoid the potentially catastrophic consequences of a war in Asia or a widespread economic collapse, we need to understand the diversity of risks the region faces and to begin thinking about how to manage those risks. Given the importance of the Indo-Pacific, we have little excuse for being taken by surprise by an Asian crisis. Nothing in this book predicts or presupposes any particular dire outcome, yet the very act of identifying dangers and thinking them through can lead to wiser investment decisions, policies, and intellectual engagements. This is risk analysis on a broad palette.

This book is based on a quarter-century of engagement with and study of Asia, and years of travel throughout the Indo-Pacific region, including three major research trips and several shorter trips starting in 2010. During these journeys and afterward, I interviewed dozens of politicians, military officials, academics, business leaders, media figures, and ordinary citizens. In addition, I have sought to pull together as much publicly available information as possible about Asia. Stylistically, I have not followed Asian nomenclature, which is to put surnames first followed by given names, except in the case of China and Korea, which is standard practice in American media. All monetary amounts, unless otherwise specified, are in U.S. dollars. For Chinese, I generally follow the current Pinyin transliteration style, but switch into the traditional Wade-Giles when talking about pre-twentieth-century eras.

As for terminology, I use the terms "Asia," "Asia-Pacific," and "Indo-Pacific" interchangeably, the way we use both "United States" and "America." Our traditional definition of Asia needs to be expanded, and "Indo-Pacific" is a far better term for the region covered in this book. Yet it is to some degree a neologism, less familiar than "Asia-Pacific." The reader should keep in mind that the terms all refer to the same geographic space: that great arc sweeping from southwest to northeast, from the Indian Ocean to the Bering Sea. By the end of this book, I hope readers feel as comfortable with the concept of the "Indo-Pacific," and will use it as interchangeably with "Asia," as I do.

As always, any errors in interpretation, misstatement of facts, or confusing or misleading phrasing are my fault alone.

ACKNOWLEDGMENTS

I was trained as a historian to work primarily with documents, not people. Historical records are unchanging in themselves, though new discoveries and interpretations always let us refine our picture of the past. This book has been an entirely different experience for me and, in that sense, an experiment as well. Over the five years it took me to research and write, so much changed in Asia that in some ways, parts of the region are unrecognizable. Moreover, dealing with living actors required an entirely different set of analytic and interpretational skills.

Perhaps because of this, my debt to those who helped me is greater in this book than in my previous books. From Washington, D.C., to Tokyo, Beijing, New Delhi, and Jakarta, and many other places in between, I learned how to ask for interviews, approach individuals, and deal with rapidly changing data and regular news-making crises. Moreover, because of the scope of this book, I undoubtedly missed talking to certain experts or practitioners whom others would have contacted, and ignored data and even issues that would have featured prominently in other books.

Nonetheless, the following is as comprehensive a list as I can make of all those who offered their time and expertise, some by letting me interview them, others by attending roundtables or providing me opportunities to give presentations on this book, others by reading chapters or parts thereof, and many just by listening to my ideas and asking helpful questions. Public officials and military officers made it clear they were speaking for themselves and not for their governments. For anyone whose name I inadvertently left out, my sincere apologies.

I must begin with Arthur Brooks and Dany Pletka, of the American Enterprise Institute, who supported this project and allowed me the travel and time to complete it through its various incarnations. I am particularly grateful to the Smith Richardson Foundation, whose generous financial support made possible my research trips and writing time.

My thanks go to Ambassador Takeo Akiba, Dewi Fortuna Anwar, Yusuke Arai, Claude Barfield, James Barker, Admiral Uday Bhaskar, Karan Bhatia, Dan Bob, Max Boot, Ernie Bower, Shawn Brimley, Meredith Broadbent, Anne Marie Brooks, Kurt Campbell, General Hawk Carlisle, Sandeep Chakravorty, Chen Dongxiao, Guangcheng Chen, Sujan Chinoy, Kang Choi, Mark Clifford, Eliot Cohen, Patrick Cronin, Da Wei, Sudhakar Dalela, Dorothy Delahanty, Lieutenant General Dave Deptula, Sadanand Dhume, Major General Mark Dillon, Tom Dodd, Peter Dutton, Geoff Dyer, Nicholas Eberstadt, Ralf Emmers, Andrew Erickson, Martin Fackler, Robbie Feldman, Isaac Stone Fish, Gordon Flake, Richard Fontaine, Foo Chi Hsia, Representative Randy Forbes, Jim Della-Giacomo, Paul Giarra, Matthew Goodman, Euan Graham, Christopher Graves, Michael Green, Louisa Greve, Arvind Gupta, Ha Duy Tung, Admiral Harry Harris, General Tan Sri Mohamed Hashim bin Mohd Ali, Ambassador Tim Hitchens, Lucy Hughes, Tim Huxley, Frank Jannuzi, Kenneth Jarrett, Ku-hyun Jung, Fred Kagan, Harry Kamian, Ambassador Nobukatsu Kanehara, Robert Kaplan, Ambassador Ryozo Kato, Admiral Tim Keating, Kent Kedl, Colonel Khanh Do Mai, Jun-Ki Kim, Jonathan Kindred, Mary Kissel, Daniel Kliman, James Kralik, James Kraska, Daniel Kritenbrink, Desmond Lachman, Jeffrey Lapin, Ambassador Frank Lavin, Richard Lawless, Le Dang Doanh, Le Dinh Tinh, Le Hai Binh, Chung Min Lee, Dong-Soo Lee, Phil Levy, Satu Limaye, Weimin Liu, Justin Logan, Walter Lohman, Luo Zhaohui, Satoshi Maeda, Thomas Mahnken, Terry Markin, Richard McGregor, Admiral Raja Menon, Mark Michelson, James Miles, Ambassador Ashok Kumar Mirpuri, C. Raja Mohan, Christian Murck, Henry Nau, Senior Colonel Nguyen Anh Duong, Senior Colonel Nguyen Hong Quan, Ni Jianping, Anthony Nightingale, Rosita Noer, Joseph Nye, David O'Rear, Ambassador Ted Osius, Major General Pan Zhenqiang, Rajaram Panda, Pham Quang Minh, Michael Pillsbury,

Raja Reza Bin Raja Dato Zaib Shah, Evan Ramstead, Ely Ratner, Ambassador John Roos, James Rosen, Admiral Gary Roughead, Eric Sayers, Jim Schoff, Derek Scissors, Constance See, General Tan Sri Dato Seri Mohd Shahrom bin Nordin, Ambassador Dave Shear, Noriyuki Shikata, Ambassador Arun Singh, Jeff Smith, Daryl Sng, Scott Snyder, John Starr, Juwono Sudarsono, Dato Syed Sultan Idris, Sun Xuefeng, Phil Swagel, Ta Minh Tuan, Nobushige Takamizawa, Ashley Tellis, Jonathan Tepperman, Sue Mi Terry, Jim Thomas, Greg Torode, Tunku Varadarajan, Hans Vriens, Richard Vulyesteke, Emma Wade-Smith, Gareth Ward, Jessica Webster, Jennifer Hendrixson White, Enders Wimbush, Ambassador Paul Wolfowitz, Thomas Wright, Shigeo Yamada, Joseph Young, Dato Husni Zai bin Yaacob, Ambassador Zainol Rahim Zainuddin, and Robert Zoellick. Many of those I interviewed in Asia asked for confidentiality, but I am happy to acknowledge their help here.

Adam Garfinkle, Harry Kazianis, Rich Lowry, Seth Mandel, Benjamin Pauker, John Podhoretz, Avik Roy, and especially Hugo Restall provided venues for me to publish articles covering many of the issues discussed herein. In producing this book, I relied on the excellent work of my research assistants, Lara Crouch, Eddie Linczer, and Shannon Mann. Claude Aubert and Olivier Ballou came up with the artwork, while Judy Mayka and her team helped with publicity. My interns Olivia Blanchette, Zhelun Chen, Justin Davis, Lauren Forman, Jack Guen-Murray, Mamoru Higashikokubaru, Allison Kim, June Kim, Peter Liu, Emma Murphy, Gabriel Noronha, Madison Sparber, and Peter Wood all provided much needed assistance.

My agent, Don Fehr, taught me how to navigate the world of nonacademic publishing, and Bill Frucht of Yale University Press gave me my first experience of working with an editor who cared deeply about my project and carefully read the draft, offering suggestions on how to improve nearly every line. Karen Olson, also at Yale University Press, helpfully guided me through the production process, as did Kim Giambattisto. I owe Robert Dilenschneider special thanks for his encouragement and support. On a more personal note, I continue to be grateful for the friendship of Ted Bromund, Nick Schulz, and Sean Todd. I also would like to thank David and Caren Grossman, Aric and Judith Kabillio, Richard and Barbara Marcus, and Gregory and Marina Shmunis for keeping an eye out for my family during my many travels.

My family, as always, proved a bastion of support. My mother, Myra Auslin, kept up her interest, even when it was unclear exactly what I was doing, and my brother, Dan, shared his bemusement at my profession. Not all about writing a book is enjoyable. Unlike in the past, my research on this project kept me away from Ginko and Ben during months of travel over several years, yet they never complained and always were eager to hear about my adventures. Their support and love made it all seem worth the effort.

1

MAPPING RISK IN ASIA

Ever since Japan emerged as an economic juggernaut in the 1970s, the world has anticipated the "Asian Century." Predictions of America's and Europe's inevitable decline and Asia's inexorable rise have been staples of books, newspaper and magazine articles, and news shows for decades, what former secretary of the Treasury Larry Summers has called "Asiaphoria."[1] In a tectonic shift in global power similar to the one that took place in the early twentieth century, we are told, the countries of the Indo-Pacific will begin to dominate global economics, politics, and security.[2] From dystopic 1980s movies like *Blade Runner* to visions of Shanghai's twenty-first-century postmodern skyline, Asia's economic, political, and cultural dominance has embedded itself in the world's collective imagination.

Such claims seem merely to reflect reality. Over four billion people live in the great geographic arc from India to Japan, and one in every three persons on our planet is either Chinese or Indian. The formerly war-ravaged and impoverished countries of the Indo-Pacific now export 40 percent of the goods bought by consumers around the world.[3] The world's most populous countries and largest militaries are in the Indo-Pacific, and millions of Asian immigrants are changing the societies to which they have moved. Asian art, cuisine, and pop culture have spread around the globe. Whether you care about the Indo-Pacific or not, it is a part of your world.

Meanwhile, more Asians than ever in history are benefiting from economic growth and political stability. The region has not seen a real war since the Sino-Vietnamese clash of 1979. Since the mid-1980s, democracy has spread to Taiwan, South Korea, the Philippines, Mongolia, Indonesia, and elsewhere. Hundreds of millions of Chinese, Indians, Vietnamese, and others have been lifted out of poverty. Life spans throughout the region have increased, and the standard of living in Asia's major cities now rivals (sometimes exceeds) that of the West. Scientists and scholars from Asian countries play leading roles in research institutes, laboratories, and universities around the globe. Some of the world's most advanced industrial factories are in countries like Japan, South Korea, and Taiwan.

Perhaps most important, when compared with the strife-torn Middle East, aging Europe, or crisis-beset Africa, the Asia-Pacific region looks like the one major area of the world where opportunity, economic growth, and political development are still possible. In short, the global future looks increasingly Asian.

But no place, of course, is free of economic challenges, conflict, and adversity—certainly no place as large and crowded with diverse peoples as Asia. The region's new stature means these conflicts, once safely distant from the West, now have worldwide consequences. The collapse of Chinese stock markets in 2015, for instance, echoed throughout the financial world, while a nuclear-armed North Korea with ballistic missiles is becoming a potential threat to any nation on earth. Under its dynamic surface, Asia is at risk of economic stagnation, political upheaval, war, and other dangers.

Many of the threats to Asia's future are consequences of its rapid growth; others, deeply rooted in the region's history, have taken on new importance. They are no longer merely regional. An economic or security crisis originating in Asia would reverberate around the globe, while domestic political upheaval could set off regional conflict and economic collapse. Much of the world's attention in the coming generation will be devoted to managing and mitigating the consequences of negative events in Asia.

Yet because the world has focused on Asia's successes—and there are many—even knowledgeable observers are unlikely to have a comprehensive view of the various risks Asia faces and how they are intertwined. Thus, many predictions are misleadingly rosy. Among the suspect assumptions are that China's economy will continue to grow for decades, that war won't break out over disputed island territory, and that the turn away from liberalism in parts of Southeast Asia won't result in greater cross-border tensions. Given Asia's importance to the global economy and its military potential, if the world's prosperity and stability are to be protected and nurtured, we have to get ahead of the risk curve in Asia.

The first step toward understanding the reality of risk in Asia is to change our mental approach to the region. We have all been taught to think of the Indo-Pacific in traditional geographic terms: countries, borders, oceans. It is fair to say that when they think of Asia, most Americans think mainly of China, Japan, and Korea, while India is sliced off as a separate region and Southeast Asia is often overlooked entirely. This pretty well replicates how universities, businesses, and governments divide up the region: Northeast Asia, Southeast Asia, South Asia, Central Asia. It's how I taught the region when I was a professor at Yale.

Yet when I sat in a conference room in Chennai talking with Indian businessmen about their export of small Honda trucks made in India to Indonesia, I realized that we have been drawing the wrong boundaries. Similarly, when the Japanese prime minister is the guest of honor at India's national military parade because both countries fear China's growing military strength, that is a signal that traditional relationships are breaking down and re-forming. Not only are there no dashed lines in the ocean or on the land, broad borders in Asia are being redefined even while political identities are strengthened.[4]

We in the West have not yet caught up mentally with the way globalization has transformed the Asia-Pacific. When we think of political cooperation or free trade, we misread Asia if we limit ourselves to smaller slices of the pie. Anyone who travels through the region can tell you that nationalism and ethnic pride now coexist with a growing sense of "Asianness." When Asians think of business, threats, or allies, they increasingly think of them in common terms. The rest of the world must do the same, and understand that the Indo-Pacific today is an increasingly integrated region. Once we expand our geographic frame to this "dynamic crescent," we can better perceive and more accurately calculate the tensions and dangers that ripple throughout the area.

But opening up our critical field of vision requires more than just flying higher to take in more territory. Even seeing Asia as an integrated whole is still a fairly conventional, if important and more accurate, approach. Our analytical frame needs to be more revolutionary. We need to think differently. No one has yet employed such an integrated view to map out the region's risk factors, not just country by country but across the Indo-Pacific.

Mapping Risk in Asia

This book presents that "risk map," incorporating economic, political, social, and security dimensions. Granted, many places have unique threats—tribal unrest in the Indonesian archipelago, or the divided Korean peninsula. But when we talk about demographic collapse or political unrest, we can best understand them as broad categories of risk that affect the entire region, and thus the world. This type of diagnostic approach can supplement, but not supplant, traditional cartographic maps.

This book will map out five discrete yet interrelated risk regions. The first such region is the threat to Asia's growth from the end of its economic miracle and the failure of reform. Thousands of headlines and dozens of books continue to proclaim the economic miracle as if it were destined to last forever. Yet dig beneath the headlines, and you find major problems, many of which national governments are failing to solve.

From Japan to India, the nations of Asia struggle to maintain growth, balance their economies, and fight slowdowns. For most of these countries, the days of high-flying growth are long over, while for others, they never began. It is past time for the rest of the world to pay attention to the threats to Asia's economic health. Uneven development, asset bubbles, malinvestment, labor issues, and state control over markets are just some of the features of economic risk in the Asia-Pacific. And because Asian economies are increasingly interlinked, problems in one country spill over to others.

This region of Asia's risk map, economic slowdown or collapse, directly concerns non-Asian nations. Global stock markets tanked in the summer of 2015 and the beginning of 2016 when China's stock exchanges collapsed. Even if Asia's economies manage to muddle through, the world must ask what will happen to global trade and investment if growth in Asia simply cools off. It is increasingly prudent to prepare for a far less economically energetic Asia than we are used to. And we must account for both long-term structural stagnation, as in Japan, and the style of

Asia's Risk Map. Artwork by Olivier Ballou.

house-of-cards capitalism currently practiced in China. There is little doubt that the world must prepare for a China whose growth has dramatically slowed if not stagnated, and for mature economies like Japan's never to recapture their former vibrancy. As for the developing states, the risk is that they will never attain the growth needed to ensure the modernization of their societies.

Economics, being about people and wealth, leads us directly into the second region of Asia's risk map: demographics. All of the Indo-Pacific faces a Goldilocks dilemma: either too many people or too few. I once visited Tokyo right after spending nearly a month in India; I received a palpable culture shock in going from a seething kaleidoscope of people in Delhi and Calcutta to the rapidly aging Japan.

Most of Asia's developed countries, including Japan, South Korea, Taiwan, and Singapore, are facing or will soon face unprecedented

demographic drops. China's one-child policy and horrendous environmental pollution will also bring a population decline in the world's most
populous nation, at a time when the country is not yet rich enough to
deal with the resulting dislocation. On the other hand, India has a growing surfeit of young people and needs to improve educational standards,
expand its urban and rural infrastructure, and find them all jobs. Much
of Southeast Asia is in India's situation, offering opportunity along with
challenge.

The costs of Asia's rapid modernization have long been ignored, fore-
most among them environmental damage. The polluted skies and waters
of Asia affect demographics as much as do fertility rates. The horrors of
Japan's Thalidomide babies during the 1950s may seem a relic of another
era, but images of the darkness of Chinese cities at noon, thousands of
dead pig carcasses floating down major rivers, and towering garbage heaps
reveal the almost inconceivable environmental harm that now threatens
the future of youth in some of Asia's major countries. Demographics will
put enormous pressure on Asia's domestic political and economic systems;
understanding this is a must for understanding risk in the region.

The third enormous region of risk on our map comprises Asia's unfinished political revolutions, in both democracies and autocracies. How
political leaders respond to economic and social challenges will ensure
domestic tranquility or produce civil unrest. Ever since the last Chinese
emperor left his throne in Beijing's Forbidden City, Asia's political history has been one of unfinished revolution.

Given the ongoing struggle for the political soul of Asia, Americans
should not be complacent about the future of democracy there. The fight
is far from over. Hundreds of millions of men, women, and children have
been freed from oppressive governments but have not completed their
journey. The gains of democracy continue to be put at risk by corruption,
cliques, protest, cynicism, and fear of instability. The spread of democracy, which has succeeded so well in recent decades, may be reaching a
limit—how temporary is impossible to say. Even mature democracies, like
Japan and India, face a crisis of political confidence and a "political ar-
thritis" that leaves vital problems unsolved.

Autocracy maintains its grip on China, North Korea, and other Asian
nations. The cold stares of security forces in Tiananmen Square and the

empty chair of Liu Xiaobo at his 2010 Nobel Prize ceremony showed Chinese and foreign observers alike that China remains decades, perhaps generations, away from political freedom. As long as China remains unfree, democracy and autocracy will remain in a stalemate.

Yet autocratic regimes face their own grave dangers. There is probably no more important risk factor for Asian politics in the coming years than China. Talk to ordinary citizens in Beijing or Shanghai, and their pride in their country's economic growth quickly turns to silence about its political future. Despite its economic successes, the Chinese Communist Party has become ever more isolated from the citizenry and is seen as corrupt, inefficient, and often brutal. With over two hundred thousand protests of varying sizes every year, China's society is at more risk than most people realize. The party has kept a lid on dissent, but it has been able to do so in part because of the country's huge economic gains. As growth starts to wane, unrest will very likely increase.

Visitors to Southeast Asia come away with similar concerns for long-term social stability. Talking to politicians and students in Jakarta and Kuala Lumpur, I had the impression that they felt their societies were more fragile than any headlines show. Liberals in the region fear that democracy has only a limited capacity to respond to social demands and the growth of militant Islam.

The question of whether to allow greater political participation is central to the politics of Indonesia, Malaysia, and Singapore, where the ruling parties are all grappling with how to maintain power while defusing popular demands for more open electoral systems. On the other hand, democracy can be swept aside, as in Thailand, whose continued instability appears to be a quasi-permanent threat to democratization. For Vietnam, how to ensure Communist Party control yet provide continued opportunity for business, as in China, is the overriding concern. The ultimate test will be how governments and their societies react to growing pressures and unmet expectations.

Although Asia's nations face many of the same problems, there is little that links those nations together. Beyond a rudimentary sense of "Asianness," there remains no effective regional political community. There is no NATO, no European Union in Asia that can try to solve common problems in a joint manner or to address bilateral issues in a broader framework. This lack of regional unity constitutes the fourth region in our risk map.

Stand in front of the Palace of Heavenly Purity in the center of Beijing's Forbidden City, and you can feel the centuries of political order, both theoretical and real, that shaped Asian history. In some ways, Asia has never recovered from the fall of the Last Emperor, the Qing ruler Puyi, in 1911 during the Chinese Revolution. The fall of the China-dominated political order that was taken for granted for centuries left a vacuum throughout nearly half the world.

Americans often forget that the concepts of sovereignty and equal relations between states are still relatively new in the Indo-Pacific region. For centuries, India and China dominated areas far beyond their current borders. From 1895 to 1945, Japan created a sprawling empire that was both land- and sea-based. A century of European colonization of Southeast Asia and parts of China introduced Western-style imperialism, which both France and Britain briefly attempted to re-create after Japan's defeat in 1945. In short, until just a few decades ago, Asia's collective history was one of hierarchy and empire, either indigenous or imposed from outside. Perhaps that is one reason that today Asia is filled with the type of distrust and dislike of neighbors that used to bedevil Europe. To hear just how tenuous political cooperation remains in Asia, try talking with a Korean or a Chinese about his or her feelings toward Japan.

The danger is that there are no mechanisms for mitigating such deep antipathy, certainly between major players such as India and China or Japan and Korea. A nation like China is all too ready to threaten economic or political action in response to its antagonists. The various nations have few working relationships that can help defuse crises. Nor is there a core of powerful liberal nations committed to playing an honest broker's role or trying to set regional norms. How well can Asia weather another regional economic crisis like the one in 1997, or a major border dispute?

This litany of economic and political risks might be enough to cause observers to alter their long-term assumptions about Asia's prospects. Yet there is a fifth risk to be mapped, the most dangerous of all: war and peace.

How close is Asia to seeing conflict erupt, and where? Not every dispute threatens peace, but today, the Indo-Pacific region is regressing to a nineteenth-century style of power politics in which might makes right. With the world's largest and most advanced militaries other than the United States, and including four nuclear powers, a conflict in Asia could truly destabilize the global economy and spark a conflagration that might spiral out of control.

If you are lucky, you might be near Pearl Harbor in Hawaii when one of America's aircraft carriers is in port. One afternoon not long ago, I watched the USS *Ronald Reagan* slowly steam out of Pearl Harbor into the vastness of the Pacific Ocean. The *Ronald Reagan* is an apt symbol of how security risk has been managed in Asia: the United States has underwritten regional stability since 1945. Today, however, the post–World War II order instituted by the United States is increasingly stressed, at the very time when Washington is finding it difficult to respond to crises in Europe and the Middle East. The economic and political risks discussed here are not isolated from these security trends.

The immediate cause of rising insecurity is simple: as China has grown stronger, it has become more assertive, even coercive. Beijing has embraced the role of a revisionist power, seeking to define new regional rules of behavior and confronting those neighbors with which it has disagreements. Japan and Taiwan, along with many countries in Southeast Asia, fear a rising China, as does India, though to a lesser degree. That fear, fueled by numerous unresolved territorial disputes in the East and South China Seas and by growing concern over maintaining vital trade routes and control of natural resources, is causing an arms race in Asia. The region's waters have become the scene of regular paramilitary confrontations.

These fears and responses are triggering more assertive policies on the part of all states in the region, which only raises tensions further. At the same time, governments feel pressured at home to demonize neighbors, encroach on territory, and refuse to negotiate on security disputes. This is clearly what has happened in recent years in the Sino-Japanese relationship. We have already gone through two turns of a "risk cycle": uncertainty and insecurity, driven over the past decade by China's growing power and increasingly assertive and coercive behavior, and by the emergence of a de facto nuclear North Korea. A third turn, to instability, could cause conflict and even war.

The "Asian Century" thus may not turn out to be an era when Asia imposes a peaceful order on the world, when freedom continues to expand, or when the region remains the engine of global economic growth. What it imposes may instead be conflict and instability. The nations of the Indo-Pacific and the world must prepare for the possibility of economic stagnation, social and political unrest, and even armed conflict. The emergence of those would mark the end of the Asian Century.

Managing Risk in Asia

Any goal of mitigating risk needs a strategy. As this book will show, the most promising way to reduce risk is to push for greater liberalism and a strengthened rules-based order in the Indo-Pacific. No one believes that such a goal is easily reached or is a panacea. Yet democratic nations are both more cooperative and more peaceful in their dealings with other nations than are authoritarian ones. Unleashing the power of women and minorities and promoting entrepreneurialism offer a better future than tighter state control. True, nationalism can be a threat, but the cooperative bonds that liberal societies usually forge help pacify their region. The question is how to work toward those ends. One way is to increase America's role in the region as a partner and catalyst for further liberalization.

For a country that traditionally identified itself as an Atlantic nation, America's role in Asia has often been an afterthought. All that must change. From any angle, America is the most important external player in the Indo-Pacific. American corporations long ago shifted their attention to Asia, which now represents the country's largest area of bilateral trade in goods. With European economies now shrinking, trans-Pacific trade will likely eventually overtake trans-Atlantic trade in importance, just as Asia's legions of well-trained scientists and engineers will be increasingly important to future innovation and entrepreneurship. Hundreds of thousands of Asian students study each year in the United States, and increasing numbers of American citizens are of Asian heritage. Lately, the U.S. government has begun catching up with American private business and the flood of personal connections across the Pacific. In response to Asia's challenges and opportunities, the Obama administration has attempted to "pivot" its economic, foreign, and security policies away from its twentieth-century focus on Europe and the Middle East.

Yet America's role in Asia cannot be taken for granted. A severe, long-term slowdown in Asia would lead U.S. corporations to look for other partners, while increasing instability and the threat of armed conflict could strain America's alliances and unbalance political relations in the region. Thus the end of the Asian Century could also spell the end of America's involvement in Asia, or at the least, a dramatic reduction of its role there.

Whether in Beijing or New Delhi, people in Asia focus on America. Some envy its strength, like the businessmen I talked to in Calcutta, which was just throwing off its three-decade Marxist leadership when I visited. Others fear it, like the scholars in Shanghai I debated on whether America was a destabilizing force in Asia. Dozens of nations in the region depend on America for trade, political support, and security assistance. The American consumer market is crucial to the health of nearly all of Asia's economies, which is why even Communist Vietnam desperately wants to get into the proposed Trans-Pacific Partnership. American-style democracy, though not replicated anywhere in Asia, still remains an inspiration for those dreaming of liberalization.

This unique set of relationships and intertwined interests puts the United States in the best position to help the Indo-Pacific reduce risk. Updating Washington's half-century-old alliance system, promoting a community of liberal interests, and further tying the American economy to Asia's through free trade will deepen our leverage and enhance our stake in the region. It also will be a means for working with America's European partners to forge a truly global liberal community and trading system. Creating an Asian future more firmly tied to liberal principles and rules is the best hope for a world in which every nation benefits.

Only by having an integrated and comprehensive approach to Asia can America hope to help the region mitigate its enormous dangers. In doing so, Americans will also enhance the enormous opportunities the nations of the Indo-Pacific have to become richer and more stable. We will live up to our oft-professed values of encouraging and supporting democracy and liberalization. Deeper engagement will help unleash even more productive and innovative energies, benefiting millions in Asia and around the world. Such an unabashed approach can also help steady U.S. relations with China, as Chinese leaders take note of our steadfast commitment to liberalism in Asia. Ultimately, they may realize the benefits of pursuing cooperative behavior that upholds international norms, rather than remaining a revisionist power intent on suppressing its own people and challenging stability abroad.

Ultimately, U.S. engagement will help harness the energies, knowledge, and interest of the American people, who will come to appreciate that their future is increasingly, and inextricably, tied to a successful and growing Indo-Pacific. That will help ensure that the rest of the twenty-first century is indeed a global one, and not a replay of the breakdown in global order that brought such catastrophic suffering to the last century.

2

THE ASIAN MIRACLE AT RISK

When trading opened on the Shanghai Composite Index on Monday, June 15, 2015, China's stock exchanges were the best-performing markets in the world. Riding a three-year bull run, the Shanghai stock market's value had skyrocketed 106 percent since the summer of 2014. At $5.9 trillion, Shanghai now had the world's third-biggest market capitalization, behind only the New York Stock Exchange and the NASDAQ. That very morning so invincible did the juggernaut seem that a CNN story blared, "China's stock market is now worth over $10 trillion."[1] An accompanying graph showed the Shanghai Exchange soaring above the flat S&P 500. That day, the bubble popped.

Fueled by fears of a slowing economy, a weakening currency, and artificially high prices driven by hundreds of thousands of new investors using borrowed money, China's markets began a free fall. By that Friday, the Shanghai market had dropped 13 percent from its June peak. A week later, on June 26, it dropped 7.4 percent in a single trading session.

Despite emergency measures by the central government to limit short selling and provide funds to brokerages to buy stocks, the market continued to fall. On August 24, "Black Monday," the Shanghai composite cratered, falling another 8.5 percent, and the impact affected the rest of the world, with the Dow Jones Industrial Average sinking 588 points. By the end of the summer, Shanghai's market had lost over a third of its value. In just a matter of weeks, the world began to ask whether China's economic miracle was over.

The psychic shock over China's financial troubles struck at our strongest-held beliefs about the future of the global economy. The miracle of Asia's economic growth has transfixed the world for the past four decades. Once derided as a region known for producing low-quality goods with minimal technology and cheap labor, Asia has become indispensable to the lives of billions of consumers around the globe. The entire concept of globalization, which has shaped economic and political debates since the 1980s, is inconceivable without Asia.[2]

In one of the most profound shifts in economic history, the region has taken over the mantle of "the world's workshop" from Western countries. And yet this extraordinary transformation has been driven not by one country or one set of policies, but by many. The Indo-Pacific uniquely benefited from the post–World War II evolution of global politics, economics, and security. Today that economic miracle is at risk from the failure of economic reform to deal with the costs of growth, whether in advanced countries like Japan or developing nations like India and Indonesia. The global community has yet to accept that Asia's economic future really is at risk, and to consider what a less dynamic or even stagnant Asia-Pacific would mean for prosperity and stability.

In trying to discern the contours of economic risk in Asia, it is crucial to recognize that the region has benefited from a unique historical moment, a decades-long stretch of general global stability, combined with the explosive rise of the middle class and a technological revolution. As I will discuss in chapter 6, security has been the cornerstone of Asia's postwar history. Regional stability allowed countries like Japan and Indonesia to modernize their economies and begin integrating into larger regional and global trade networks. Even South Korea and Vietnam, which saw destructive wars within their borders, took advantage of that regional trend once their wars ended.

Asia is perhaps the first beneficiary of a new era in world history. Previously, most technological innovation and expansion of productive capabilities took place during wartime or periods of quasi-military conflict, like the Cold War.[3] But in the half-century since the Asian economic miracle took off in the 1950s, the majority of global growth has come from supplying peaceful Western consumer societies with much of their needs.[4]

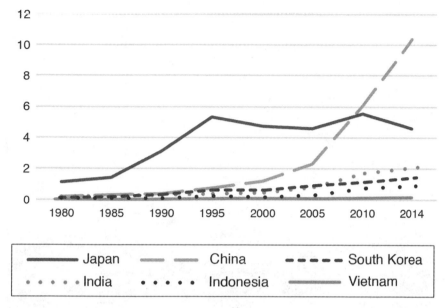

GDP at Market Prices in Select Asian States, 1980–2014 (in trillions of current US$). World Bank data. Artwork by Olivier Ballou.

Most global consumers could hardly imagine a world without Asia as its workshop. China and Japan are two of the world's three largest economies, and the majority of clothing, textiles, and consumer electronics are produced in Asia.[5] A massive building boom accompanied the decades of post–World War II growth, as capital investment in plants, ports, roads, airports, and office buildings transformed rice paddies into business parks, while sleepy capital cities became financial and industrial magnets. Urbanization has erased traditional villages across Asia, and megacities like Tokyo-Yokohama, Shanghai, Jakarta, and Mumbai now burst with tens of millions of people, from the world's wealthiest tycoons to its most poverty-stricken strivers. Today, eighteen of the world's twenty-five largest container ports are in Asia, including all of the top eight, while the largest U.S. port, Los Angeles, is ranked only nineteenth.[6]

No city is more symbolic of Asia's economic rise than Shanghai. In just two decades, Shanghai's skyline has become an iconic image around the world. While most of the city's twenty-four million people live far from the vibrant downtown, its core is a microcosm of Asia's economic past and

A general view of Shanghai's financial district of Pudong in 1987. Reuters/Stringer.

future. The famous Bund, with its shimmering elegance of Art Deco hotels, banks, and office buildings, is a living reminder of the humiliating subordination suffered during the region's colonial era. Across the Huangpu River, the magical growth of Pudong into a global economic center, from swampy flats and scattered villages to a jungle of neon and steel twisted into fantastic *Blade Runner*–like skyscrapers, parallels Asia's stunning economic rise over the past half-century. But the steel, glass, and neon deflect attention from the dangers that threaten these extraordinary achievements.

For too long, observers both within the region and outside it have downplayed failures, stubborn problems, and enduring weaknesses. Few ask inconvenient questions, such as, how resilient are Asian countries to economic shocks? How adaptable are leading economic sectors and government policies? Will Asia really continue to innovate, or is it easier to

A general view of Shanghai's financial district of Pudong in 2013, with the Shanghai Tower (right). The 632-meter-high (2,073 ft) Shanghai Tower, completed in 2015, is the tallest skyscraper in China and the second tallest in the world. Reuters/Carlos Barria.

piggyback on foreign breakthroughs? This is a surprisingly unmapped region of risk. We should have begun asking those questions after Japan's bubble popped in the early 1990s. Now, China's travails are giving us a second chance to understand exactly what is happening, and to prepare for further trouble.

Asian countries, developed and developing alike, face significant challenges maintaining their economic health over the next generation. Demand from Western countries will possibly level off as those societies age and as incomes remain stagnant. Domestically, corruption, malinvestment, and waste eat away at economic efficiency. As Asia's economies reach the natural limits of intensive development schemes, the prospect for their continued growth may be far murkier than what the world has come to expect.

Within this large region of risk, four areas stand out. The first is the apparent end of China's stampeding growth; the second is the difficulty mature economies like Japan have in transitioning to a postindustrial future; the third is that the countries of Southeast Asia may never become stable, middle-class societies; and the last is India's continuing development drama, which will shape the lives of over one billion people.

Is It All about China?

After the summer 2015 stock collapse destroyed over $2.8 trillion of wealth, governments and media around the world convinced themselves that the worst in China was over.[7] Yet unnoticed by many of those observers and commentators was the snowballing downturn in China's economy. Not only did Beijing continue revising downward its growth estimates, investors voted with their feet. Although the central government committed as much as $235 billion to propping up markets, by the end of 2015, an astonishing $500 billion, and possibly as much as $675 billion, of capital had fled China, underscoring deepening doubt about the overall health of the economy.[8]

The beginning of 2016 proved that the summer stock collapse was no fluke, as Chinese markets again crashed, falling 6.9 percent on the first trading day of the year. The Chinese government halted trading twice the first week of 2016, and stock exchanges around the world followed China sharply downward. As during the previous summer, stunned investors worldwide asked themselves what it meant. Was it simply the return to earth of an overheated market that had become separated from the real economy? Or was this really the beginning of the end of China's economic miracle? What few wanted to acknowledge is that China's problems go far deeper than its stock markets.

The story of global economic activity for the past two decades has been the story of China. In the space of one generation, China has become the largest or second-largest trading partner of seventy-eight countries around the globe, including the United States, Japan, and South Korea.[9] By some measures, China is now the first-, second-, or third-largest trading partner of nearly every nation on earth. According to the International Monetary Fund, it is central to the entire world economic structure, as its imports help prop up the economies of major players such as Germany, smaller ones like Australia, and fledgling countries in Africa.[10] The world

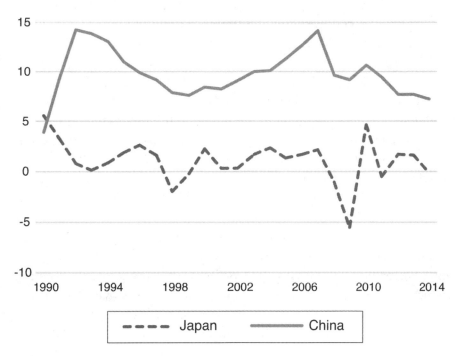

China versus Japan: Annual GDP Growth Rates, 1990–2014 (%). World Bank data. Artwork by Olivier Ballou.

has grown used to miracle stories of people like Jack Ma, the founder of e-commerce giant Alibaba, who became China's richest man in a few hours when his company's initial public offering on the New York Stock Exchange netted him $13 billion.[11] Shelves of books have been written about China's economic explosion and how it is transforming the world.[12]

But now, after nearly three decades of unparalleled growth, it is time to start paying attention to the Chinese economy's failures, its growing weaknesses, and the central government's inability to fix looming problems. The deep-rooted risks to China's economy stem from unbalanced, government-driven development. What some see as strength may instead be an inability to adapt for the long run, while false statistics hide worse development numbers than what the headlines portray. Western observers assumed in the 1980s that Japan would continue to grow forever; a similar assumption still dominates many discussions of China. Both businesses and governments in the West should be prepared for the possibility of continued and significant disruptions in China's future.

The big story in China is the dramatic slowdown in GDP growth. Once boasting annual growth rates of 10 percent or higher, the Chinese government has steadily lowered expectations in recent years. Yet in 2014, after the economy missed its target of 7.5 percent by 0.1 percentage points, Chinese officials revealed the increasing difficulty of making firm predictions, instead vaguely aiming at growth in 2015 of "around 7 percent." Yet even with this wiggle room, the economy underperformed expectations, as growth slipped under 7 percent in the third quarter of the year.[13] China's actual growth may be even slower—maybe already stagnating.[14] Only now are observers willing to talk openly about their distrust of the official numbers, so no outsider can have real confidence in what is happening, unless they have extensive ground networks throughout the country, which few do. But what no one disputes any longer is that China needs significant economic reform to keep its economic miracle going.

As the country's leaders struggle to implement the reforms they have proposed to keep the economy growing, they and the world need to ask three questions: First, what is really happening on the ground? Second, where is the greatest threat: from a stock market collapse, bank failures, massive debt, labor issues, or loss of global trade? Third, how far can growth fall before the social reaction threatens political stability?

Today's China has not yet spawned a subculture of humor the way the late Soviet Union did. Endless jokes helped expose the reality of life behind the propaganda façades put up by the Kremlin. If China had inspired such jokes, one of them might go something like this:

> An American and a Chinese economist are arguing with each other. "Our economic statistics are the best in the world," boasts the American. "Once we get all the numbers, we can refine the growth rate to one-tenth of one percent."
>
> "That's nothing," replies the Chinese. "Our economic forecasting is so superior that the government sets a numerical target and the economic growth rate exactly matches it!"

As suspicion of official numbers grows, so too does a reassessment of the connection between economic policy and Beijing's political priorities.

The traditional story accompanying China's economic reforms is that the Chinese Communist Party (CCP) learned from the experience of Mikhail Gorbachev in the Soviet Union during the mid-1980s.[15] In an effort to maintain the legitimacy of the Communist Party and save the Soviet economy, Gorbachev embraced a policy of perestroika, or "restructuring." But first he loosened the Kremlin's political control so as to gain the people's trust before attempting to reform the economy. The unforeseen result of this moderate liberalization was the collapse of Soviet power. That China would take a different road became clear in 1989, when the leadership under Deng Xiaoping used the Chinese military to crush a massive pro-democracy student movement in Tiananmen Square. When Deng relaunched his economic reforms in the early 1990s, centered on special economic zones along the country's eastern seaboard, it was only two years after the fall of the Soviet Union, and Deng ensured that the CCP retained strict control of politics.[16] The result is the China we know today.

The most important insight into China's predicament is that the last thirty years have been easier than the next thirty will be. As a late-developing nation, China was able to take advantage of proven technologies, an open global trading system, and neighbors who needed its raw materials and cheap labor base. There is little question that the CCP, for all its flaws and brutality, did an impressive job shepherding China through the early stages of its modern development.

Beginning from such a low base, growth was relatively easy to attain once the state lifted some restrictions and promoted trade policies. As late as 1990, just before Deng made his famous push to revitalize economic reform, per capita GDP in China was just $340. Ten years later, it had almost tripled, to $945, and in 2014, the World Bank estimated it to be $7,590, more than a sixteenfold increase in twenty years.[17]

Yet China's rise has been uneven and remains incomplete, a tension that is certain to worsen in the coming years. Some authors see not one but many Chinas coexisting; one such description is of the "Nine Nations of China," each both geographically and economically discrete.[18] Other taxonomies are also possible, but at a minimum, let us conceive of two Chinas: one modern and developed, and integrated with the outer world; the other traditional and still developing, and still largely isolated from global trends.

No visitor to Shanghai, for example, can come away unimpressed by its dynamism and creature comforts. It may be hard for that visitor to keep in mind that China is still a developing country that has barely reached middle-income status. After three decades of national growth, rural villages throughout China share almost none of Shanghai's or Beijing's wealth, safety, and convenience. Farmers and day laborers in poor areas like Yunnan live in villages with no running water or electrical grids, and have few educational or economic opportunities.[19] Even in major cities, a visit to some areas such as Beijing's or Shanghai's slums can feel like a trip back to the nineteenth century.

Having concluded the first phase of its modernization, China must now transition from simple growth to sustainable development.[20] Yet the trade-off between economic development and political stability will remain. Beijing has crafted policies to benefit manufacturing, labor, and better use of land, yet much of China's modernization is still new and often incomplete. For example, only in 2004 was the holding of private property recognized as a right.[21] Sustainable development will require, at the minimum, a rule-of-law system in which the government and courts are widely trusted as impartial arbitrators. All such reforms have political implications, which is why China today is very far from this, a subject we will revisit when we discuss its unfinished political revolution in chapter 4.

Some of the recent slowdown has been engineered by the government itself, such as raising interest rates and reducing bank lending so as to prevent inflation, restrain the pace of investment, and deal with the excess capacity that emerged after the world financial crisis of 2008. Yet just as the world seemed blind to the possibility of a slowdown in China, China's economic planners seem to have been surprised by the severity of the downturn. Now the worry is that the economy must keep growing enough to absorb the millions of young adults entering the labor force each year and fulfill the expectations among middle-class urban workers for increasing wages. The downward revision of official GDP growth from the blisteringly fast pace of the 2000s to less than 7 percent in the mid-2010s raises questions about whether Beijing can maintain the standard of living of a middle class that has grown accustomed to a consumer lifestyle, while also creating opportunities for the urban and rural poor.

China is pursuing only some of the reforms it badly needs. Reducing the number and size of state-owned enterprises (SOEs) is vital to expanding the private sector, yet appears to be something that the government is unwilling to do. While Westerners often see China as a freewheeling, Western-style economic actor, the truth is that many economic sectors are dominated by SOEs like the China National Petroleum Corporation, the telecommunications company China Mobile, and the Industrial and Commercial Bank of China. All of these play an outsized role in vital economic sectors. By some estimates, China's SOEs account for over 40 percent of total business profit.[22]

Certainly, China's economy today is far more market oriented than it was before liberalization. But there are still 155,000 state SOEs of varying sizes in China, and the influence of the state-run sector has been increasing over the past decade as privatization slowed and in some cases even reversed.[23] Of the ninety-eight Chinese companies on *Fortune* magazine's 2015 "Global 500" list, only twenty-two are private, while all twelve of the largest Chinese corporations are state owned.[24] State ownership assures control over major enterprises in strategically important economic sectors, and provides an invaluable source of patronage for the central or local governments to use to keep elites and the middle class happy. Yet it can also result in a less rational allocation of resources and an ability to avoid tackling inefficiencies in production.[25]

The firms still under state control are increasingly the larger economic players in their sectors, and the government has made moves to increase their power.[26] Early in 2015, for instance, Beijing was said to be considering a merger of China National Petroleum Corporation with its domestic rival, China Petrochemical Corporation, both of which are controlled by the government, to create a massive state-owned oil company that would dominate the domestic market.[27] The fear is that such moves signal a continuing turn away from market-based activity, with the result that smaller firms face regulatory and financing roadblocks while larger firms continue to expand.

Companies not owned by the state are in a delicate relationship with Beijing. Outside the SOEs, there remains among major firms a gray line between state influence and private economic activity. It is unclear how much influence the Communist Party retains over leading private companies like telecommunications giant Huawei or the computer manufacturer Lenovo. Formally, they are largely private and the state owns just a small percentage of shares. But while these businesses are largely run by their managers, they continue to receive favored treatment and financial help from either Beijing or the provinces where they are located.

The opaque governance of many of China's leading corporations raises questions not only about state control and influence but about how their activities may benefit Beijing as much as the companies themselves. Huawei, for example, was founded by a former officer in the People's Liberation Army (PLA) and has long been suspected of maintaining ties to the PLA. This wound up derailing Huawei's planned purchase of an American information technology (IT) company in 2011, when the Committee on Foreign Investment in the United States did not allow the sale to proceed.[28]

There are other concerns about the relationship between the Chinese government and private business. In part because of inefficiencies introduced by government interference, China's regulatory environment is another area needing reform. The special deals offered to favored domestic companies hurt smaller Chinese businesses as well as foreign entities, reducing competition and innovation. Cumbersome licensing procedures, widespread corruption, and an underdeveloped system of commercial law all impose unnecessary costs. Foreign companies and small entrepreneurs are both subject to an intrusive and murky regulatory regime. In my conversations with foreign businessmen, I heard constant complaints about the lack of regulatory reform in services, telecommunication and information technology, and banking.

While much of the regulatory and corporate governance picture is hidden from the public, other economic problems are not. China suffers from significant macroeconomic imbalances that threaten its future growth, which are made worse by government policies. During the 2008 global financial crisis, the government committed some $600 billion to stimulus spending in an effort to avert a collapse at home.[29] While China's leaders and many commentators claim that this strategy succeeded, it also added to the country's huge government debt.

Foreign observers largely ignore this debt, but it may be one of the greatest risks the government faces. By some estimates, China's total government debt is 200 percent of GDP, approximately $22 trillion.[30] This is, in percentage terms, less than Japan's, which is around 240 percent, but it is growing, and the lack of transparency in China's case makes it a particular concern.

Local indebtedness in China spiked thanks to stimulus programs in the wake of the 2008 financial crisis. A significant proportion of the estimated $2.9 trillion in official local government debt is a result of government housing and construction projects.[31] Official government estimates from 2011 stated that some 30 percent of this would not be paid back, but some Western analysts believe the percentage is more like 80 or 90 percent.[32] An additional $400 billion to $1 trillion of underground financing is kept off the books and is not subject to any type of regulatory control.[33] When combined with the lack of transparency in the accounting methods of China's biggest banks, the indebtedness of local governments raises serious questions of the underlying stability of China's financial system. A significant part of that indebtedness is connected to real estate development, and a collapse of property prices has the potential to wreak havoc throughout the economy.[34]

China's property bubble takes various forms. In the largest cities, like Beijing and Shenzhen, housing prices have moved out of the reach of many ordinary workers. But in the "smaller" cities (those with up to three million people), massive overdevelopment has resulted in as many as forty-nine million empty apartments and homes.[35] These eerie "ghost cities" haunting China have lately become a popular topic for foreign media: apartment blocks, roads, and parks, all built according to plans drawn up by bureaucrats jostling for more central spending, and all completely uninhabited.[36] Other high-profile projects, like the Phoenix Island resort on the southern island of Hainan, have stalled out, leaving half-finished luxury hotels and empty convention centers.[37]

With housing accounting for nearly 13 percent of China's GDP in 2011, the overinvestment in real estate casts doubt on many banks' balance sheets.[38] In the first quarter of 2013, China's National Bureau of Statistics (NBS) reported that real estate as a portion of GDP grew by 7.8 percent compared with the first quarter of 2012.[39] Should the housing industry suffer a significant collapse, millions of laborers would be thrown out of work and hundreds of construction firms would fall into bankruptcy, while local governments and banks could collapse.

This unbalanced development, driven by government policies, threatens China's macroeconomic picture, but it is just one element that threatens the future. Capital goods investment in China totaled nearly 48 percent of GDP in 2011, far higher than in other countries,[40] while Chinese households saved just over half of their income during the same period. This shows that GDP remains driven by the state and private business sectors and not yet by consumers. The result is chronic overproduction.[41]

This investment strategy also means that China remains dangerously dependent on exports to maintain GDP growth. In 2012, China became the world's biggest trader in goods, exporting nearly $2 trillion. Exports of goods and services accounted for 23 percent of its GDP.[42] Not surprisingly, its vulnerability became clear during the 2008 global financial crisis, when a sharp fall in overseas demand compelled the state to unleash its multibillion-dollar stimulus program. Global economic weakness remains a danger: China's exports to the European Union fell by 1 percent in 2012, putting pressure on manufacturers to find markets at home.[43] But China's citizens still do not consume enough and the state exports too much, keeping it stuck in an export-led model better suited to a developing country. This may change as the population ages and spends more while saving less, but for now, China's economic growth depends too much on markets overseas.

In the early morning hours of June 2, 2013, a fire broke out at a poultry processing plant in rural northeastern Jilin province. As the thick, black smoke rolled through the plant, three hundred panicked workers were trapped by locked doors, with only one side exit open. In the chaos, 121 of them died. It was China's version of the infamous Manhattan Triangle Shirtwaist Factory fire of 1911: a brutal reminder that the country's economic miracle was built on the backs of an often overworked and vulnerable labor force.

China's growth has long depended on rural workers flooding into the cities, located mostly on or near the coast, to work in sweatshops or on spartan campuses. These facilities, which combine a Dickensian atmosphere with twenty-first-century technology, can be huge: iPhone assembler Foxconn's compound in Shenzhen employs 240,000 workers.[44] Those in less skilled sectors work in atrocious conditions, while their more skilled counterparts benefit from the internationalized part of China's economy. This situation is not unique to mainland China but exists throughout much of Asia, in countries like Indonesia, Vietnam, and India. In many cases, conditions outside China are worse, as shown by deaths of over one thousand Bangladeshi garment workers in the collapse of a commercial building in April 2013.[45] Yet China faces significant labor problems that will make its other macroeconomic challenges more difficult.

Much of China's early economic success after the reforms of the 1980s and 1990s was based on exploiting cheap domestic labor. Chinese companies were not alone in taking advantage of this: foreign manufacturers from Japan and Taiwan opened factories on the Chinese mainland. In 2010, foreign-owned enterprises employed 18.2 million Chinese.[46]

Yet as China has moved up the wage scale, its workers, especially along the coast, are no longer as affordable. Average wages for blue-collar workers during the last decade rose by over 10 percent annually. Many other countries in Asia now have lower labor costs. Vietnam's labor costs, for example, are just two-thirds China's.[47] Moreover, China's labor force is shrinking—by nearly ten million in the first half of the 2010s alone—and this also puts upward pressure on wages. The foreign companies that flocked to China in past decades have begun moving some of their low-value production elsewhere. Even Chinese companies are looking abroad for more affordable labor.[48] This is a problem that will grow in the coming years.

Still, Chinese workers' wage gains have been unequally distributed, and those at the low end remain vulnerable to global economic trends. In the depths of the economic downturn in 2009, at least twenty million migrant laborers lost their jobs. Many returned to the countryside, where they waited for opportunities to move again to the cities.[49] This population is increasingly discontented. As export markets shrank in the spring of 2011, a series of clashes between police and mostly migrant laborers rocked major industrial cities such as Tianjin. The authorities called out paramilitary forces to disperse rioters.[50]

Issues of health and safety, wages and job security were manifest even when the economy was stronger. According to the state-controlled *China Daily*, nearly 1.3 million labor disputes were filed with local courts or arbitration centers in 2010, triple the number from 2005.[51] While this might be a sign of growing trust in the legal system, it also indicates the degree of dissatisfaction among the working class. Violent clashes like those in Tianjin are still rare, but unrest simmers below the surface, tied to land appropriation, corruption, and access to public services. All this puts continued pressure on national leaders to respond to labor complaints, put the legal system on fairer footing, and make it easier for migrants to live legally in cities where they work, so that they can register for social services and place their children in school.

Such demands on the part of laborers will continue as long as China has some of the world's worst income inequality. Official statistics are notoriously unreliable (some say hopelessly corrupted), but there is abundant evidence that the income gap is worsening. In 2012, laborers in the countryside made roughly one-third that of urban workers, with median wages of around $1,000 and $3,000 per year, respectively.[52] Meanwhile, according to some analyses, as much as $1.5 trillion in hidden income is added each year to the pockets of China's rich, all of it under the tax radar and outside the formal banking system.[53] Little of this money finds its way to lower-income laborers.

For the last decade, China's gini coefficient (the standard measure of income distribution in a society) has stood above 0.4, the threshold for severe inequality.[54] What this means in practice is that the top tenth of China's households received close to 60 percent of the country's income.[55] Some estimates show that the top 10 percent of households receive sixty-five times as much as the poorest 10 percent. This level of inequality goes far beyond the gulf between coast and countryside. In China's main cities, you can be on a street cluttered with Mercedes Benzes in front of brand-new towering skyscrapers, and just blocks later find yourself looking at hovels fronting dark alleyways. Moreover, the persistently low incomes in rural areas are another hurdle to getting China's consumer sector to contribute more to the country's growth.

China's leaders are well aware of the dangers the economy faces. President Xi Jinping, who took power at the end of 2012, is the first leader of the so-called fifth generation of Communist Party rulers. He has staked the regime's legitimacy on reforms, including a broad set of reforms unveiled at the end of 2013 at the party's Third Plenum.[56] Among the most important are initiatives to allow greater private use of state-owned agricultural land, to make SOEs more market oriented, and to reform parts of the financial system. In addition, Beijing has pledged to liberalize the household registration (*hukou*) system, which officially identifies the region where an individual and family live, thereby determining who is allowed to work where, which children can go to the local schools, and what social services they can receive.

These proposals—there were some sixty altogether—do not solve the country's broader structural problems. Nor do they do much to increase confidence that the economic playing field is becoming any fairer. For example, the reform plan for the household registration system, designed to allow rural migrant workers access to state benefits in urban areas, does not apply to some of the country's largest cities, including Beijing and Shanghai. The reform of the financial system, moreover, does not fully address informal lending practices, which account for a vast number of loans. Even so, these limited measures face resistance from entrenched interests.

The reform program is designed to last through 2023, but repeated government demands that changes be implemented more quickly suggest that little concrete change has occurred, even as China's economy continues to slow down.[57] The reason, as we shall see in later chapters, is that the CCP fears that too much reform will spill over into the political arena, an outcome it has shown itself willing to prevent through the use of deadly force against its own citizens, as it did in Tiananmen Square in 1989. That leaves the leadership walking a tightrope: pursuing reforms that can bolster economic growth without threatening their hold on power.

At the same time that China's internal problems are growing, doing business in China is becoming more difficult for foreign companies. After years of feel-good stories about economic opportunity for foreign firms in China, a different narrative is slowly beginning to take hold, and foreign businesses are speaking out about the problems and pressures they face. This already is leading to foreign companies reassessing their activities in China. There is a danger that, as China's economic woes deepen, foreign companies will decide it is increasingly not worth doing business in the country, which will only exacerbate the problems, and potentially lead to a new era of economic inwardness. For this, China has only itself to blame.

When I began visiting Japan in 1990, just as its economic bubble was bursting, other Americans, far more adventurous, were heading to China. I recently met one of them in Shanghai, a lanky Midwesterner who has been in China for over two decades. He works for a corporate security firm, and although I expected to talk about cyberhacking, he had a different, more low-tech story to tell. When a Chinese company is worried about foreign competition, he said, "they send goons to your door. This is old-fashioned intimidation. It comes from the companies that are moving into international trade but aren't as sophisticated as the older ones. They play by Chinese rules." Rural firms trying to work their way up to the global trade rung in particular fall back on such methods.

From talking with others in business, I learned that this is part of a broader trend, even if Mafia-style arm-twisting isn't necessarily the main danger foreign companies face. The costs of doing business in Asia are not measured solely in labor and transportation costs, or tariffs and ad campaigns. Bribery, legal capriciousness, and old-fashioned intimidation are just some of the problems that foreign businessmen deal with in Asia.

Theft of intellectual property and complex fraud are increasingly a point of contention between foreign businesses and their local partners. This problem is not exclusive to China: the first wave of American expansion into Asia in the 1960s and 1970s also resulted in bribery cases and intellectual property theft, particularly in Japan. China made commitments to protect intellectual property rights (IPR) when it joined the World Trade Organization in the 1990s, but Beijing has failed to follow through on these commitments, and there has been no significant reform to IPR law that has increased business confidence. A study by the National Bureau of Asian Research estimated that American firms lose over $300 billion per year from intellectual property theft in China.[58]

The issue is made worse by the opaque nature of Chinese businesses, where controlling interests and shadow management structures are not understood (or meant to be understood) by outsiders. American and European businesses in China are subject to numerous pitfalls. Perhaps the most prevalent is pure IPR theft, through hacking, trademark infringement, or old-fashioned stealing of secrets. At the most basic level, anyone who has traveled through Asia is constantly exposed to knock-offs and fake brands, be they "Gucci" handbags or "Rolex" watches, at a fraction of what the real thing costs. U.S. movies and CDs are likewise pirated and sold cheaply in open-air carts throughout Asia.

The theft goes all the way up the value-added scale. Microsoft, for example, estimates that 90 percent of the Windows operating systems currently used in China are either pirated or illegally shared versions and that Microsoft loses $4 billion a year to illegal copying.[59] According to a 2011 U.S. International Trade Commission report, U.S. "intellectual property intensive" firms that reported IPR theft "accounted for 58.1 percent of the total sales of firms in the U.S. IP-intensive economy conducting business in China."[60] In 2009 alone, IPR theft in China cost U.S. firms $48 billion in sales, royalties, and licenses.[61]

At a more sophisticated level, Chinese businessmen in the United States have been arrested for attempting to purchase industrial secrets.[62] This has long been an issue in corporate relations around the world. Japanese companies were accused in the 1970s and 1980s of stealing from American competitors, as well as regular infringement of copyrights during the years they were building global brands and beginning to dominate various technology markets.[63] The same cycle is repeating itself in China, yet with an economy far larger, the theft is correspondingly bigger.

Of even greater concern is cybertheft, which in recent years has become a major political irritant between Beijing and Washington. A report by the computer security firm Mandiant in 2013 revealed massive penetration of U.S. corporations by a hacking unit of the PLA based in Shanghai.[64] The report showed how one PLA cybertheft unit had penetrated over 140 U.S. firms, stealing terabytes of information, for periods as long as four years. The thieves used a network of at least one thousand servers manned by hundreds, perhaps thousands, of military specialists. Far from being random phishing operations, the activities of China's elite hackers can compromise companies for months or years. Millions of pages of proprietary information are being siphoned off, including many of America's taxpayer-funded defense industrial trade secrets.[65]

There are other, unexpected effects of taking the easy and illegal route. All this theft of intellectual property, from handbags to software, also means that Chinese companies are focusing comparatively less on original research and development. Without investment in innovation, China's own competitiveness and production efficiency are weakened over the long run.

Fraud and illegal activities to capture markets is another way in which Chinese companies harm U.S. and foreign counterparts. Corporate security professionals in major Chinese cities like Shanghai argue that traditional fraud, blackmail, and strong-arm tactics have been increasing in recent years. Chinese companies increasingly attempt to muscle out foreign competition or look for shady ways to hold their own against better-organized foreign companies. Blackmailing foreign executives is a time-honored way to force overseas companies out of contested markets, though such sordid episodes rarely are publicized by the victims.

As more Chinese business moves away from the coastal regions into the relatively less developed, less regulated, and less cosmopolitan interior of the country, this activity appears to be on the upswing. Many of the heads of these new companies are the first generation to work with Westerners and are unfamiliar with international business norms. The downturn in global trade after 2008 abetted this trend. According to corporate security specialists I spoke to in Shanghai, as Chinese companies working on thin margins aren't able to weather dips in trade or increased competitiveness, they turn to illegal means, such as intimidation, to stay afloat.[66]

Old-fashioned fraud is also prevalent among Chinese companies listed on U.S. securities exchanges. According to the *Wall Street Journal*, over 170 Chinese firms listed in the United States have been charged with embezzlement, theft, and other crimes. These activities have cost investors hundreds of millions of dollars.[67] Yet the U.S. government so far refuses to demand that Chinese firms going public on American exchanges abide by the Securities and Exchange Commission's auditing rules. Again, the prevalence of fraud means that Chinese companies are not maturing and adopting Western norms of doing business. This will increasingly be a drag in the future, dampening competitiveness in an environment where companies from other countries are seeking to eat away at China's global position.

Another pressure on U.S. companies is coming increasingly from failed joint ventures and trade promotion policies. In both these cases, what appear to be accepted, normal business practices actually provide unfair if not illegal benefits to Chinese companies. The Chinese government policy of "indigenous innovation," adopted in 2006, aims at providing "preferential support to Chinese companies, technical standards, government procurement, and technology transfers that seek to absorb foreign technology and apply it to spur Chinese technological advances."[68] Little different from IPR theft, this policy encourages Chinese firms to initially partner with foreign companies. The targeted foreign firms are generally those with intensive intellectual property stakes, thus higher up the value chain and creating greater return on investment. Some of the key sectors for Chinese adoption of indigenous innovation practices, according to the U.S. International Trade Commission, were in wind energy, telecommunications equipment, software, automotive production, and civil aircraft.[69]

U.S.-Chinese joint ventures have also been used to steal trade secrets and technology or to push a competitor out of the market. On the face of it, joint ventures should be the most beneficial type of economic exchange, but the rate of failure is high, and many American firms complain about illegal pressure tactics that force them out of China. One high-profile case involved the U.S. office equipment maker Fellowes, Incorporated, whose decade-long partnership with a Chinese machinery company to produce high-end paper shredders abruptly ended when the Chinese demanded that the American firm surrender machinery and other assets.[70] When the intimidation failed, the Chinese locked down the factory in April 2011 and stole much of the manufacturing equipment, costing Fellowes $100 million.[71]

Other major foreign companies, such as health-care product maker Kimberly-Clark and automotive parts producer Borg-Warner, saw joint ventures sunk by their ostensible partners, who used the relationships as stepping-stones to establishing rival operations. The more such intimidation and theft occur in an environment of a slowing economy, the less that U.S. and foreign firms will be willing to enter into cooperative partnerships with Chinese firms, as the U.S. Chamber of Commerce has already pointed out.[72] As with IPR theft and fraud, Chinese companies are only hurting themselves in the long run, and will become increasingly inefficient and uncompetitive against foreign rivals. That will further depress growth, just when China needs to move away from the economic models of the past.

The world is just waking up to the fact that China is entering a new economic era, one that will be dramatically different from the success story of the past quarter-century. Until recently many foreign observers believed that in the near term the government would be able to respond to economic problems and manage challenges but that the leadership runs a grave risk in the longer term by putting off fundamental reforms. Yet with mounting evidence of economic problems, it is increasingly clear that the party leadership, concerned with the balance between a more open economy and maintaining political control, has been deterred from attempting bold moves, and may not have the answers needed to forestall even more serious problems. Xi Jinping has focused on consolidating his own political base rather than pushing more robust structural reform or allowing market forces to play a "decisive" role, as he promised in the widely touted reform rolled out during the 2013 Third Plenum of the Communist Party.

Xi is faced with a herculean task, and his reforms so far appear unequal to the challenge. It is not surprising to find numerous economic problems in a country as large and diverse as China. Yet too many of the risks it faces are being ignored or tackled only hesitantly, often because of state interests and entrenched groups. Already, Chinese leaders warn that growth in the mid-single digits is the "new normal," but without a meaningful liberalization of state control over the economy and a rooting out of waste, inefficiency, and fraud, China's economic woes are certain to grow.

As China's economic picture worsens, moreover, pressure will be put on Xi Jinping and future leaders to insert the government ever more directly into the economy, as was seen in the aftermath of the summer 2015 stock market crash. This will make it even harder to pursue the reforms that are needed. Already, the slowdown is increasingly affecting nations throughout the region that are dependent on Chinese demand for their products or raw materials. China's economic problems, then, are also Asia's problems.

The End of Asia's "Dynamic Crescent"?

Despite the worldwide headlines, it is a mistake to focus solely on China, for all its importance. There are more than two billion non-Chinese living in the Indo-Pacific, and their economies are a vital part of the global system. Asia's extraordinary economic diversity, along with the enduring problems stretching from India to Japan, cannot be adequately tackled in one chapter or even one book. This section instead seeks to give the reader a very broad view (what some in business or government like to call the thirty-thousand-foot view) of the risks to Asia's ongoing modernization. The differing landscapes include mature economies like Japan and South Korea; unified modernizing states like Vietnam; less developed, sprawling countries such as Indonesia; and the kaleidoscopic environment of India.

When the ground began to ripple in northeastern Japan on March 11, 2011, earthquake-sensitive Japanese braced themselves for yet another temblor. But this one was different. Hundreds of miles away from the epicenter, Tokyo's skyscrapers began to sway, and near the origin, the quake spawned a massive tsunami that raced ashore in just minutes. The flood inundated hundreds of miles of coastline, completely obliterating whole towns and drowning some twenty thousand people. Television broadcasts showed rivers of flaming debris engulfing mile after mile of farmland.

The tsunami flooded the cooling system of the Fukushima nuclear power plant, causing the world's worst nuclear crisis since the Chernobyl disaster in 1986, and resulting in a national emergency. The bungled political response eventually brought down the government when Prime Minister Naoto Kan resigned five months later, while the scale of the damage meant years if not decades of costly reconstruction. For many, "3/11," as it came to be called, seemed yet another sign that Japan's once-dominant position in Asia would never be recaptured.

In many ways, Japan remains the test case for Asian modernization. In the late nineteenth century it became the first Asian nation to begin moving away from being an agriculturally dominant society, as it dramatically transformed itself from a feudal system to an industrialized, constitutional democracy. Starting with the Meiji Restoration of 1868, Japan modernized its educational system, provided government support to budding industries, and imported technical and scientific talent.[73] Its population was almost entirely literate by the early twentieth century, and at the start of World War II its skilled workforce was decades ahead of that of any other Asian nation. After its defeat in World War II, it not only rebuilt itself but grew to become the world's second-largest economy in just a few decades. Just as dramatically, it fell into a funk of stagnation in the early 1990s, from which it is still struggling to emerge.

Japan is all too easily caricatured as a has-been nation. It catapulted to its dominant status on the basis of traditional industrial manufacturing, including steelmaking and shipbuilding. It then concentrated on consumer electronics and automobiles, aiming at capturing ever-larger market share regardless of initial profitability.[74] In the process, it became one of the world's richest nations, and by the 1990s, its per capita GDP ranked just below those of the United States and the larger western European countries. From the 1960s to the 1990s, Japan seemed to be an unstoppable economic force, the one country pointing toward a high-tech, industrialized future based on lean manufacturing processes, close management-labor relations, and an almost-too-laudable work ethic.

So what happened? Just as today with regard to China, investors and a media looking for the next "hot thing" too often ignored Japan's weaknesses. Few observers in the 1970s or 1980s took seriously the country's malinvestment, its onerous regulation, and the unsustainable asset bubble on its horizon. Dreams of Japanese economic prowess hid the system's lack of resilience, its resistance to adaptation, and the lack of effective government policy to promote structural reform.

Eventually, these ills converged to throw Japan into stagnation.[75] Successive governments failed to embrace meaningful reform. Stimulus schemes that poured hundreds of billions of yen into dead-end public works projects simply wasted money and added to the country's enormous debt. An asset and property price bubble nearly brought down Japan's financial system in the 1990s before measured deregulation and government intervention to reduce bad loans and clean up the books of Japan's leading banks restored some stability. Tight money policy brought interest rates near zero but also caused the country to skirt deflation throughout the 2000s. Perhaps most damaging was a continued reliance on export-driven growth; this provided some years of economic expansion during the early 2000s, but the country was hammered when the global financial system crashed in 2008.

Japan has steadily seen its once-dominant position fade. Even if its economy had continued to grow throughout the 1990s and 2000s, it likely would have lost ground to the young and hungry Four Asian Tigers of

Hong Kong, Singapore, South Korea, and Taiwan, as well as China as they followed Japan's path toward modernization. Previously the world's largest shipbuilder, Japan was overtaken by South Korea in 2003 and then China in 2009.[76] Its electronics manufacturers, who transformed the world of personal entertainment with inventions such as the Sony Walkman, have been surpassed by those of the Koreans and the Chinese. No longer the centers of innovation that they once were, Japanese companies like Sony, Panasonic, and Sharp have lost two-thirds of their value in the past decade, and lost competitiveness as well.[77] The Taiwan Semiconductor Manufacturing Company and South Korea's Samsung have also knocked Japan from its perch as the world's leading producer of semiconductor chips and silicon wafers.[78] Only in the automobile industry has Japan maintained, and even expanded, its lead. Toyota became the world's largest carmaker in 2012, and both it and Honda have been leaders in hybrid technology and electric car development.

Japan's fall from manufacturing grace has reverberated throughout its economy. One of the country's great transformations has been in labor policy. Once lauded as the land of permanent employment and almost fanatically hard-working "salarymen," today's Japan has a far different labor market. Through the 2000s, its wage growth was essentially flat, and temporary workers grew to constitute nearly one-third of the labor force,[79] undermining the Japanese tradition of "lifetime employment." These workers were the first to be let go during the global downturn in 2008–9. The erosion of workers' purchasing power was reflected in Japan's per capita GDP, which began to slip behind the Asian Tigers in 1993. It now lags behind Singapore, Hong Kong, and Taiwan, and may be overtaken by South Korea before 2020.[80]

Japan's negative economic trends were exacerbated by the Fukushima crisis of March 2011. As a result of the reactor's near-meltdown after the earthquake and tsunami, prefectures throughout Japan shut off all of the country's fifty-four nuclear power reactors, which at the time supplied 30 percent of Japan's electricity. This significantly damaged industrial output: manufacturers throughout the nation were forced to ration electricity, shut down production lines, and pay exorbitant costs for oil and natural gas on world spot markets. Increased dependence on imports cost the country $250 billion in 2012. Even three years after the

Fukushima incident, Japan paid over twice the price for liquefied natural gas that America did.[81]

Half a decade after the 2011 crisis, many manufacturers continue to face uncertain energy supplies. A pickup in economic activity conversely means paying more for energy. Only a handful of Japan's nuclear reactors have been reopened, and large companies continue to discuss the possibility of locating their manufacturing operations offshore so as to ensure access to uninterrupted energy supplies. While the government focused on disaster relief and long-term reconstruction of the region affected by the tsunami, a greater challenge to Japanese economic health remains the issue of stable energy supply, especially given Japan's vulnerability to global energy markets in oil and natural gas.

The country also has to do much more to break down old habits that stifle the broader economy. The most ambitious plan to do so in many decades is currently unfolding under Prime Minister Abe. Yet many critics believe the prime minister's gambit is too timid. His so-called Abenomics policy started with a multibillion-dollar stimulus and a move to increase the money supply, but there has been less movement on meaningful structural reform, despite widespread recognition that it can no longer be put off. Only in February 2015 did the government begin to propose changes to Japan's highly protected agriculture market, most notably by reducing the power of the central agricultural union over farm cooperatives, and by making it easier to sell or transfer land. The energy industry has been deregulated, and the corporate tax rate lowered. But the effects of these reforms will take years to work their way through the economy.[82] Serious reform is still needed in the telecommunications and pharmaceuticals sectors, where fear of foreign competition has blocked bold measures.

Just as important, Japan's labor market needs significant reform. One of the most glaring inefficiencies in the Japanese economy is the gender disparity: Japanese women remain disadvantaged in the workplace and underrepresented in the labor force. According to the Organisation for Economic Co-operation and Development (OECD), Japanese women are among the most educated in the world, with 42.5 percent of them having some postsecondary education. But just 67.5 percent of Japanese women have jobs, including part-time work.[83] A 2010 report by Goldman Sachs estimated that if women in Japan could be employed at the same rate as men (about 80 percent), it could add as much as 15 percent to overall GDP.[84] Yet the cultural resistance to having female CEOs and other executives remains extremely strong in Japan, as in most Asian countries.

After returning to office in 2012, Prime Minister Shinzo Abe raised the issue of gender imbalance to national prominence and offered suggestions for enabling more female workforce participation. But these proposals carry the risk of new and intrusive government regulations. Abe's "womenomics" goal is to raise the number of employed women between the ages of twenty-five and forty-four by 5 percent by 2020. An even more ambitious target is to have at least 30 percent of corporate "leadership and management" positions filled by women. To achieve this, Abe proposes a law requiring large companies to craft and make public their plans for increasing the role of women in their businesses. This top-down government approach risks setting unrealistic targets and shoehorning Japanese companies into a one-size-fits-all policy. It also goes against Abe's stated goals of freeing up Japan's economy to be more competitive.

If women face an almost impenetrable glass ceiling in Japan, so do foreign workers, especially in professional or executive positions. Here, the economic problems owe as much to cultural norms as to intrusive government regulation of immigration and the labor market. Japan would benefit from having high-ranking foreign executives who will bring with them best practices from around the world and from a variety of industries. Yet the former CEO of one of Japan's largest global trading firms, a man well known for his cosmopolitan outlook and flawless English, once told me that it was difficult to hire foreigners for top positions at Japanese companies because "they aren't able to understand Japanese culture." This timeworn excuse typifies the rigid thinking that prevents Japanese firms, even highly internationalized ones, from successfully adapting to a new global economy.

So rare is the foreign top executive in Japan that when the French-Lebanese-Brazilian executive Carlos Ghosn became the head of carmaker Nissan in 1999, his penthouse apartment in one of Tokyo's most prominent buildings was regularly pointed out to foreign visitors. There are few leading Japanese companies like Takeda Pharmaceuticals, which hired Christophe Weber, a Frenchman, in 2014 to take over as president. Still, the announcement of Weber's hiring was protested by over one hundred shareholders and employees, who opposed the company's "hijacking by foreign capital."[85] This resistance to globalization must change for Japan to restore its competitiveness.

In addition to gender and nationality issues, the ossified nature of the corporate-labor compact needs to be reformed. Perhaps most importantly, it must be made easier for companies to fire permanent workers. So far, the Abe government has put off such controversial moves, preferring instead to focus on increasing wages, which have been largely stagnant over the past decade.[86] Flat wages means that consumer purchasing power hasn't improved, and so the short-term benefit from tinkering with the money supply and increasing government spending wore off after Abe's second year in office, leading to a renewed slowdown in growth.

The underlying, and politically endemic, problem is that Japanese governments of all political stripes are unwilling or unable to take on the country's entrenched special interests, including the aging farmers' lobby, the often-corrupt construction business, and the titans of industry. Meaningful reform would cause significant, even severe, dislocation over the short and possibly medium term, most likely ending the career of any politician who promoted it. So the politicians play a shell game with the country's wealth, trying to find the alchemic solution that will reignite growth without forcing pain on major sectors of society.

But in a free society, not every reform must come from the government. If Japan's politicians are unwilling to make the hard choices, what about its private businesses, which cannot ignore their shrinking market share, growing inefficiency, or lack of innovation?

Business in Japan has embraced reform unevenly. Back in the 1980s, at the height of the asset bubble, it was front-page news when Japanese interests bought trophy properties like Rockefeller Center or the Pebble Beach Golf Club. Such conspicuous consumption sparked American fears of being overtaken by Japan and spawned racially tinged conspiracy thrillers in print and on screen.

Today, however, Japan's mergers and acquisitions splurge is being driven by firms focused on expanding market share in their sectors. Japanese companies are now more likely to avoid flashy but unsound investments. Instead, firms such as Takeda Pharmaceutical are soberly looking to diversify outside Japan; the drug giant bought Swiss-based Nycomed in

2011 for $14 billion, the biggest Japanese merger and acquisition purchase ever, and gobbled up some U.S.-based start-ups as well. However promising, this new era of responsible acquisitions is still in its infancy.

There is still far more to be done. By some estimates, Japan's companies have over $2.5 trillion in liquid assets that are sitting unused.[87] Too many companies avoid taking risks, adopting global best practices, pursuing innovative research, or adding foreign managers to their top ranks. At best, the examples of a few leading companies will create a new cultural acceptance of risk and entrepreneurship for which Japan's skilled workers, infrastructure, and technology base will be well positioned to take advantage. That, however, is not yet widely evident.

To one degree or another, the rest of the Indo-Pacific shares successes and faces challenges similar to those of China and Japan. The presence of nations at differing levels of development has actually benefited the region. From high-end producers like Japan down to emerging manufacturing centers like Vietnam and Malaysia, the law of comparative advantage has worked to raise the standard of living in any nation that has tried to integrate itself into the world economy. Yet as these economies modernize, the drag of excessive regulation, questionable legal systems, and subpar educational systems, along with ongoing infrastructure needs and financial reform, highlight the risks to Asia's economic future.

Some countries, like the Four Tigers—Taiwan, South Korea, Singapore, and Hong Kong—long ago chose the path of modernization and continue to reap the benefits of early industrialization. South Korea leapt from third-world nation to major economic player in just one generation.[88] More impressively, it did so while democratizing its political system.[89] It is now poised to be a major exporter to the American and European markets for at least a generation. Korean carmakers such as Hyundai now compete with Toyota and Honda, and Samsung is the world leader in selling smartphones. Though Japan got there first, Korea now dominates the flat-screen TV market, and it is becoming a significant exporter of prepared foodstuffs. Its low unemployment rate and highly skilled labor force make it a benchmark for other Asian countries.

Yet South Korea hosts some of its own unique risk factors. At the top of the list is the *chaebol* business conglomerate system, in which industrial activity is tightly concentrated in a few family-run mega-firms.[90] These massive industrial, financial, and trading combinations ironically are part of the reason for South Korea's phenomenal success; they have conquered world markets in shipbuilding, smartphones, flat-screen TVs, and other products, but they also are regularly accused of bribery, false accounting, and buying political influence. Their size and protection by government sponsors prevent smaller firms from playing a fair role in Korea's market. Another risk factor in South Korea's system, one already faced by Japan, is that the larger and more important giants like Samsung become to the economy, the more important it is that they not make bad bets. A mistake in investing in emerging markets, or a big gamble on a product that fails (like the Japanese bets on plasma TVs or the Betamax video tape recorder system), could have widespread consequences throughout South Korea's economy.[91]

South Korea, like almost every country in the Indo-Pacific, has a skewed ratio of investment to consumption, usually abetted by government policies favoring the former. This is naturally changing in Japan, because of its aging society, but the export-dominated growth strategy that catapulted Japan and the Asian Tigers to economic success is hard to dislodge. As noted before, it caused a severe downturn in Japan after 2008, when exports fell by nearly 50 percent at the height of the recession. South Korean exports fell by more than fifteen percent in 2008–9, but its quick recovery masked that structurally it is even more at risk. Its exports are close to 50 percent of GDP, far higher than Japan's (16 percent), leaving it dangerously exposed in the event of prolonged global trade disruption.[92]

As with all of Asia's exporting nations, South Korea's very success in integrating itself into the global economy paradoxically raises the risk of destabilizing spillover effects. The ups and downs of global trade affect the entire economy. Seoul also has one of the world's most volatile stock markets. This is partly a result of the size of its derivatives market, and partly a result of its financial openness, which led to major foreign currency outflows during the 1998 Asian Financial Crisis and again in 2008.[93] Over the past several years, instability and inflexibility have combined to give South Korea a growth rate of roughly 3 percent annually, only slightly better than Japan's. But there is as yet little support for the types of major reform that would challenge special interests and ensure innovation and reduce the dependence on exports that holds back a rebalancing of the economy.

As China's growth falters and as Japan and South Korea struggle with the problems of maturing industrial societies, global business and investors are looking for the next big thing. Many believe that Southeast Asia offers the best opportunities to find that elusive growth.

Asia's smaller economies face a different set of risks from those of their giant neighbors. Not just lower levels of development, but endemic corruption, lack of social trust, dangerous labor conditions, and underdeveloped financial and legal systems all hamper growth in Southeast Asian nations. Countries like Vietnam and Malaysia, which drew global attention by offering cheap labor for offshore manufacturers and as suppliers of natural resources, are finding it difficult to escape the low-income trap, while others, like Cambodia and Laos, have yet to reach the "takeoff" stage. Many Asian leaders are focusing on the tension between the centralizing tendencies of growing governments and the recognition that state interference and inefficient regulation hamstring native industries. They also fear opening up their economies fully to global trade.

A visit to Vietnam, for example, exposes the challenges facing a homogenous, unified country that is starting to modernize. "We think we can be Asia's largest logistics hub," a senior official in Vietnam's Ministry of Industry and Trade tells me. "Look at our coastline and access to the seas. We just need the investment to build harbors and ports." While the desire to grow is laudable, it may not be quite that simple.

Despite the iron grip on political freedom held by the Communist Party of Vietnam (CPV), the country's political and business elites radiate confidence when asked about their future. Riding through Hanoi on the back of a motor scooter, I saw firsthand the dynamism they describe to me in our meetings. Rushing past old French colonial buildings, whose washed-out yellow façades blend into the background, I watched crowds of young people shopping, selling goods, and drinking in cafés. There is a hum of activity in Hanoi, a palpable sense of movement.

On paper, there is good reason for optimism. Vietnam currently has a population of ninety-four million, 86 percent of whom are under fifty-four years old.[94] Its two thousand miles of coastline provide the basis for developing export-oriented industries or even, as my government interloc-utor dreams, becoming a logistics hub for Southeast Asia. The state has relaxed restrictions on mom-and-pop businesses, so that the streets of major cities are lined with clothing shops, informal kitchens, odds-and-ends stores, and entertainment shops. Urban roads winding around often aging apartment blocks are crowded with Japanese motor scooters and cars, while bicycles, though still numerous, are increasingly squeezed to the curbs. All this combined to produce nearly 7 percent GDP growth in 2015.

The country's business leaders believe it is Vietnam's destiny to play a more influential role in Southeast Asia, and perhaps beyond. Unlike in China, the CPV is still respected by the populace, and the country faces nothing like China's degree of social unrest. Yet of the many officials and business professionals whom I visited in Southeast Asia, those in Vietnam seemed the most aware of the difficulties ahead.

The state remains a large part of the problem in Vietnam's economy. As in China, the most important sectors of the economy, such as energy and telecommunications, are run by SOEs. Vietnamese business leaders point out that the number of SOEs has dropped from twelve thousand in 1990 to only one thousand today, in part due to consolidation, but major liberalization still waits.[95] Moreover, because the government lacks transparency on such subjects as foreign direct investment and public-private partnerships, it is hard to assess its progress in privatization.

Vietnam's Ministry of Finance has struggled at times to tame the country's inflation, though falling oil prices helped drive inflation lower in 2015.[96] The banking system is plagued by bad loans, especially in the real estate sector, thus hampering the efficient flow of credit. The country is eyeing nuclear and green energy to ease its shortage in power generation, yet it remains wedded to inefficient oil, coal, and gas sources, with no real changes in sight.[97] Perhaps most worryingly, the country's main source of strength, exports, means that a global downturn risks stalling out the Vietnamese economy. Just like China and South Korea, Vietnam needs to rebalance its economy, or face the danger of being exposed to foreign trade disruption.

Despite some high-level foreign investment in the past decade, particularly by Japanese manufacturers, Vietnam is only slowly becoming an attractive environment for foreign direct investment (FDI). In 2012, the latest year for which numbers are available, the United States had only $1.1 billion invested in the country, even though Vietnam's labor costs were just two-thirds of China's.[98] Much of the difficulty in attracting even more investment comes from domestic businesses, which resist liberalizing the service sector or developing the IT industry. Ho Chi Minh City (the former Saigon) is a modern urban zone, but infrastructure in the rest of the country is decidedly backward. Vietnam continues to be low on the value-added chain in manufacturing, and eighteen percent of its exports are agricultural products such as rice and pepper.[99]

One of the bigger risks facing Vietnam, as with other Southeast Asian nations, is its education deficit. One reason it struggles to develop its productive sector is its low standard of post–high school education. Leading institutions of higher learning like Vietnam National University in Hanoi are woefully underfunded, with spartan facilities and not nearly enough computers. When I visited that university, enthusiastic students showed me around the crowded concrete campus, with its aging buildings that gave off an air of decay.

Compared to some of its neighbors, however, Vietnam has many advantages. A different example of the challenges of economic reform is provided by Indonesia, which is neither as socially homogenous nor as unified as Vietnam. Few in the West grasp the enormity or complexity of Indonesia. The world's fourth most populous nation, with 255 million people scattered across six thousand of its sixteen thousand islands, Indonesia is lower down the value chain than many of its neighbors, with a per capita GDP of just $3,500.[100] Over 40 percent of its population works in agriculture, and along with neighboring Malaysia, Indonesia accounts for nearly all the world's supply of palm oil, the harvesting of which is a major cause of deforestation. Growth in palm oil exports has tracked population increases in Asia, making Indonesia's economy ever more dependent on its continued export.[101]

For a while in the 2000s, there was hope that Indonesia might turn out to be Asia's next giant-in-waiting. Its location and population made it seem a natural for economic takeoff. As perhaps the most influential country in the Association of Southeast Asian Nations (ASEAN), it has been touted as the next China: a growing country with increasing influence.[102] Size confers economic benefits, but for Indonesia it also imposes extraordinary challenges. Building reliable infrastructure and logistics throughout the nation's six thousand inhabited islands has sadly lagged, and even the main island of Java, where the capital Jakarta is located, lacks sufficient roads, bridges, and ports.[103] Traffic in Jakarta is among the world's worst: complete standstills of thirty minutes or more are routine. Repeated infrastructure initiatives by the central government have fallen prey to corruption and inefficient planning.

A visit to Indonesia reveals an eager population hampered by a protectionist government and a sense of drift in public policy. Indonesia's former president S. B. Yudhonyo, who served from 2004 to 2014, made economic reform a centerpiece of his policies, yet he left office having failed to achieve many of his reform goals. The state had sought, and failed, to sell off its controlling interests in some of the country's major telecommunications and construction companies.[104] During Yudhonyo's second term, corruption allegations and political maneuvering took the wind out of the reformers' sails.

Indonesia's biggest problems are an economy that is largely closed to foreign investment and a protected agricultural sector run by powerful business interests intent on avoiding global competition. One of the common complaints heard in Jakarta is that the China-ASEAN Free Trade Agreement, signed in stages in the 2000s, has destroyed Indonesia's native textile and handicraft industries by flooding the country with cheap machinery and other equipment. The almost visceral backlash in Indonesia against free trade is a reminder that exhortations about the benefits of open economies do not always resonate in newly industrializing countries. A nation like Indonesia must tread a fine line between opening itself up to foreign competition and maintaining local economic viability.

For its part, the government has promoted economic nationalism, and even President Joko Widodo, a populist former mayor of Jakarta who came to office in 2014 promising economic liberalization, has embraced protectionist measures that call into question how much he can liberalize the economy. Indonesia's litany of corruption, malinvestment, and unresponsive government was echoed in my talks with business leaders and academics throughout the Indo-Pacific.

In Jakarta, as in all Asian capitals, however, conversation about economic challenges regularly returns to China. The economic fortunes of Asia's countries appear inextricably tied to China, as opportunity, threat, or most commonly both. Already the China downturn is depressing exports of raw materials and forcing down the price of commodities worldwide. In advanced economies such as Japan, exports for machine tools and advanced industrial parts slumped in 2015, crimping corporate profits and reducing national growth to barely 1 percent. Australia, to give another example, has gone nearly twenty-five years without a recession, caused in no small part by massive Chinese purchases of its minerals. Canberra now watches China nervously as its own growth slowed to under 3 percent in 2015. The effect of China's troubles on developing nations in Southeast Asia is even more pronounced. Both the Philippines and Indonesia saw growth estimates revised downward in 2015, thanks to China's troubles. They know that a sustained weakening of China would mean a radical revision of their own economic plans, and the likelihood that their ability to modernize will be dramatically slowed down.

Just how large the shadow of China looms over Asia's economic future becomes clearer with each round of bad news. Yet as one moves toward Asia's western edge, a different country begins to dominate the discussion, and the true economic diversity of the Indo-Pacific, along with the manifold risks to its future, towers into sight.

Nothing in Asia, not even China, quite compares with India. This sprawling patchwork of ethnic and linguistic groups, rightly described as a subcontinent unto itself, will soon be the world's most populous country, with economic growth that in 2015 surpassed China's. Yet India's promise has always been hampered by its extraordinarily complicated present.

From its independence from Great Britain in 1947 through 1991, India's ruling Congress Party imposed socialist-style central planning. Its byzantine system of regulation was derided as the "license raj," hamstringing innovation and entrepreneurship and preventing Indian businesses from either growing at home or participating in the global economy.[105] This disastrous policy brought the country almost to bankruptcy in 1991, when New Delhi was forced dramatically to airlift India's depleted gold bullion reserves to London as security for an IMF loan.[106] With its back against the wall, New Delhi embarked nearly a quarter-century ago on an economic liberalization plan that helped give it some of the world's most impressive growth during the 2000s.

In response to the near default, then–finance minister Manmohan Singh instituted a dramatic reform plan that included policies to reduce regulation, lower tariffs and taxes, break up state monopolies, open the country to foreign trade, and ease investment rules.[107] India's GDP grew in the high single digits annually during the mid-2000s before dropping by nearly half later in that decade. After years of reform, however, its 2014 GDP was only $2 trillion, far behind China's and just half of Japan's.

India's diversity makes it more difficult to deal with its extraordinary challenges. Although New Delhi began to reduce state interference in the broader economy in the 1990s, it still retained significant regulation in crucial areas like labor and agriculture. Many inefficiencies were not tackled, such as the huge subsidies paid to consumers for daily goods, nor were special interest groups challenged. Unlike China, India did not establish special economic zones (SEZs), free from most government oversight, until 2005, and its SEZs remain much smaller than those in China.[108]

India's less ambitious approach was partly a result of the natural give-and-take of democratic politics. Elected officials tried to shield their constituents from the pain of reduced government subsidies or the economic dislocation of freer trade. Heavy government subsidies for electricity and oil, including kerosene and diesel fuel, continue to skew India's markets while adding to government fiscal imbalances, producing one of Asia's higher debt-to-GDP ratios, 70 percent in 2012.[109]

India began its reforms from an even lower economic base than China, and parts of the country barely existed beyond subsistence farming. No country in the world has greater income inequality. There is a stark difference between the relatively wealthy coast and India's impoverished inland areas. At the start of economic reform in the 1990s, over one-third of the population lived in "absolute" poverty (defined as a standard of living at least 25 percent below the official poverty line).[110] Images of slums in major cities such as Calcutta were immortalized in films like 1992's *City of Joy* and drew attention through the charitable work of Mother

Teresa. After two decades of economic reform and strong growth, India's per capita GDP in 2011 was still only $1,500, less than half that of China. Worse, 20 percent of the population—some 260 million Indians—still live below the poverty line ($1.90 per day).[111] In any city, town, or village, the streets are clogged with peddlers eking out a living amid the cacophony of carts, scooters, cars, cows, and buses. Everything from machinery to haircuts and fruit is sold on roadsides.

By themselves, these vast extremes can create unique risks. India's richest families possess staggering wealth, far greater than China's millionaires and billionaires. One of the most glaring examples is Mukesh Ambani, India's wealthiest person, whose personal residence is a twenty-seven-story glass tower in Mumbai with amenities that include three helipads, a health club, a mini-theater, and nine elevators.[112] From its top floors, Ambani can gaze down on debris-filled slums that contain millions of people surviving on a few dollars a week.

Yet surprisingly, despite their enormous personal wealth, the business conglomerates that India's magnates control are often of modest size in global terms. They are hampered from growing because of continuing regulation and economic inefficiencies at home. Some Indian companies, such as Tata and Sons, Mittal Steel, and Infosys, are global brands with a large exposure to foreign markets. Yet even they are overwhelmingly focused on the domestic market. The country's largest firms also represent a proportionally larger chunk of India's economy than in other countries. By some estimates, 70 percent of India's stock market value lies with its top one hundred firms, which *The Economist* magazine nonetheless labels global "middleweights" by comparison to foreign multinationals.[113] Moreover, among those top one hundred companies, SOEs make 40 percent of the profits. Firms run by independent management or institutional owners earn less than 20 percent, and the rest comes from family-owned firms. Such concentration is one explanation for the dearth of small and medium-sized companies in India, including start-ups, and helps illustrate why manufacturing accounts for only 15 percent of the country's output, compared with 60 percent for services.[114]

India's underdeveloped industrial sector is one reason its bilateral trade with the United States stood only at $66 billion in 2015, a fraction of America's trade with China or Japan.[115] India remains low down the production value chain: it sends the United States textiles, precious stones and metals, pharmaceutical products, and mineral fuel and oil. But in the services sector, both at home and abroad, it has been more successful. Because English is the subsidiary official language of India, the country has found a comparative advantage in offering back-office services to American, Canadian, and British firms. Indian-run call centers are ubiquitous. Only in a few other areas, however, such as IT, is Indian business carving out a global market share.

Acutely aware of their country's shortcomings, Indian policymakers are obsessed with building "national power," which translates into modernization and higher growth. The southern part of the country, in particular, has embraced global manufacturing and is emerging as a regional hub for production and export. More educated than the north and less concerned about security challenges from Pakistan, cities like Bangalore and Chennai (Madras) are pushing India into the forefront of global IT and regional manufacturing.

Bangalore, India's Silicon Valley, attracts the country's best engineers, computer scientists, and entrepreneurs. It is the center for India's aerospace and biotechnology industries, the home of global software giants like Infosys and Wipro, and a magnet for India's young, educated elite. Many relocate from the northern part of the country, drawn by the intellectual infrastructure and sense of entrepreneurship.

If Bangalore is Silicon Valley, Chennai, on India's southeast coast, is its Detroit. Centuries ago, kingdoms located near Chennai served as the gateway to Southeast Asia, and their impressive stone carvings in Mahabalipuram draw thousands of visitors a year. In the seventeenth century, the British East India Company set up its first trading post there, at Fort St. George, and made the city part of its global trading network. Today, a visitor to the fort's bucolic grounds can run into a Frenchman helping build a new $1 billion tire plant for Michelin and a Japanese auto executive who runs the passenger car production division for Honda.

Chennai is home to one-third of India's automotive sector and 40 percent of its auto components industry.[116] Ford, Nissan, Renault, Hyundai, and Michelin have factories there.[117] Chennai's location makes it a natural export center, and companies like Ford are using it both as a production hub (in Ford's case for its light trucks) and as the shipping point to markets throughout Southeast Asia. While not the mecca that Bangalore is for IT, Chennai also hosts leading electronics manufacturers and telecommunications companies. Some observers expect its economy to more than double by 2025, to perhaps $100 billion a year.[118]

Bangalore's and Chennai's success has not reached the rest of India, however. After nearly a decade of solid economic growth, its economy began to slow in the 2010s. The half-decade from 2010 to 2015 saw a significant drop in investment in India, causing the stoppage of major infrastructure and manufacturing projects.[119] Economic reform seemed to stall out, and India's parliament torpedoed major international deals, such as one with the United States to build civilian-use nuclear reactors. Corruption scandals over the auctioning of telecommunication licenses damaged former prime minister Manmohan Singh's government, a development made more dispiriting by the fact that Singh was the father of economic liberalization in the 1990s.

The sense of drift and missed opportunities led to an electoral landslide in May 2014 for Narendra Modi, former chief minister of Gujarat state and the leader of the populist Hindu National Party. Modi promised to make economic reform his priority. Yet in his first budgets, he showed himself to be a cautious reformer, leaving intact much of India's entitlement spending, lowering some business taxes but not others, avoiding difficult land and labor reforms, and maintaining costly subsidies on daily-use items like fuel.[120]

While economic growth ticked up in the mid-2010s, hitting 7.5 percent in 2014, India's structural problems nonetheless remain enormous. Great strides have been made in literacy, a prerequisite for a skilled workforce, but nearly 30 percent of the population is functionally illiterate.[121] Not surprisingly, the eradication of poverty remains the government's primary goal, but the task of pulling hundreds of millions of citizens out of subsistence-level living is overwhelming, especially for a democratic government continually influenced by special interest groups.

As elsewhere in Asia, one of India's main problems is an underdeveloped and fragile system of infrastructure. The country desperately needs more roads, bridges, rails, and ports to facilitate internal trade. Throughout northern India one can see piles of fruit and vegetables rotting at distribution centers, waiting for trucks to bring them to local markets.

Cities like Delhi are choked with cars and trucks, yet have completely in-adequate road systems; outside the major metropolitan centers, roads are even worse, and highway networks are still rudimentary. Despite its huge population and its location astride the most important international trade routes, not one of the world's twenty-five largest ports is in India.

The country's electricity production and distribution system has, if any-thing, grown worse. Over 35 percent of Indians lack access to a secure supply of electricity.[122] The inadequacy of the country's electrical grid was put on shocking display in July 2012, when a massive power outage in the north left an estimated 680 million Indians—nearly the population of Europe—sweating through two hot summer nights in the dark.[123] Part of the problem is that the country depends on coal for 70 percent of its energy needs, but energy output by the inefficient state-owned pro-ducer, Coal India, continues to fall far behind demand.[124] On the supply side, state-owned electricity boards distribute power at subsidized rates (especially for rural areas), and fail to prevent massive amounts from be-ing siphoned off illegally or diverted to the black market.[125] Building the roads and electrical grids that India needs requires liberalizing the finan-cial sector so as to more efficiently collect and allocate resources, but politics has prevented a rational freeing up of the country's biggest banks.

The ways that Indians have taken around these roadblocks are not en-tirely beneficial. Corruption is a massive drain on the economy and in-fests all major industrial sectors. A recent report concluded that just the corruption cases reported in the media cost India nearly $6 billion in a single year.[126] Much, of course, went unreported. Corruption also causes political scandals, which will be discussed in chapter 4. Recent estimates by a number of Indian think tanks put the size of the "black money" economy at up to 30 percent of GDP.[127] The fact that a huge proportion of the labor force is employed in the underground economy means that the government misses out on tax revenue and cannot effectively enforce labor laws or control off-the-books transactions.

Like much of Asia, India has made impressive strides in recent years, yet it faces daunting challenges. It must rationalize public policy, reduce regulation, reduce poverty and corruption, and place the economy on a solid footing to take advantage of global economic trends. India's enor-

mous size introduces unique problems that lessen the prospect of significant economic development reaching those who need it most. The greatest
risk facing India is that it simply will never create an economy strong
enough to change the lives of the vast majority of its citizens.

Despite decades of economic growth and development, the nations of the
Indo-Pacific face a common challenge. Whether an advanced yet aging
society like Japan or a young and underdeveloped country like Indonesia,
each must find a way to keep its people reasonably prosperous and content.
Yet we have seen the common denominator of failed economic reform
across the region, even as that failure takes slightly different forms in each
of the countries we have surveyed. In Japan, and to a large extent in South
Korea, for example, the unwillingness to challenge special interests, and
the consensus-oriented nature of society provide stability at the expense
of dynamism. The regulatory environment in Japan and India stifles innovation and increases inefficiencies throughout the economy.

Even in today's globalized world, autarkic tendencies remain in the
Indo-Pacific. The region's most developed economy, Japan, continues to
maintain barriers against the world, as do the region's most developing
economies, such as Indonesia. FDI was essentially flat in South Korea from
1999 to 2014.[128] The fear of opening up to global market forces and resistance to FDI and foreign ownership of companies threaten competitiveness and innovation throughout the region.

Even if not inwardly focused, the economies of some Asian nations are
not diversified enough to ensure continued development or weather disruption. Indonesia and Vietnam, for example, along with the countries
of the Mekong Valley, continue to rely far too much on the export of raw
materials, and they struggle to build up their production capacity. Even
Australia is overly dependent on sending its minerals and other raw materials to China. Greater economic diversification is a must for developing and even some advanced nations to ensure continued growth.

A shadow on the economies of many Asian nations is the political resistance to adopting reforms or opening up to the world. Especially in authoritarian nations like China and Vietnam, the fear that greater reform
will bring demands for political liberalization hampers attempts to deal

with growing economic problems. This is a major factor in the Mekong Valley nations, not to mention North Korea, a country whose economy survives only through Chinese support and illicit activities.

The economic risks in Asia are manifold, but no one can predict with confidence how they will play out. Thanks to its rapid growth over the past several decades, China has made itself perhaps the most important single factor in Asia's economic picture. The deeper that China's troubles run, the greater the effect on its neighbors, at least until they are able to diversify their trade and investment.

While the threats are real, a dramatic collapse into regional or country-specific depression seems less likely, thanks to the development of trade networks, the establishment of currency swap agreements, and integration into the global economy. However, there is a real danger that the era of high and possibly even medium growth is rapidly coming to an end. The Western image of the Asian miracle will be tested as the region potentially suffers years of tepid economic expansion. Some slowdown is inevitable, ironically, as Asia modernizes and becomes wealthier. But an era of sluggish growth will not be enough to deal with the aging populations of China or South Korea, nor will it provide enough opportunity for Vietnam and India.

Just as important as the bare figures, the risk to Asia's economic future will intimately affect not just how people in the region live, but how their countries develop. We turn now to the second risk region on our map: Asia's demographic and social picture.

3

THE GOLDILOCKS DILEMMA

I first fully grasped Asia's demographic crisis while wandering around Istanbul's Topkapi Palace. The famous promontory jutting out into the Bosphorus was packed with foreign visitors, everyone trying to cram centuries of art, architecture, and religion into one sunny afternoon.

Outside the magnificent jewel room with its spectacular Topkapi Dagger, crowds swirled around, little children running on the grass among the trees. A small group of elderly Asian tourists rested on benches near the sultan's bedchamber, under the eye of a middle-aged tour guide. I didn't have to hear them speak to know they were Japanese. Behind me came a raucous group of younger Asians, ranging from their twenties to their forties. These were Chinese. Memories of quiet side streets in Tokyo and mobs of teenagers lazing away Sunday afternoons in Jakarta flashed through my head.

There is no more diverse anthropological region on the globe than the Indo-Pacific. By some estimates, over 3,500 languages are spoken in the region.[1] Its various races, ethnicities, and cultures support vastly different political systems, the world's poorest or least developed societies, as well as its richest individuals. Like crashing tectonic plates, this diversity creates a new topographical risk region. Asia confronts a Janus-faced demographic crisis: either too many people or too few. Each threat has political and economic implications, demanding both political and economic solutions, and no country in the vast Indo-Pacific is unaffected. Yet because the changes wrought by demographic trends are so slow to become visible, they are all too easy to miss.

This chapter explores Asia's demographic picture. It will do so by focusing on three nations, each of which represents a different facet of demographic risk: Japan, which has too few people; China, which is making a transition from too many people to too few; and India, whose population is still growing. These are just rough categories. The demographic challenge presents a shifting constellation of overlapping similarities and differences.

For example, two of Asia's largest states, Japan and China, are facing demographic decline, while India continues to add population. Japan and India, however, are both democracies whose people expect their governments to answer to the popular will in addressing demographic problems. Unlike India, though, Japan has the resources to deal with its problems and plan ahead. China and India showcase how modernizing countries are trying to deal with demographic challenges, often creating significant fiscal and political pressures, even as they continue to pursue economic development programs. In short, there is no one-size-fits-all demographic picture in Asia.

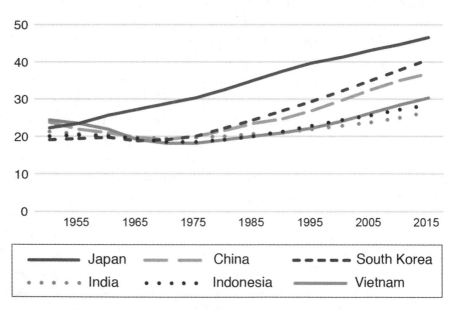

Median Age in Select Asian States, 1950–2015 (in years). U.N. Population Division data. Artwork by Olivier Ballou.

Unlike the other risk regions this book explores, demographics could be treated solely from an anthropological or sociological perspective, independent of business or policy concerns. In a way, Asia's demographic risk region is narrower and sits between the much larger areas of economic reform and political revolution, while belonging to neither.

Demographics, then, can be considered "contested territory," in that it spills over into two neighboring risk areas. Think of it a bit like Alsace-Lorraine, situated between France and Germany before World War I: its existence has an impact on both, but it has its own distinct boundaries. This chapter will explore the terrain of Asia's demographic risk region in light of both its economic and political challenges.

Japan Leads the Way Down

Haruko Miyagiyama, an eighty-nine-year-old widow, quietly spends her days in in a small village in the mountains of Japan's southern island of Kyushu.[2] Her husband long dead, she lives in one bedroom in the house of her seventy-year-old younger son, Hiroshi. Her other son lives in the neighboring house, and nearby in the village are a number of cousins, most of whom are only a few decades younger than she. The entire village has the feel of a retirement community, but without the bingo games, and it is far from an anomaly. Japan is the world's most rapidly aging society. In 2014 it counted over 58,000 centenarians, the most on the planet.[3]

Japan has few American-style retirement communities, despite its aging population. Elderly people like Haruko depend on their families for support and often for ensuring timely access to basic medical care. Yet Haruko spends most of her time alone, relegated to a dark room, largely unattended during the day while her son is out working. She is understandably thirsty for companionship, and even a casual visitor finds himself eagerly engaged in conversation. Haruko is neither abused nor abandoned; rather, she is simply one of millions of elderly in a society just beginning to grapple with its aging problem.

Since the nineteenth century, for better or worse, Japan has led the way in Asia. It was the first country to throw off its feudal past and modernize its political system, economy, and society. It also was the first Asian nation to create a Western-style colonial system and impose its rule over far-flung lands. After World War II, it was the first nation to become an industrial and then postindustrial power, and then the first to see its economic miracle sputter to a halt. Now it is poised to record another first: the first Asian-Pacific country to suffer demographic collapse.

Some estimates indicate that over half of the world's elderly will live in the Indo-Pacific by 2030, and by 2050 a full 20 percent of Asia's population may be over sixty years of age.[4] We barely grasp what such a demographic shift will mean. Even the most basic questions are just beginning to be asked: How will economies survive the disappearance of a large pool of robust, young workers? Can governments prevent entitlement programs from destroying their fiscal balances? How will militaries fill their ranks? Can innovation continue in a society dominated by the elderly? Japan will be the first society to provide a rough draft of the answers to these questions.

Japan's crisis was long in the making. The population dropped for the first time in 2004 and now has entered a period of year-on-year declines that will continue for decades. In 2014, the population shrank by 268,000 persons, while the number of births barely topped one million.[5] Fully 26 percent of its population is now sixty-five or older. The sociocultural effects of this change are already visible, especially outside metropolises like Tokyo and Osaka. In a scene repeated around the country, the local elementary school in Haruko Miyagiyama's village closed down in 2010, and its handful of children are now bused to a larger town a half-hour away. Meanwhile, because her village is too small to support any shops and the nearest sizeable town is too far away for those who do not drive, a "grocerymobile" comes by once a week, selling fresh fruit, vegetables, meat, and fish.

By some estimates, Japan's population, which stood at 127.3 million in 2013, will drop as much as 30 percent by 2060, to as low as eighty-six million, which is smaller than Vietnam today.[6] In just two years, from 2011 to 2013, its population shrank by around five hundred thousand. In some scenarios, as many as 40 percent of Japanese will be over sixty-five in just a few decades. This would be the largest peacetime demographic drop in modern world history.

The cause of the decline is simple: Japanese couples are having fewer children, and Japanese women are marrying later than ever before. Japan has had one of the world's lowest birthrates for decades, which first dropped below replacement level in the 1950s before temporarily recovering; it fell below the replacement rate again in the early 1970s and has not recovered since. In 1975, the fertility rate for women was 1.91 babies; by 2007 it had dropped to 1.34.[7] This has led to a natural increase rate of -0.1 percent. Calculations by demographer Nicholas Eberstadt indicate that in the half-century between 1947 and 1997, Japan's birthrate decreased by an astonishing 55.6 percent—a record unequaled in modern history.[8]

It is not merely that the gross numbers are decreasing. The average age of women having their first child rose from 25.6 years of age in 1970 to 29.4 in 2007. More dramatically, in 1970, half of all babies born in Japan were to women in their mid- to late twenties, while today, 36 percent of babies are born to women in their early thirties. Starting childbearing so late translates into fewer babies per female.

A few other fertility-related factors are rarely noted by outsiders, though they contribute to Japan's baby deficit. Japanese society still frowns on unwed mothers, and a stable, two-parent family remains the norm. Only 2 percent of Japanese births are to single mothers, versus 40 percent in the United States.[9] Teen pregnancy is almost unheard of and when it does happen, often results in a scandal. In addition, the country has a high divorce rate, having quadrupled in number in the half-century since 1960, and estimates indicate that over one in four marriages end in divorce.[10] But anecdotally, while it seems that a significant number of divorces among couples with children take place after the offspring have left home, Japanese government statistics show that the majority of divorces happen between five and ten years after marriage, possibly before such couples have children. While such cultural preferences help maintain Japan's social stability, they also depress the birthrate.

Statistics tell only part of the story. Sex, or the lack of it, is another, often hidden part. Surveys and studies suggest that young Japanese are simply not as interested in sex (and relationships) as either their global contemporaries or their predecessors. One recent poll revealed that 45 percent of women between the ages of sixteen and twenty-four "were not interested in or despised sexual contact."[11] Even higher percentages of men reported that they are not in, or rarely ever have, romantic relationships. Some of these young Japanese are celibate, some engage in fleeting sexual trysts, and others fuel the country's multibillion-dollar pornography industry.[12]

At a busy lunch counter in downtown Tokyo recently, I take the foreigner's privilege of engaging my countermate in conversation. A woman who, I learn, has just turned forty, Akiko is representative of her demographic group. Living with her parents, she works steadily as a temporary employee. She is comfortable in her material circumstance, like most urban Japanese. Yet when I ask her what is her greatest fear for the future, whether a sluggish economy or the fear of terrorism, she answers simply, "I don't want to grow old alone."

Long-term visitors to Japan sooner or later observe that there is an enormous cohort of unmarried women in their thirties, something that was unheard of a generation or two ago. Perhaps the lack of interest in sex is one reason that the average age of marriage in Japan is steadily increasing, up to 29.3 years of age for women and 30.9 for men.[13] This has led an entire generation of women to marry later, if at all. In the early 1970s, over one million couples wed annually; today under seven hundred thousand tie the knot each year, a drop of fully one-third.[14]

Those who remain unmarried are referred to as "parasite singles," since they often live at home with their aging parents.[15] Government statistics show that over thirteen million unmarried Japanese between the ages of twenty and thirty-four lived with their parents in 2013. A further three million unmarried Japanese between the ages of thirty-five and forty-four—a stunning 16 percent of that age cohort—also still lived at home.[16] These parasite singles not only earn less than their married counterparts; they purchase fewer durable goods because they are not buying houses, major appliances, or (often) automobiles. Still, they account for a significant segment of consumer spending on clothing and accessories, travel, dining, entertainment, and other services.

Parasite singles are just one end of the unmarried spectrum, however. Single-person households overall are increasing rapidly in Japan, from just six hundred thousand in 1975 to over four million today. The majority of these households consist of single elderly women who live alone until no longer able to care for themselves.[17] Ironically, then, Japanese domestic patterns flip over the lifespan of an individual: older adults live with their parents until they finally marry; once they become aged themselves, they often then move into their own grown-up children's homes near the end of their lives.

The wages of such demographic trends are now clear. Currently, a quarter of Japan's population is over sixty-five years of age, making Japan the world's most aged country.[18] Haruko Miyagiyama and the rest of her age group are often dependent for their housing and daily needs on a shrinking number of younger relatives, despite their government pensions. This aging effect is multiplied by the fact that Japan has the world's longest female life expectancy—eighty-seven years—of any major country, while male life expectancy ranks eighth, at eighty years.[19] Some segments of Japan's workforce dramatically reflect these trends; for example, the average farmer in Japan is now sixty-six years old.[20]

No modernized society has ever faced such a challenge. This growing social burden raises fundamental questions about how to maintain a labor force, ensure productivity and competitiveness, fund entitlement programs, and reshape society to deal with a majority-elderly population. With full basic pensions providing approximately $7,000 per year and social assistance totaling approximately $10,000 per year to over-sixty households, Japan's total social entitlements currently cost $250 billion annually.[21] These numbers, which will only grow in coming decades, create an unsustainable pressure on public finances.[22]

While clearly the most dramatic and challenging demographic issue for Japan, aging is only one of Japan's significant social changes. More and more young people are essentially opting out of education and careers. There is the strange, if minor, phenomenon of "shut-ins," usually young men, who spend months or even years inside their parents' homes, doing little besides watching videos and reading *manga* comic books.[23] More serious is the problem of what the government calls "NEETs": no education, employment, or training.[24] These are young people in their late teens and twenties (estimated a few years ago to number at least 640,000) who are not enrolled in any academic program, hold no job, and are getting no vocational training.[25] The proportion of young people working in low-skilled service jobs has also risen steadily through the past decade, but even now Japanese fast-food restaurants, for example, cannot fill all their vacant positions, a function of the combination of a declining birthrate and NEETs who opt out of the labor market.[26]

Such choices are not entirely surprising for a generation that has known little but political paralysis and economic stagnation. Where their parents saw Japan becoming a world power, today's Japanese youth have watched China's economy eclipse theirs and sense South Korea nipping at their heels.

Even those young Japanese who remain engaged in society appear to have turned away from the outside world. When I first lived in Japan, in the early 1990s, the buzzword of the day was *kokusaika*, or "internationalization." This meant in particular educational exchanges and a focus on foreign language study, as well as bringing in foreigners, especially from English-speaking nations. This attitude was in part a recognition that Japan at that time was a magnet for foreigners due to its economic strength.

Yet the number of Japanese students studying abroad, particularly at the undergraduate level, has plummeted since the 1990s and the bursting of the economic bubble. More than 40,000 Japanese students studied in the United States two decades ago, versus less than half that number today. In my time teaching at Yale, I encountered only a handful of Japanese students outside the professional and graduate schools. Nor was Yale exceptional; in 2010, just one Japanese student matriculated in the undergraduate class at Harvard.[27] Meanwhile, Chinese enrollment in American colleges rose 164 percent from 2000 to 2010. In 2013–14, almost 275,000 Chinese students, over 100,000 Indian students, and nearly 70,000 Korean students populated America's colleges and universities.[28]

It is probably an overreaction to suggest that this drop-off in foreign study portends an isolationist future for Japan, what some call the "Galapagos syndrome." The real danger is that coming generations will be less informed about the world; less comfortable participating in global economic, social, and political networks; and less fluent in the international language of English. That would make it far harder for Japan to maintain its international role in the face of increased competition from its Asian neighbors.

How will a developed, democratic country deal with unprecedented shrinking of its population, and the specter of hundreds of thousands of others dropping out of the labor force or turning their backs on the wider world? There have been few studies of how a smaller population affects business, society, or the military.[29] What path will Japan forge to maintain its standards of living? Perhaps it will become the world's first robotic country, with automatons doing everything from driving cars to cooking food; or even field the world's first robot military. Whatever path it chooses, it will become a model for other developed Asian societies.

Japan's economic success since 1945 makes it better placed than any other Indo-Pacific country to change the way it does business—but only if its politics rises to the challenge. It retains a highly skilled, universally literate workforce and an advanced technological base unmatched by most countries in the region. The danger is that both government and society have postponed tackling difficult decisions.

Take, for example, the debate over how to raise Japan's birthrate and whether to loosen immigration restrictions. No amount of government prodding has much changed the fertility rate, in part because of social resistance to working mothers or employer-provided childcare. Similarly, fears over the influx of foreign cultures have thus far hindered real immigration reform. No Japanese politician has found the courage to openly call for the loosening of immigration restrictions, yet the Japanese economy has long depended on foreign day laborers in construction and service positions.[30] Today, most convenience stores and fast food restaurants have several if not a majority of foreign workers. Even if winked at by employers and the government, this is not a tenable long-term solution to the problem of labor shortage. Prime Minister Shinzo Abe has called for a modest easing of the entry of skilled labor into the country, but not for permanent immigration.[31]

Yet this unprecedented challenge also offers opportunities. The question is whether Japanese society and its political leadership will be bold enough to embrace pathbreaking measures. Given its demographic plunge, Japan will be forced to innovate and liberalize in order to survive, but it has been slow to grasp the challenge of a radically different demographic environment.

There are only mild indications of change in Japan. For example, the question of how to keep an elderly population mobile is driving companies such as Honda to research self-directed vehicles equipped with radar, cameras, and lasers.[32] Similarly, while the elderly have traditionally lived with their extended families, Japan must now dramatically expand its assisted living and nursing home sector to provide more meaningful lifestyles for its legions of aged. That, in turn, could lead to significant economic benefits, from construction to the hiring of specialized caregivers to growth in the pharmaceutical industry. Yet such plans are just beginning to be drawn up, and those elderly who lack family support or are too weak to live on their own must contemplate moving into grim nursing homes like those that dotted America in the 1970s.

As for robotics, even though Japan already is the world's leader, its shrinking workforce will force it to invest even more heavily in this area, and in next-generation automated manufacturing processes. Its industrial base could even benefit from the need for unmanned defense systems such as remotely piloted aircraft and autonomous undersea vehicles, which are increasingly taking the place of humans in combat.

Accelerated robotics research is partly an attempt to get ahead of the demographic curve. Japan once relied on robots to automate expensive labor tasks and thus bring down production costs. Increasingly, the motive will be simply ensuring that production can continue.

My visit to Toyota's main automobile production plant, outside of Toyoda City, gave me a dystopian vision of Japan's future. While a few humans could be seen scattered throughout the enormous facility, the visitor gallery of the chassis assembly area resembled something out of *Terminator*. Dim light illuminating a steadily crawling production line was punctuated by silver and purple starbursts, as spindly mechanical arms dipped and whirled over the metal skeletons of car beds. It resembled a soulless ballet, and when the machines fell silent for a scheduled break period, I felt an inexplicable urge to applaud.

Both Japan and South Korea are racing to become the world leaders in robotics, and declining populations are increasingly part of the reason. The Japanese government has initiated a policy clumsily named the "Realisation of a Robot Revolution," which aims at doubling the size of the industrial robot market to 1.2 trillion yen ($11.2 billion) by 2020. Prime

Minister Abe also expects that demand for service industry robots will rise twentyfold in the same period, until it is as large as that for industrial robots.[33] Here is the path by which day-to-day life will change, though no one can say how. Already, robots are taking on customer service roles in stores, while in Nagasaki, the world's first robot-run hotel is using androids that work as maids, waiters, and reception attendants while speaking four different languages.[34] As much as it seems like science fiction, Japan's robotic future may also be the seeds of a national survival strategy.

Japan's demographic problems today will become those of South Korea, Hong Kong, Taiwan, and Singapore tomorrow. Each faces a similar demographic future. To take just one example, the direst scenarios for South Korea's population predict a drop from fifty million today to just ten million in 2100, thanks to a record low fertility rate of 1.19 babies per woman.[35] Morbid studies conducted by a parliamentary committee have actually calculated when the last South Korean will die (currently the year 2750). Such dystopian visions are beginning to find their way into public consciousness, though perhaps not fast enough to stave off encroaching problems.

Each of these countries has a fertility rate far below replacement level, but each is approaching the problem differently. Some will face significant social and economic dislocations but will have a good chance of surviving, thanks to long-standing immigration practices. Hong Kong and Singapore, for example, are relatively open despite recent attempts in both cities to restrict the inflow of unskilled labor. But neither South Korea nor Taiwan readily accepts immigrants. Seoul and Taipei will have to deal with the growing entitlement demands on the state and will be forced to rebalance domestic consumption away from areas like education toward more care for the elderly.

At the same time, they will have to deal with the socioeconomic changes driven by a declining population. Above all, they will need to focus on maintaining a labor force large enough to preserve if not expand their manufacturing output. Yet they, like Japan, will also face pressures on their rural and urban infrastructures, as a smaller population ultimately means abandoned villages and shrunken cities. In contrast to the last half-century's breakneck urbanization, the next fifty years will see cities shrinking, entire neighborhoods going dark, more expensive main-tenance thanks to a smaller labor force, and other issues no one has yet thought about. Rather than a *Blade Runner*–like vision of impersonal, neon-lit megalopolises filled with towering spires, Asia's urban future may more resemble retirement communities, uncrowded cities of elderly pensioners.

The social consequences of demographic decline are unknown, but states around the region have begun to follow the lead of Japan, which instituted a national healthcare service after World War II. Such programs are uneven and still evolving, and they only partly answer the larger ques-tion of what aged societies will look like. South Korea, for example, spends the least among developed nations on social entitlements, which account for just over 9 percent of GDP. Yet it ranks first in elderly pov-erty, with a stunning 48.6 percent of those sixty-five and older falling be-low the poverty line.[36] Such declines in living standards will become a major driver of economic and political change in South Korea, with the potential for social unrest if the needs of an aging society are not met.

One of the hallmarks of Asian culture is that the elderly are usually cared for by their extended families. This tradition helped preserve the social stability of Asian nations during the disruptive period of economic modernization and decolonization that followed World War II. Many ob-servers thought that this type of family structure reflected the veneration of elders and the sense of generational belonging in societies that derive many of their ethical beliefs from Confucianism. But as Asia confronts the twin problems of aging and economic slowdown, tradition will clash with the needs of today, and long-standing social patterns will be at risk of being overturned. Nowhere is this more evident than in China.

The Worst of Both Worlds: China's Coming Demographic Decline

Few bureaucrats make headline news around the world, but China's nondescriptly named National Health and Family Planning Commission did just that in late October 2015. An understated announcement released by the commission ended nearly forty years of one of the greatest social experiment in modern history: the infamous one-child policy. The world's most populous country finally admitted that it soon would begin shrinking, raising fears of economic decline and political instability.

Stroll through a park in Beijing on a Sunday afternoon, and you might be forgiven for briefly thinking that you are in Japan. The language is different and the surroundings are not as nice, but the overwhelming number of three-person families seems eerily familiar. Mother, father, and single child, all picnicking under trees or sitting on benches, just like their Japanese counterparts. The difference, of course, is that the Chinese for decades were forced to stop at one baby.

At the same time that the Communist Party was building up China's economic power, it was also creating numerous social problems, including a huge demographic one. While the world is finally becoming aware of the environmental and social costs of China's breakneck modernization, its demographic puzzle has been barely noticed by Western media or business: the world's most populous nation will soon face a demographic decline, thanks to the one-child policy instituted in the late 1970s. Popular demands for a better standard of living, greater mobility, and social safety nets will quite likely present the Chinese Communist Party (CCP) with its greatest challenge over the coming decades, as it will have to improve the nation's economic performance despite a falling population. Before we examine China's demographic future, however, it is worthwhile to take a brief look at just how dramatically life in China has changed in the last few decades.

A nineteenth-century British observer once said of the frenzied pace of change in Meiji Japan: "To have lived through the transition stage of modern Japan makes a man feel preternaturally old; for here he is in modern times . . . and yet he can himself distinctly remember the Middle Ages."[37] The same could be said of twenty-first-century China. Its modernization has occurred largely within a single generation.

In 1953, just 13 percent of China's people lived in urban areas. In the 2010 census, that figure stood at 49 percent and had grown by 13 percentage points in just the previous decade.[38] China's largest cities have exploded in size, and the country now boasts 170 cities with over a million people, as well as five with over ten million.[39] Shanghai holds close to twenty-five million inhabitants, while Chongqing, China's largest city, has over twenty-eight million.[40]

From Beijing down to the southern coastal city of Guangzhou, skylines have been transformed. Urban sprawl is no less stunning, as cities stretch for dozens of miles across the landscape, pierced by endless roads and highways. For people who visited in past decades, perhaps the most noticeable aspect of modernization is that China's tens of millions of bicycles have been replaced by automobiles. The once-iconic scene of thousands of people pedaling past the Forbidden City has given way to traffic jams worthy of Los Angeles or Atlanta. Car ownership reached 154 million vehicles in 2014 and is expected to grow for several more decades.[41] In response, China doubled the length of its roadways between 2000 and 2004 and now has the third-most miles of roads in the world.[42]

The newly mobile residents of China's large cities increasingly live like their counterparts in Japan, South Korea, and Europe. Gucci jostles with Zara in tony Shanghai neighborhoods, while fast food restaurants and coffee shops dot cities and towns. While shopping or eating, China's upwardly mobile are electronically connected to each other and the country's Internet. China had nearly one billion mobile phone users in 2011, with millions of new users signing up every month. Sina Weibo, the world's biggest social networking site, attracts a large percentage of China's nearly six hundred million Internet users.[43]

Urbanization in China will not slow down for several decades. The American Chamber of Commerce in Beijing expects that fourteen million people—1 percent of the rural population—will move to the cities each year through at least 2025. These expectations are one reason for the phenomenon of "ghost cities" mentioned in chapter 2, though the economic costs of building those cities have not yet been offset by the predicted urban migration. Betting on such an internal migration means that China's massive infrastructure and building projects will continue for another decade.[44] The demand for clean water, electricity, hospitals, supermarkets, and other amenities for urban living will be a major driver of China's domestic economic growth, but also a major political issue.

China's unprecedented growth has come at a horrific social cost that is just beginning to get serious attention. The political leadership of China, like Japan and South Korea before it, put economic growth far above environmental protection or health concerns, and the country now faces a catastrophically polluted countryside. Nearly all aspects of China's environment are affected, and the true economic and health effects are only now becoming apparent.

Pollution in China is now at an unsustainable level. The cost in lives and the cost of cleaning up China's ruined rivers, lakes, skies, and soil are staggering. Just as significant will be the economic cost of changing the way business is done in China to prevent further environmental destruction. While a risk region of environmental effects could easily be a separate part of our map (and therefore a separate chapter in this book), the clear and undeniable social and demographic consequences of pollution lead me to map it here.

The lack of industrial regulation, the burning of dirty coal, and the rapid growth in private ownership of cars have combined to create one of the world's worst air pollution problems. On one of my first trips to Beijing, as our plane touched down in early afternoon, the sky looked as though it was dusk, a phenomenon universally noted by visitors. The rare sunny and blue sky is avidly remarked on by everyone from shopkeepers to government officials—the latter, of course, off the record.

By some estimates, only 1 percent of China's urban dwellers breathe safe air.[45] During the winter of 2012–13, levels of the most dangerous type of particulate matter in Beijing's air were over twenty times the amount recommended by the World Health Organization.[46] Midday in Beijing looked like late evening, and residents were urged to stay inside. The massive scale of China's air pollution problem was dramatically exposed when Beijing was cleared of over one million automobiles for nearly a month before the start of the 2008 Olympic Games, creating a stretch of clear weather not seen in over a decade.[47] In October 2013, the city of Harbin in northeastern China, home to eleven million people, was essentially shut down for over a day because of smog that measured fifty times worse than the daily limit set by the World Health Organization.[48]

China's dark skies impose staggering demographic costs. As early as the 1990s, respiratory disease was identified as one of the country's leading causes of death.[49] Chinese environmental activists claim that in some of the most polluted cities, such as Guangzhou, residents' lungs turn black by the time they are in their forties. A 2007 World Bank study claimed that outdoor air pollution causes up to four hundred thousand premature deaths each year, and polluted air inside homes and factories causes another three hundred thousand.[50] A more recent study put the total number of deaths caused by air pollution at 1.2 million annually.[51] A 2013 study estimated that people in northern China have a nearly six-year drop in life expectancy due to pollution.[52]

Nor do China's citizens find much help in the ground. The water may be even worse than the air. Most of the country's water sources, from lakes to rivers, streams, and catch basins, are hazardous to human health. Industrial runoff, poor sewage treatment, and lack of adequate waste disposal locations, particularly throughout China's interior, have poisoned the country's water sources. Environmental groups such as Greenpeace accuse industrial concerns of dumping poisonous chemicals and other waste into rivers and lakes in and near cities. In March 2013, over three thousand dead pigs floated down a major river through Shanghai, leading to widespread fears of waterborne contamination from the carcasses.[53] Some rivers are so polluted that the fish in them have died, yet local populations still use them for washing clothes. The World Bank concluded in 2007 that sixty thousand deaths occur each year from diarrhea, cancer, and other diseases caused by waterborne pollution.[54]

One nonprofit environmental group claimed in a 2011 study that 39 percent of China's seven main river basins were too polluted for general use, including 14 percent that were unfit even for industrial use.[55] In twenty-six key lakes and reservoirs, only 42 percent of the total water was deemed fit for swimming and fishing, while 8 percent was unfit even for industrial use.[56] The World Bank estimates that the groundwater in half of China's cities is dangerously polluted.[57] That means that at least half of China's population lacks access to safe drinking water. In all, a quarter of China's water sources are too polluted for human use. The problem is growing despite government attempts to improve water quality.[58]

All this pollution is taking an enormous toll on China's citizens and its economy. The World Bank estimated that the health effects of pollution cost China's economy upward of $100 billion per year, or 3 percent of GDP.[59] Chinese business at home and abroad is also affected. Food safety issues, arising in part from lax regulation and in part from pollution, have damaged China's food exports. There was a particularly bitter spat with Japan in early 2008 after dozens of people were sickened by Chinese-produced dumplings contaminated with pesticides. Overall, as millions of Chinese continue to move to the cities, air quality worsens and local sanitation systems get overwhelmed, while back in the hinterlands, factories go on destroying lakes and rivers. Modernization clearly does not mean wealth for everyone in China, nor, despite the trappings of middle-income lifestyles, does it necessarily mean a healthier standard of living.

Not just the lives of those living, but those of future generations have been affected by political choices. China's leaders have created another looming problem that they cannot easily fix. Introduced at the same time as the environmentally deleterious economic reforms, the infamous one-child policy of 1979 was meant to control overpopulation in a country just beginning to develop a market economy. By some estimates, the policy has prevented as many as four hundred million births.[60]

The policy has always had numerous loopholes—those living in the countryside, or parents who are themselves single children have long been allowed more than one child—but it has been largely successful at the macro level. China's current fertility rate is around 1.56, putting it on par with Japan, South Korea, and Singapore.[61] The aggregate number of births in China in 2050 is expected to be 28.5 percent less than in 2000.[62] By then, China's median age will be just under fifty years of age.[63] Its population is expected to be some 2 percent smaller, and it will have more elderly than North America, Europe, and Japan combined.[64]

Finally acknowledging the disastrous consequences of the one-child policy, and increasingly worried about its economic prospects, Beijing made a startling about-face in October 2015 when it announced the end of the single birth restriction, and the right of all families to have two children.[65] Larger families, however, are still prohibited, and so the people of China continue to wait for their reproductive freedom.

Despite the change in policy, China's population will still begin its downward trend around 2025, and it is unclear if the loosening of the birth restriction will be enough to offset the social and economic stresses it has created. The effects of the one-child policy in the labor sphere are already apparent. In 2011, the total number of working-age Chinese dropped by almost 3.5 million.[66] Between 2012 and 2014, the labor force shrank by 9.6 million, and the steady flow of migrants into coastal manufacturing centers has begun to dry up, putting upward pressure on wages and straining development plans in the interior provinces, where the labor pool is becoming smaller. This trend will only add to wage pressures over time, making Chinese exports less competitive.

The future of China's labor market may already be visible. The country has employed over forty thousand North Korean workers in the past several years to help ease its labor shortage.[67] In coming decades, China may also become a magnet for cheaper labor from around Asia, reversing a 150-year trend of exporting its poor to developing economies, including to America in the late 1800s. Yet to make the country a welcoming place for foreign labor, the government will have to dramatically transform its residency and labor laws as well as deal with its citizens' endemic xenophobia. There are no plans currently to address such needs on a nationwide scale or much understanding of the social strains the large-scale importation of foreign labor may cause.

Demographic decline will bring host of other economic problems. It has become a cliché to say that the country will get old before it gets rich. China's ratio of retirees to workers will invert, as some estimates indicate that the number of twenty- to twenty-four-year-olds will be 50 percent smaller by 2050.[68] This will put increased pressure on the Communist Party to provide basic social services, such as health care, for elderly who because of the one-child policy do not have large families to support them. Like other countries, China is seeking to expand its social safety net, but the cost for a country of its size will be exorbitant. It is not difficult to imagine a future in which local and national leadership is challenged by dissatisfied workers as well as abandoned elderly in both cities and the countryside, leading to serious instability across the entire country. Here is where demographic risk abuts domestic political risk on our map. The question of how such risk may play out in domestic politics will be discussed in chapter 4.

China's demographic risk has another angle that Westerners visiting Beijing rarely see. Get out of the major cities, and you will soon notice that you are surrounded by far more men and boys than women and girls. The practice of selective abortion, intended to give families male children, has left China with a badly skewed sex ratio. Among major nations, only India is worse. Male children traditionally were prized for their ability to work on rural land, and females were seen as an economic drag. Chinese men today outnumber women by thirty-four million.[69]

A shrinking population will leave tens of millions of young men unable to find wives or partners.[70] While recent statistics suggest that the gap has narrowed slightly since 2008, the problem will persist for decades.[71] The potential dangers of a large group of young, unmarried, frustrated men are well understood. Petty crime, public disturbances, the spread of prostitution, and social alienation are all possible side effects, raising yet more risk of social instability. Governments throughout history have turned to foreign adventurism as a way to relieve social pressure at home. Doing this would pit China against its neighbors, a security risk that is mapped out in chapter 6.

In response to its demographic concerns, Beijing has begun to try to deflect future unrest. It now provides basic health insurance to nearly its

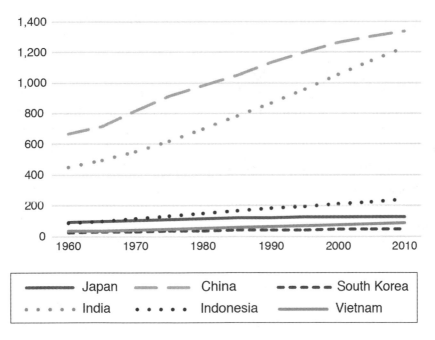

Population Growth in Asia, 1960–2010 (in millions). World Bank data. Artwork by Olivier Ballou.

entire rural population, a move being copied by other nations facing a rising demand for social services. China has only just begun basic planning for dealing with demographic change, and the process is hesitant, slow, and uneven. The same cannot be said of poorer nations whose growing populations are just beginning to move up the wealth and development curve.

Crushed by Fertility: India and Southeast Asia

The best way to get a bit of breathing space in downtown Jakarta is to go down to the waterfront and visit the old Dutch colonial settlement of Batavia, whose genteel nineteenth-century European architecture and relatively open spaces around former colonial government buildings make it a tourist magnet. Just off the main square, one can wander into decrepit Dutch houses and shops, now overrun by nature, some with giant trees arching up through broken roofs.

In one of these houses on a Sunday afternoon, I encountered a gaggle of photographers. They were all under forty years of age, and the subject of their attention was a group of even younger women, wearing skimpy dresses and heavy makeup, posing amid the ruins. I asked one of the photographers if this was a professional photo shoot. No, he answered, the men were just a group of friends who had come here because they knew these amateur models would be hanging out. Both the photographers and the models were doing something that is common in Indonesia: clustering in large groups. As I traveled around Jakarta, I began to notice crowds of adolescents and young adults gathering on sidewalks, in open spaces, and at restaurants. It is a world apart from the quiet, sometimes deserted streets of Japan.

India and Indonesia can give you a feel for the demographic crush of young Asia. These countries, as well as Vietnam, lie on the opposite end of the demographic spectrum from shrinking Japan and South Korea. Unlike China, they are decades away from a demographic slowdown. Instead, India and much of Southeast Asia face the risk of too many people. The pressures to provide education, jobs, and higher living standards for growing populations are immense. Many Asian governments facing this demographic increase have little expertise or capacity to deal with the needs of their citizenry.

Indonesia is the world's fourth most populous nation, with over 250 million people. Yet it has a per capita GDP of just $3,500. It struggles to catch up to its wealthier neighbor, Malaysia, or approach the political unity of Communist-run Vietnam.[72] With a median age of just twenty-nine, Indonesia faces enormous pressure to provide opportunity for the tens of millions of young people spread throughout its six thousand inhabited islands. While these age numbers do not match sub-Saharan Africa, where the median age can be as low as fifteen, Indonesians, like others among Asia's developing populations, increasingly have high economic, political, and social expectations.

Indonesia's democratically elected leaders have traditionally protected the economy from international competition so as not to see low-skilled agricultural or industrial jobs disappear. Over 40 percent of the population is employed in agriculture and the processing of natural resources for export. Along with Malaysia, Indonesia accounts for nearly all the world's supply of palm oil. Yet these are low-value-added activities. Officials I talked to in Jakarta, like their counterparts in Hanoi and Manila, are eager to develop a more educated population, so as to move up the production ladder. But the costs of improving the school system are prohibitive. A visit to Jakarta's leading university shows relatively modern buildings, but the professors there quickly let me know that most other colleges are not nearly as well funded or as well run. The demands of the agricultural sector, moreover, often mitigate against postsecondary education, as many youth from poor families are driven to enter the low-wage workforce.

Education is a major issue for Asia's demographically pressed developing countries. As a former professor, I made a point to visit as many universities as I could when I traveled throughout South and Southeast Asia. Many countries, notably India, maintain proud colonial traditions of higher education, but the institutions have struggled financially since independence.

While every official I met stressed his or her country's commitment to education, most have barely begun the task of building modern educational systems that will graduate workers able to take their place in the competitive global economy. Poor populations, underfunding, and the relentless focus on building export industries have diverted resources and focus away from higher education. One senses that particularly powerfully in Vietnam.

In Hanoi, I rode on the back of a motor scooter through heavily congested streets, my shirtsleeves sometimes brushing the sides of buses passing in the other direction. We passed what seemed like thousands of young Vietnamese sitting in cafés or hanging out in parks. This nation of ninety-four million people has a median age of twenty-nine, and the young are increasingly concentrated in the country's few large cities. On the way to the Vietnam National University, my guide took me to one of Hanoi's best-known coffee shops, on the second floor of an old colonial-era building, where raw egg is ladled onto hot coffee in a tiny demitasse cup. This has been a hangout for students since the war, I was told, and there were dozens of young people crammed into every corner, reading books, talking with friends, or texting on their phones. It looks and feels like a Berkeley hangout.

When we finally arrived at the university, it presented a vision totally at odds with the stated aspirations of the government. Hanoi might be aggressively pursuing more trade and foreign investment in order to become a major global economic player, but here, where the next generation of leaders is being educated, there were bare-bones buildings like something from Brezhnev's Russia, with students working on 1980s-era computers. Yet every inch of the small urban campus was crammed with bustling students. Restricted by the ruling Communist Party from teaching any potentially controversial political subjects, the university has the appearance of a technical campus in desperate need of resources.

Other national universities in the region, such as the University of Malaya or Universitas Indonesia, face similar problems of modernizing to serve growing student populations that by most accounts are undereducated at the primary and secondary levels. Even in India, with its vaunted technological institutes and venerable schools such as Calcutta's Presidency University, as much as 30 percent of the adult population is functionally illiterate.[73] This makes government modernization plans all the more difficult and retards the growth of national economies.

Like China, Southeast Asian nations are attempting slowly to build so
cial safety nets that may mitigate some of the future demands of their
young populations, in the absence of faster improvement in education or
labor opportunities. One major goal is to begin extending health insurance to almost all citizens. As noted by *The Economist*, this would make
welfare an integral part of the Asian state, raising questions about the financial liabilities governments are taking on just when they will also have
to expand their spending on infrastructure, education, and national defense.[74] Making such commitments, especially for a place with a growing
population like Indonesia's, will only add to the country's debt-to-GDP
ratio. Yet Jakarta's hopes of growing a larger middle class cannot be ful-
filled by an agricultural sector low on the value-added chain that mainly
provides low-paying jobs. Exactly the same problem confronts the Philippines, Vietnam, and other developing countries.

It is a situation that India, Asia's poster child for demographic pressure, knows all too well. Its population is predicted to surpass China's by
2022, according to the United Nations.[75] India's most recent census revealed an astonishing net gain of 180 million persons over the past decade. The world's largest democracy will soon be the world's most populous
nation.

While India's teeming slums are well known in the West from movies
such as *City of Joy* and *Slumdog Millionaire*, only a visit to the outskirts
of Calcutta, Delhi, or another major city can really bring home the enormity of the country's poverty and overpopulation.[76] "You don't want to
walk out there," my driver cautioned me, shaking his head from side to
side in the Indian way, as I climbed out of the car in a particularly congested slum inside Lucknow, the capital of Uttar Pradesh, the northern
state bordering Delhi. Piles of garbage marked the poorest areas, which
were strewn with rubble from which temporary housing was thrown up.
The site of a famous siege of a British colonial headquarters during the
1857 Sepoy Rebellion, Lucknow is a city of three million people, making
it modest by comparison to its giant neighbors like Mumbai. Its larger
counterparts have even worse slum conditions. In Calcutta and Chennai (colonial Madras), row after row of makeshift tents hugged crumbling
walls, their roofs jury-rigged from old carpets or plastic sheeting. I found

myself stunned that life can go on in such conditions, babies being born, families eating together, children playing.

Even outside the slums, life for many in India seems to be lived in the open, on the roadside. Barbers shave clients under the shade of trees while innumerable food and juice carts jostle with old men and women sitting on the ground surrounded by mounds of watermelons, mangoes, bananas, and other fruit, much of it rotting in the heat. Public wells are surrounded by women washing clothes and men washing their bodies. Open store-fronts and shacks crowd the roads selling every conceivable item, from san-dals to industrial fans encased in sheet-metal siding. Children run back and forth among the cars and sidewalk-dwellers, darting in and out of shanties that sit cheek by jowl just beyond the impromptu markets.

If the roadsides are pulsating, nothing can prepare one for the riot of cars, bicycles, scooters, autorickshaws, ox-drawn carts, pedestrians, and cows in the streets themselves. Tailgating and honking are so ubiquitous as to seem a part of nature. Families of three or four crowd onto motor-cycles, babies held in mothers' arms while toddlers sit in front of their driving fathers. Autorickshaws designed for a few people carry a dozen or more. Traffic rules are an absurd joke: lane markings are mere dec-orations on the pavement, and people turn wherever and whenever they like. At one point, while I was being driven on the highway, seeing a traffic jam ahead but having passed the exit to an alternate route, my driver simply turned the car around into oncoming traffic to go back to the off-ramp.

Amid the chaos, I was heartened by the energy put into daily labor, the continual striving to earn a few rupees. Even with moderate economic growth, India is expected to have a middle class of 583 million people by 2025, according to the director of the McKinsey Global Institute.[77] Such progress has its challenges, though, as it will put enormous pressure on New Delhi to create even more jobs, build better housing, and improve education, health, and other public services.

This is a staggering challenge. To take just the case of health care, Prime Minister Narendra Modi's budget for 2015 allocated only $5.3 billion, less than 1 percent of GDP, on health services. This is less than half of what even Russia spends.[78] A country of over 1.25 billion, India has just one doctor for every 1,400 people.[79] Modi's ambitious plans for universal public health coverage are running up onto the rocks of budgetary, bu-reaucratic, and social reality.

Standing out among all the problems besetting India, women face spe-cial challenges.[80] As in much of the developing world, women are seen mostly watching children or tending to domestic chores. Most of the offices, shops, restaurants, and bookstores I visited were staffed by men, who also act as drivers, waiters, hotel cleaners, and street stall operators. Many women find jobs as teachers in public schools, or as librarians and research scholars, like the ones I met while in Calcutta, but according to a 2015 study by the International Monetary Fund (IMF), India's female labor force participation rate stands at only 33 percent.[81] Not surprisingly, they also earn far less than men, and rural Indian women make less than $2 a day.

Violence against women is an endemic problem in India. The country was galvanized by the horrific gang rape and murder of a twenty-three-year-old student on a bus in New Delhi in December 2012. Such incidents are deplorably common in India. While I visited a few years ago, two young Muslim women who had eloped with Hindu men were murdered by their own mothers in an honor killing in Uttar Pradesh. While such crimes are increasingly in the public eye, other types of social pressure and discrim-ination against women remain pervasive and often hidden.

As in China, families in India routinely practice sex selection. The past decades have seen the birth of far more males than females, not only in poor areas but in richer regions as well, and the most recent census showed a widening of that sex imbalance despite the growth of the middle class. In most development models, as a country becomes richer, its sex ratio evens out. In India the gap has not narrowed, even though the rate at which it is widening did slow over the past decade. Today's sex ratio of 940 females to every 1,000 males ranks among the worst in the world.[82]

Despite this imbalance, India's colleges and universities are full of young women with professional goals. My first day in the country, at the height of a May heat wave, I visited the University of Madras, one of India's three oldest institutions of higher learning, and learned that over half of its four thousand undergraduates were female. When I reached Calcutta a week later, I stopped at the elite Presidency University to meet Professor Amita Chatterjee, then the vice chancellor of the university. Echoing the comments of her counterpart at Madras, Chatterjee told me that 60 percent of her three thousand undergraduates are women, and many of them do better than the men at their studies. Of the five hundred thousand applicants in India's national civil service examinations in 2010, for example, the top two slots were taken by women.

Yet when they have graduated, the talents of many of these young women are often not put to full use. "I'd like to be a sales manager one day," muses Sita, a young lady with whom I'm having coffee in one of Chennai's upscale hotels. "But my parents have arranged a marriage for me, and it will be finalized next year." Her disappointment is palpable, yet muted by the odd formality with which she describes her upcoming nuptials, a mood matching the sober if stylish sari she is wearing. Like many of India's young urban women, Sita is educated and holds a professional position, yet her skills and dreams come second to respecting her parents' wishes.

Similarly, when I ask a professor at the University of Calcutta what his female students will do after they leave the university, he shrugs. Some will get research jobs, he allows, but most will see their careers and aspirations ended by marriage. I met several educated young women in India, both Hindu and Muslim, who were willing to talk about their struggles to have a career in the face of family pressure to get married and start a family. Almost none of them felt they had any personal freedom to make a choice of marriage or a job, or even to influence the decision their families would make for them.

In some ways, India's women are better off than their counterparts in Bangladesh, Burma, or Laos, yet they share the same problems related to education, jobs, and family structures. There is no real movement for female emancipation in India, or throughout much of less-developed Asia. Paradoxically, the more these populations grow, the more intense the competition for resources, thus leading to pressure to have even more babies to provide in the future for the family. That keeps women out of the workforce and close to home, yet not only they feel the burden of ensuring family survival. Asia's broader social and demographic problems are also a burden to men, scraping by for a living, though they ostensibly are socially dominant.

The diversity of the Indo-Pacific's demographic picture can be grasped only sketchily in this chapter. Unlike economics or security, demographics is a less sexy subject for reporters and writers. Yet Asia's demographic challenges are an underappreciated risk, one that directly abuts other risk regions we explore in this book, specifically economics and politics.

What is clear is that whether in aging or youthful nations, Asia's demographic problems demand economic growth and more responsive governments. Yet the failures of economic reform we explored in chapter 2 make it ever more difficult to answer the needs of nations that have either too many or too few people. Without growth, however, tension from populations dissatisfied with their economic and social prospects has the potential to create political instability in countries throughout the region. It is to this risk area that we now turn.

4

ASIA'S MESDAMES DEFARGES

In the heart of Beijing's Forbidden City stands the Palace of Heavenly Purity, the mystical politico-sacral center of the traditional Chinese universe. The surrounding palaces shimmer in the summer heat, giving a sense of infinity to the smoggy horizon. Forgetting the crowds of tourists and the massive city beyond the walls, I feel as though I'm floating at the midpoint of the world. Visions of Bernardo Bertolucci's masterpiece *The Last Emperor* flash through my head, and I can almost see the toddler Puyi, the Last Emperor, playing hide-and-seek behind his massive throne just in front of me.

The vast area surrounding the Palace of Heavenly Purity is a triumph of architecture, urban planning, and political ideology. The Forbidden City was far more than a mere palace complex, more than simply the home of Chinese emperors for five hundred years. It was a symbol of a universal order that radiated from the emperor's throne, a comprehensive social and political system that encompassed civilized and barbarian alike, structuring the lives of hundreds of millions of people. In some ways, Asia has never recovered from the fall of Puyi during the Chinese Revolution in 1911. The political order that was taken for granted for centuries, often abused and ignored but never fully forgotten, was destroyed, leaving a vacuum throughout nearly half the world.[1]

The regional demographics that we explored in chapter 3 spill over directly into domestic politics. Next to the failure of economic reform, the political challenges facing Indo-Pacific nations are perhaps the largest risk area the region faces. How well its leaders deal with the demands of their populaces, be they modernized or developing, may be the most important factor determining the future of the Indo-Pacific.

The real risk from domestic politics in Asia can be boiled down to one idea: ever since the final Qing ruler abandoned his ivory-inlaid throne, Asia's political history has been one of unfinished revolution. From armed uprisings in Japan in 1867 and in China in 1911 and 1949, through decolonization in India in 1947 and in Southeast Asia in the 1950s, to peaceful popular revolutions in the Philippines in 1986 and in South Korea in 1987, Asian politics has been one of constant struggle.

It sounds odd to claim that Asia's future is still threatened by political revolution. After all, Japan seems an entirely stable mature democracy, and the Vietnamese and Chinese Communist Parties maintain an iron grip on power. But economic and social pressures inside all of Asia's countries threaten domestic political consequences.

Equally, to turn a popular advertising slogan on its head, what happens inside a country does not always stay there. An Asia whose political systems fail to provide stability, legitimacy, and growth is an Asia that will become increasingly troubled. The region's history is full of examples of domestic failure leading to wider dislocation.[2] At the same time, embattled regimes have regularly sought to defuse tensions at home by exporting instability abroad, even to the point of invading neighboring countries.

In looking at the trends in domestic politics throughout the Indo-Pacific region, this chapter will chart the challenges to democracy and authoritarianism alike. Few Westerners pay more than passing attention to Asia's politics. It sometimes may get a minute or two on the network newscasts, as when Thailand's military launched a coup in May 2014 or after the victory of Nobel Peace Prize winner Aung San Suu Kyi's democratic opposition party in Burma's November 2015 election. Yet precisely because so many are not paying sufficient attention, we should be far more sensitive to the hidden risks that roil domestic politics in the Indo-Pacific.

The question of domestic political stability leads to the larger issue of the future of politics throughout the region. Americans, whose nation originated in a war of independence from a European colonial empire, see the spread of democracy as a natural condition. They believe that, given the choice of self-determination or servitude, any people would prefer to choose their destiny.[3] Economic freedom and opportunity are believed to follow naturally from and be guaranteed by political freedom. The collapse of the Soviet Union and the rapid democratization of eastern Europe in the 1990s only reinforced the American belief in the ultimate victory of democracy.[4] While most Americans understand that political development is not that simple, the moral superiority of democratic governance remains an article of faith. Even in the face of frequent domestic political gridlock and economic crises, Americans still assume democracy is a universal good toward which most peoples on earth aspire. To acknowledge this ideological predisposition is not automatically to deny its validity.

Yet the Indo-Pacific continues to confound American understanding of the natural path of political development. From totalitarian North

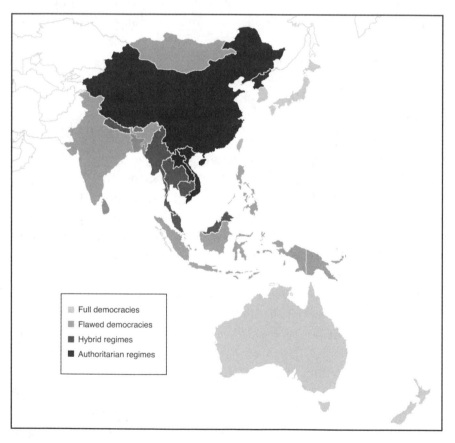

Full democracies
Flawed democracies
Hybrid regimes
Authoritarian regimes

Asian States by Regime Type. Artwork by Claude Aubert.

Korea to authoritarian China on one side of the spectrum and from India's dizzying democracy to Japan's often sclerotic politics on the other, Asia incorporates nearly every type of government known to humanity. Freedom and despotism continue to battle for Asia's political soul in another facet of unfinished revolution.

It is on this battleground that the future of the Asia-Pacific will take shape. If democracy proves successful at dealing with its domestic troubles, it will save its legitimacy, gain adherents, and more likely ensure that it becomes the norm throughout the region. But if smaller states waver in their commitment to democracy, the triumph of illiberal political regimes may be assured, and the influence of power politics correspondingly will grow.

Asia's political path forward seems to depend on whether China continues to grow at home and ultimately comes to dominate the region. That, in turn, depends on the strength of the Chinese Communist Party's (CCP) hold on society. As China's economic power has exploded, those concerned with democracy and freedom condemn its authoritarian nature, while others, like the columnist Thomas Friedman, celebrate its effectiveness and lament that America is not more like China.[5] Just as the Chinese economy faces major problems ahead, its political system must confront a host of serious challenges as it seeks to keep control over 1.3 billion people. A tour of China's political dangers is the first stop in this region of our Asian risk map.

Is China Near a Tipping Point?

"I can't give you a date when it will fall," a veteran China watcher tells me over dinner in Washington, D.C., "but China's Communist Party has entered its endgame." Such a bold prediction would be easy to ignore if its source were less experienced. While newspapers never tire of reporting that China now has the world's largest economy, the reality of its political challenges is only now becoming apparent. It is a country in stasis whose political risks are perceptibly growing.

Such beliefs are not restricted to foreign observers. "The party isn't everywhere, despite what you think," an official at one of the very few Chinese nongovernmental organizations (NGOs) dealing with labor issues tells me. "I'm not a member of the party. But the government *is* everywhere." Quietly summing up her frustration in a Beijing restaurant, she describes the lack of trust in Chinese society, the hopelessness of those trying to carve out small spheres of civil freedom, and the underlying fear and even hatred of the Communist Party.

Yet even this opponent of China's authoritarian system expresses pride in her country's economic prowess and the political respect China now commands. When I point out that this is due largely to the CCP, she nods her head. After a minute or so, she finally says, "Yes, but now we want change. China needed guidance, but now we want to make our own decisions. It's not democracy we need, but less control." It's a discussion that circles in on itself, logically inconsistent yet perfectly understandable in the context of today's China.

The People's Republic of China remains a mystery for many Americans, who know it mainly from headlines about its explosive economic growth and breakneck modernization. Yet it is, as one American academic put it, a "fragile" superpower.[6] As one peels back the layers of China's success, the brittleness of its repressive political system, the simmering dissatisfaction, and the extraordinary challenges it faces become ever more evident. For many who have dealt with China for years, sobriety long ago replaced euphoria, and China's future of risk is now glaringly evident.

Watching Chinese leaders on television, one would never think there was trouble. They seem so in control that their eternal rule seems assured, like the Qing emperor's in centuries past. Even the party's critics admire its discipline and stability. In November 2013, Xi Jinping became the latest general secretary of the CCP, and the following March, president of China. Along with Premier Li Keqiang, he heads the country's "fifth generation" of leaders. Starting with former paramount leader Deng Xiaoping, who took control of the country in 1978, China has transferred political power regularly every ten years since 1993. Unlike the contested succession for power after the death of Mao Zedong, the past two decades of political handovers have been peaceful, though not without friction between competing leaders.[7]

One reason for that stability is that since Deng's reign, the members of the Standing Committee, the CCP Politburo's highest decision-making body, have taken pains to act as a collective leadership. There are factions and fighting among them, but to the country and the world they present a bland, united front, often drawing criticism for lacking charisma and vision.[8] This may be changing, however, as Xi Jinping increasingly tests the boundaries of collective leadership, regularly overshadowing his colleagues. In just a few years, Xi has made himself China's strongest leader perhaps since Mao himself, one whose public persona grows every year.[9] Xi has encouraged attempts to describe him as China's "core leader," a symbolically potent term, and which indicates his predominance over all other top officials.[10] Newspapers laud his leadership to such a degree that some suspect another cult of personality is in the making. One of the greatest political risks China faces is the possibility that Xi will overturn the collective leadership model, ushering in a new era of strongman rule or unleashing a power struggle among the elites.

Yet even Xi is limited by political realities. The CCP's legitimacy derives almost solely from its ability to provide economic growth and rising standards of living for the millions of Chinese residing in large cities or along the country's coasts. Yet since the Tiananmen Square massacre of 1989, the party has become ever more isolated from the citizenry and is seen as corrupt, inefficient, and often brutal. Xi began his rule by trying to present a more accessible, family-oriented face to the Chinese people, even adopting the moniker "Xi Dada," or "Uncle Xi." Yet such efforts have done little to tame public dissatisfaction with the regime.

This dissatisfaction derives partly from the fact that life is so difficult for hundreds of millions of China's citizens. China remains a land of extremes. It now has more millionaires than any other country, but much of the rural populace lives in grinding poverty, as do many in the supposedly better-off cities. The country claimed 271 billionaires in 2010, but its nominal GDP per capita hovers around $7,600—and is much lower in the western provinces.[11] Furthermore, as we saw, China's demographic decline will hit the country though hundreds of millions of its citizens remain in poverty.

These issues present significant challenges for a Communist Party that is distrusted and disliked by the vast majority of the population. There is little reason to think that the party will somehow decide to democratize or reduce its social control as it attempts to deal with its economic and demographic challenges. History suggests the opposite. In the 1980s,

Deng Xiaoping carefully avoided copying the glasnost policy of Mikhail Gorbachev in the Soviet Union, so as to avoid losing control of the country's internal politics. Deng and his successors maintained a tight grip on political power and concentrated instead on building up the middle class while co-opting the educated and elite sectors of society.[12]

The moment of truth for the CCP was the 1989 Tiananmen Square demonstration, in which tens of thousands of university students and workers gathered just outside the gates of the Forbidden City, demanding political reform and liberalization. The party's decision in early June to send in the People's Liberation Army to put down the demonstration set China clearly on a path whereby economic reform was permitted but political dissent was not.[13] To this day, no one knows how many students were killed by army gunfire or crushed to death under the wheels of tanks and armored personnel carriers. What is abundantly evident, however, is that the CCP has seen little, if any, significant organized opposition since the massacre.

Today, over a quarter of a century after Tiananmen, it is only the rare political dissident in China who comes to the world's attention. Thousands more oppressed by the state are left to wage their battles alone. Yet that does not mean that China's discontented are entirely powerless. They have little chance of affecting national politics, but their activism and opposition to the CCP are of grave concern to Chinese leaders in the Zhongnanhai fortress next to Tiananmen Square, who fear that uncontrollable forces could result in mass unrest. They have reason to be worried: each year brings, on average, 180,000 reported demonstrations against the party, ranging from a handful of people in rural villages to hundreds or thousands on the streets.[14] Those activists, however, will almost never speak to foreign visitors, even if they are involved with one of the country's few monitored NGOs. Fear of official reprisal keeps China's discontented largely isolated from the broader international community of human rights or legal activists.

Despite constant official harassment, the sheer variety of protest in China reveals many of the problems the CCP faces. Government incompetence, elite corruption, refusal to grant more autonomy, and the suppression of ethnic minorities all fuel resentment that risks possible upheaval.

Maybe we should begin charting the country's domestic political risk map by defining China as a political entity.

Westerners usually don't think of China as an empire, but what we today call "China" is the product of centuries of ethnic Han encroachment on and assimilation of other nationalities.[15] China is an uneasy collection of distinct regions with strong local identities and customs, where nearly 300 languages and dialects are spoken. What binds them all together is unwavering central control, driven by Beijing's fear that the country's imposed unity would be shattered should these various nationalities assert their independence.

Next to calls for more democracy, perhaps the clearest political redline for the Chinese government is the issue of regional autonomy. Beijing remains unshakably committed to preventing any geographic area from splitting from the country at large. This dynamic drives the government's policy toward Taiwan, Tibet, and Xinjiang, and is rooted in the knowledge that these regions would readily sever ties with Beijing if they could. A China riven by fissures among its parts is the central leadership's greatest fear.

Westerners who work or travel in China cluster in familiar, developed areas, such Beijing, Shanghai, and the eastern coast. Yet the country stretches for more than 3,000 miles westward across the Eurasian landmass. Along the fabled Silk Road in China's remote western regions, far from the centers of power in the country's east, Beijing's control is tested amid constant ferment. Here, China's imperial project has run into longstanding opposition from formerly Muslim majority regions that border central Asia. While there may be up to twenty million Muslims throughout China, they are concentrated in just a few provinces, primarily Xinjiang, Gansu, Ningxia, and sparsely populated Qinghai. Since 9/11, Beijing has feared religiously inspired opposition to its secular Communist control and oppression of local communities.

The key flash point is Xinjiang, once known as Turkestan, in the country's northwest.[16] Recent years have seen numerous clashes between ethnic protesters in Xinjiang and internal security forces. Locals claim that dozens, if not hundreds, of protesters have been killed by the Chinese, most recently in June 2015.[17] The Turkic Muslim Uighur minority is at the epicenter of this resistance, which has spread outside the borders of Xinjiang itself. In October 2013, resistance struck the heart of Chinese power when a car bomb detonated in Tiananmen Square. Chinese authorities accused five Uighurs of carrying out the attack, which killed five people. Radical Uighurs also went on a rampage at a railway station in the western city of Kunming in March 2014, knifing to death twenty-nine commuters; almost exactly a year later, ten more train passengers were cut down by knife-wielding attackers at a station in eastern Guangzhou.[18] The central government's repression of these western provinces, which the militants use as justification for their acts, is abetted by their isolation from the coastal region, and restricting the flow of information from them ensures that the government's actions are hidden from outside eyes.

The unrest among Uighurs is an extraordinarily sensitive issue for the government, almost as explosive as the question of Tibet, which has been under de facto martial law for decades. In this romantic, mountainous region, another religion struggles against Communism. Home of the world's most famous Buddhist monastery, in Lhasa, and a favorite cause of Hollywood celebrities, Tibet has been under Beijing's firm control since an aborted rebellion in 1959. In recent years tension and violence alike have increased. Since 2009, over one hundred Tibetans have immolated themselves protesting Beijing's tightening control. The exiled Dalai Lama continues to draw attention to the Tibetan occupation, further straining relations with the central government. In 1995, he caused a minor crisis by selecting a successor for one of Tibetan Buddhism's highest lamas (the Panchen Lama) without Beijing's approval, thus raising fear in the capital of revived separatist feeling. While the Dalai Lama may be a global media star, it is ordinary Tibetans' resistance to Chinese control that has led to abuses by central security forces, including widespread surveillance, torture, and imprisonment.[19]

The antigovernment movements in both Xinjiang and Tibet raise the specter of uprisings by other nationalities inside China. In response, Beijing has essentially imposed martial law and news blackouts in other far western regions. Foreigners who try to visit Xinjiang often find their visas denied.[20] Even writing about the tensions there can get one onto Beijing's blacklist. The lengths to which the Chinese government will go to silence dissent on Xinjiang was shown by its September 2014 decision to impose a life sentence on Ilham Tohti, a Uighur academic and activist who, though opposing Xinjiang separatism, had criticized Beijing's heavy-handed response to the previous year's Tiananmen Square car bombing.[21]

Beijing's fear of autonomy or independence movements is not limited to underdeveloped western regions of China. Even in the most cosmopolitan parts of China, opposition to any type of independence is sufficient to cause the Chinese leadership to crack down and even break international agreements. In September 2014 the government announced that Hong Kong voters would not be allowed a free election for their next chief executive, which had been scheduled for 2017. This decision repudiated China's 1984 joint declaration with Great Britain which was intended to govern the status of Hong Kong after the 1997 transfer of the colony back to Beijing. It also sent a clear message to Xinjiang, Taiwan, and other regions that in Beijing's calculation, central control would always trump local rights. Given Hong Kong's international status as a showcase for capitalism, the government's action attracted global attention, though only mild condemnation.

China's decision set off weeks of student-led demonstrations that occupied much of Hong Kong's business and government district in October 2014. The police used tear gas against the protesters and arrested hundreds, while pro-Beijing agitators were filmed attacking the peaceful students.[22] Meanwhile, Hong Kong's business community, irked by the disruption to commerce caused by the "Occupy Central" movement, sided with the government against the students. In the end, police cleared out protesters and tore down their barricades and tent cities, even as students vowed to continue their protests, which they did sporadically in 2015.

Hong Kong's pro-democracy movement riveted the world's attention but did nothing to shake Beijing's influence over the island's government or weaken its determination to restrict political liberalization. Hong Kong is a particularly sensitive issue because it, too, combines the questions of democratization and territorial cohesion. Beijing's ruthless attitude was underlined in late 2015 and early 2016 when five Hong Kong booksellers who had published works critical of Xi Jinping and the party went missing, two of them in Thailand. Suspicion that Chinese authorities had ordered them abducted seemed confirmed when one of the publishers, who also held British citizenship, appeared on Chinese television to ritually deny that he had been kidnapped. The affair may have reeked of Cold War–era skullduggery, but it revealed the brutal methods Beijing was willing to employ even outside its own borders to clamp down on criticism of the party and government.

Keeping its diverse land unified under central control may be a priority for China's leaders, but geography is only one element of political risk. Another danger to political stability is the culture of Chinese governance. A party that has held onto power by proclaiming its success in modernizing and developing China loses its legitimacy when it is seen as incompetent or unable to respond to crises, not to mention openly brutal in its suppression of criticism.

A powerful example of social discontent came in May 2008, when rural Sichuan was devastated by an earthquake that killed nearly seventy thousand people.[23] In the days following the disaster, public outrage erupted over lax construction standards that were blamed for building collapses. Shoddy construction led to the collapse of several schools, killing an estimated ten thousand children; worse, the local government was later accused of bribing or intimidating distraught parents to drop any claims against the state and to stop making public statements critical of government officials.[24]

In similar fashion, a high-speed rail crash in Wenzhou, in eastern China, in July 2011 killed forty passengers and injured nearly two hundred. In the highly publicized aftermath, the party faced intense criticism for trying to cover up the accident by hurriedly shutting down the crash investigation and burying the crumpled rail cars even before all the victims' bodies were recovered.[25] Such callous high-handedness has undermined public support for the intertwined party and government, leading both officials and citizens increasingly to hold an us-versus-them mindset.

Yet anti-party protests also occur for more traditional reasons, such as the desire for more responsive and competent governance. For example, in late 2011, Wukan, a city of twenty thousand people in southeastern Guangdong Province, revolted over a land dispute and the local government's choice of a new administrator.[26] The townspeople barricaded the village off from the outside and declared their independence, holding off officials for several weeks until the regional party office relented and allowed the town more latitude in selecting officeholders. Not surprisingly, such victories are rare. Few groups reach a sufficient level of organization to effectively push for their rights or get abuses corrected. Usually, local government officials are able to overwhelm and suppress any significant opposition without real disturbance to the political system, if needed with the help of police and paramilitary units.

Similarly, Xi Jinping has unleashed a wave of repression against urban activists and nongovernmental organizations, shuttering some, while capriciously arresting legal advocates and others pushing for moderate reform. Many Chinese visitors abroad now privately describe the atmosphere of fear pervading the country, and argue it is the most repressive Beijing has been since Tiananmen Square a quarter-century ago.

It would be a mistake to think that only the dispossessed are unhappy with CCP rule. Though the party has tried to co-opt social and economic elites over the past decades by giving them preferential treatment and allowing them to amass enormous fortunes, it remains distrusted by the privileged, even more so as Xi cracks down on any type of dissent. Both the middle class and the rich make their dissatisfaction felt in different ways. Numerous media outlets have reported, for example, that the overwhelming majority of China's rich, including members of the elite National People's Congress, hold foreign passports for themselves and their families.[27] The same elites send their children to foreign schools, often in America and Great Britain, where many choose to buy residences and live at least part-time.

Investing in overseas property is also a way for the rich to protect their assets from the government. In just one calendar year, from March 2013 to March 2014, Chinese buyers spent $22 billion on U.S. real estate.[28] Polls indicate that nearly half of China's millionaires living on the mainland planned to move overseas by 2020, while more than a quarter of those worth at least $16 million (100 million RMB) had already done so.[29] Such actions reveal a corrosive cynicism at the heart of Chinese society. Even those who have benefited most from the unequal system do not feel their wealth is safe, nor do they see a productive future in China for themselves and their families.

The middle class has a different set of grievances. What particularly undermines support for the government among ordinary citizens is the awareness that modern China is built on graft and corruption. An avaricious nexus of government officials and economic elites squeezes the middle class, for whom trying to operate a business or get help from local governments means under-the-table payments, trumped-up regulation, and worse. Bribes, kickbacks, and shady dealings pervade economic and political life in China. From the local village headman to the highest reaches of the party's Standing Committee, the underside of China's economic miracle is the amassing of fortunes for a few and the disempowerment of tens of millions.[30] There is no way to know the true level of corruption, but several recent glimpses into the personal lives of top Chinese officials have revealed hedonistic excesses and almost untrammeled power.

Just months before he stepped down as China's second-most-powerful official in 2013, the then prime minister Wen Jiabao was reported to have used lucrative economic connections and preferred treatment from the government in the awarding of no-bid contracts to build a family fortune of nearly $3 billion.[31] Wen had cultivated an image of a down-home, folksy "uncle" whose main concern was the welfare of the Chinese people. Once his vast wealth was exposed, the hypocrisy of his public persona caused a wave of cynical reports inside the country and out, blasting the lifestyle of top leaders. Stung by the exposé and resulting condemnation, the Chinese government harshly criticized the foreign reporters responsible for the story.

Even more sensationally, the political dismissal of a major Communist Party boss and the murder trial of his wife in the summer of 2012 drew back the curtain on the seamy and sometimes fatal underside of power in China. Until his stunning fall from grace, Bo Xilai was considered a candidate for China's highest council of power, the Standing Committee of the Communist Party Politburo, and was party boss of Chongqing, China's largest city. A populist who favored Mao-era slogans, Bo was suddenly dismissed from his posts for suspected abuse of power after his former police chief fled the city amid tales of skullduggery.

That alone would have been shocking enough, but then the news took on the aura of a spy drama. Bo's wife was arrested and convicted of the murder of a British business associate who had worked as a middleman for the family, providing access for foreign companies and introducing the couple to social and political elites abroad. Reports that Bo and his wife had accepted a $3 million French villa and that their son drove a Maserati and was sent to Harvard to study fueled further outrage. Bo was convicted of criminal activity and sentenced to life in prison, but most in the middle class believed that Xi Jinping and the rest of the party leadership were merely protecting themselves from a potential power grab by a popular politician. The revelation that a web of connections had allowed Bo to amass a fortune and control hundreds of millions of dollars was taken as confirmation that China's leaders regularly abuse their positions for personal gain.[32]

As the Bo drama and the reporting on Wen revealed, corruption is perhaps the greatest threat to the party's remaining legitimacy. Scholar Minxin Pei calls it the "glue that holds [the party-state] together."[33] On assuming the presidency in 2013, Xi made cleaning up corruption his first priority. Indeed, the CCP has instituted numerous purges of corrupt officials over the years, particularly after the 2003 SARS debacle, in which senior party officials were accused of hiding information about the influenza epidemic. Since 2008, the party has penalized nearly 670,000 persons for "discipline violations," and over one hundred thousand officials were punished in Xi's first year in office alone, with thousands more under investigation.[34] Yet doubts about Xi's intentions and prospects for success are rife. Many believe his primary concern is to shore up his own political position and remove any potential challengers to his power; others assert that no crackdown can deal with so massive a problem that goes to the very core of party power.[35]

This points to a yet larger political problem. In recent years, technology has made it harder for the party to control the news or suppress information about the inequalities in China. There are an estimated 688 million Internet users in China, and competition among service providers is intense, as are government attempts at censorship. Sina Weibo was once the country's dominant digital provider, claiming an astounding six hundred million users, many of whom used its offerings to trade news and gossip that the government wanted buried. By 2014, Sina Weibo had dropped down to just sixty million subscribers, as other platforms gained popularity, even though Chinese Internet usage continues to grow at nearly 10 percent a year.[36] While good economics, it makes for bad politics, at least from the government's point of view.

China's ubiquitous social media play a major role in spreading information about scandals such as the Bo case or the Wenzhou rail crash. The government makes repeated attempts to censor information, hamstring search engines, and shut down sites it considers dangerous. In response, China's users resist through microblogging and tweeting. More recently, the government has tried to prevent citizens from using virtual private networks (VPNs), which can break through official firewalls to overseas social media sites like Google and Facebook.[37] These overt attempts at online censorship reveal a party nervous about what its citizens can know and share.

The lack of trust between citizen and state is probably the single greatest risk to the CCP's continued rule. Francis Fukuyama has identified "social trust" as the core ingredient for the development of successful, modern liberal nations. Government transparency, an independent legal system, and private civil society bonds increase social trust, allowing people to believe in their government and communities and to take entrepreneurial and social risks.[38]

All that is sorely lacking in today's China. Visitors to Beijing or Shanghai see modern cities of soaring glass skyscrapers, and the more adventurous may briefly wander around some of the less prosperous parts of these cities. They are taken to world-class factories and educational institutions, and are often treated by government officials as VIPs worthy of personal conversations in cavernous meeting rooms. The official China shown to visitors is one where the trains run on time and business can be done.[39]

But if you try to talk with ordinary Chinese, whether in universities, NGOs or businesses or on the streets, you quickly sense a deep cynicism that brings to life the middle class's acidic comments in social media and explains the rush by China's rich to secure foreign passports. It is not merely distrust of the party and the government, but rather a deeper absence of the normal social bonds that undergird an effective community. Omnipresent security forces and the knowledge that authorities are monitoring conversations add to the sense of permanent oppression. Beijing's wealthier areas, where the elites have successfully cocooned themselves from the resentments and demands of the struggling poor and uncertain middle class, can have the feel of dancing on a bubble. As a visitor, I had an uneasy sense that the hard shock of revolution or even revolt could sweep these precarious elites away in the chaos of a failed society.

Given all these risks, not to mention its literate, hardworking populace, why hasn't China developed a reform movement that could exert enough pressure on the government and the party to secure some liberalization and thereby possibly relieve some of the growing frustration in society?[40] Fundamental change in China would likely require the emergence of several different grassroots movements, from Western-inspired liberals to nationalists and regionalists interested in breaking up the unitary state. In a country where the gulf between elites and commoners remains so large, the lack of even moderate political reform raises the risk of unleashing widespread disorder and competing ideologies, not unlike that during the Chinese Revolution of 1911.

This situation leaves China in political stasis. The party cannot evolve without risking its hold on power. Yet the longer it resists change, the more dissatisfied the people become and the more sclerotic its governance. It is hard to see how the party can maintain control over the long term without becoming even more repressive, even though such repression could easily spark the unrest that might sweep it from power. Thus the comment I heard in Washington that the party is entering its endgame. It might take decades, but social repression and economic challenges are funneling it down an increasingly narrow path. China's unfinished revolution and the risk of massive social instability will keep it and Asia on edge for decades.

Democratic Doldrums: The Risks of Mature Democracies

Is Asia's future inevitably Chinese? To read the past decade's newspapers, one might think so. When popular Western writers downplay China's government repression in favor of its economic successes, the message is that however unpalatable, this is the right path for the Indo-Pacific.[41]

There is another option. The alternative to Chinese-style authoritarianism is democracy, in all its imperfection. Creating and nurturing liberal domestic political systems is a difficult and complex task, involving many trade-offs and inefficiencies. Asia's stable democracies, like those throughout the world, are those that willingly chose that path. None had it imposed on them, and even Japan, which had its current political system mandated by America in 1945, was a democracy before the war. Some continue to qualify Asian liberalization, using terms like "Confucian democracy" to explain Asia's unique democratic path.[42] Where the academic debate falls short, however, is in describing how even Asia's liberal successes are at risk from challenges that threaten democracy's future stability.[43] To assess such a claim, we turn to what many consider Asia's leading democracy, Japan.

In a coffee shop in Tokyo, an educated midlevel business executive in his early thirties sighs as he stirs his drink. "We are very comfortable, but there's no real future to look forward to," he tells me. "China is already ahead of us, and our politicians can't figure out how to change things. Even [Prime Minister Shinzo] Abe[44] is mostly just words. Why even try to participate?" After two decades of economic stagnation and political gyration, his pessimism is widespread and only partially dispelled by the activist administration of second-time premier Abe.

Even with the risks of economic stagnation and demographic decline discussed in the last chapter, few observers believe Japan is heading for significant social or political instability. Yet my friend's pessimism, which is hardly unique, presents a long-term danger to Japan's body politic. Just like its economic system, Japan's political system appears too rigid to deal meaningfully with the country's problems. This failure undermines citizens' confidence in democracy, even though no one expresses a desire to give up their freedoms. Instead, many Japanese simply lack passion for the political process and feel a sense of hopelessness. Consistently low voter turnout is but one sign of their growing political apathy among a people at once largely content with their material conditions yet worried about the future.[45]

There was a time, not long ago, when many around the world assumed Japan would supplant the United States as the leading global power.[46] For some, Tokyo stood for everything hip and modern. For others, it hinted at a fantastical, *Blade Runner*–like future. Japan's success in rebuilding from the devastation of World War II made it Asia's leading nation. From bombed-out cities and black markets, it built the world's second-largest economy by the 1980s, turning itself into the model of democratization and modernization.[47] Once its bubble popped, life in Japan did not get noticeably worse, but the country struggled to regain its political confidence as much as its economic strength.

For a while in the early 2000s, Japan seemed to have turned the corner, thanks to the unique leadership style of Junichiro Koizumi. Koizumi became the country's prime minister in 2001 and served for a half-decade, becoming one of postwar Japan's longest-serving leaders. A maverick and radical politician with wild, wavy silver hair and a penchant for Elvis Presley, Koizumi was unlike anything the country had ever seen. He was intent on reforming the economy and making Japan a more powerful and respected player around the world. *The Economist* called him "the man who remade Japan."[48]

For all his uniqueness, Koizumi was part of a much larger evolution in Japanese domestic politics, albeit a peaceful and seemingly sedate evolution. For much of its postwar history, democratic Japan was in essence a one-party state, ruled since 1955 by the Liberal Democratic Party (LDP), the party to which Koizumi belonged. The country's domestic political gyrations began in 1993, when the LDP briefly lost power to a coalition of opposition parties. While the LDP soon restored its position through a series of its own coalitions, Japanese politics were roiled over the next two decades by growing voter dissatisfaction over economic stagnation, leading to the formation and dissolution of numerous small parties and the slow crumbling of the LDP's primarily rural voter base.

Despite Koizumi's efforts, the go-go Japan of the 1980s never returned, and a string of failures among LDP prime ministers finally upended the ruling party in 2009. The new power, the upstart Democratic Party of Japan (DPJ), at first seemed to be a breath of fresh air, promising a bold plan for revitalizing the economy and society.[49] Yet the DPJ soon found that ruling was far harder than campaigning. Its first two premiers each resigned within a year of taking office, its reform plan never materialized, and its response to the 3/11 earthquake and nuclear disaster was widely criticized. Within just two years, the party of the future had become the party of incompetence.[50]

In December 2012, only three years after taking power, having failed to deliver on its campaign promises, the DPJ was thrown out of office in

as big a landslide as that which had brought it in.[51] The LDP returned
with a massive mandate. Even more surprising was the leader who brought
it back from the wilderness: Shinzo Abe, whose precipitous resignation
in 2007 after just one year in office set the stage for the succeeding years'
upheaval.

While Abe returned almost immediately to his favored project of building Japan's military strength so as to play a larger role both regionally
and around the world, his greatest challenge remains reviving Japan's
economy and ending the country's sense of drift and malaise. Touting his
economic reform program as "Abenomics" and increasing Japan's diplomatic activity abroad were designed to send a message of purpose, power,
and optimism. Yet years of crony capitalism, economic distress, and the
emergence of China as the world's second-largest economy have created a
social malaise not easy to dispel. As the comments of my coffeehouse acquaintance reveal, Japanese still suffer from an identity crisis after having
once seen themselves as the benchmark of Asia's political and economic
development.[52]

Amid all the strengths of a socially stable, highly educated, culturally
and ethnically homogenous society, Japanese are growing undeniably pes-
simistic about the future and cynical about politics. Not a small part of
that comes from its declining birth rate and the successes of its closest
neighbors. Talking to Japanese young and old alike, they express the fear
that their country faces seemingly unsolvable problems that could con-
sign it to permanently reduced power and influence. A government that
cannot figure out how to mitigate its ongoing demographic decline is flirt-
ing with economic and social disaster. Combine that with the extreme
pessimism of Japanese youth, and doubts about the shape of Japan's future
do not seem out of place.

Underneath all this, the fundamental source of Japan's malaise is simple:
the country's leaders have failed to give its citizens a compelling vision
of their future in which economic health is restored and Japan plays
an important role in the world. Nor have academics or business leaders
stepped into the gap. The days when an Akio Morita, former chairman of
Sony, could symbolize the country's can-do spirit are long gone. There is
instead in Japan a complex intermingling of satisfaction with a too-stable

status quo and concerns about the lack of dynamism and direction for the future.

It is precisely this gap in political imagination that Prime Minister Abe sought to fill on his return to power in 2012. Yet Abe's openly expressed nationalism and apparent questioning of Japan's guilt over wartime atrocities make him a controversial figure.[53] As we shall see in chapter 5, his plans to increase Japan's military activities abroad and his December 2013 visit to the controversial Yasukuni Shrine threw Japan's relations with China and South Korea into a deep freeze from which they only began to recover with his formal apology for wartime comfort women at the beginning of 2016. The tight connection between domestic politics and foreign policy often puts the two at odds with each other. Abe's attempts to give Japan's citizens a sense of purpose have at times come at the risk of isolation from its neighbors. His historical perspective, moreover, has deepened domestic splits between the left and the right.[54]

Adding to concerns is the feeling that Abe, for all his limitations, has no obvious successor. Revered or reviled, he is the only politician in mid-2010s Japan with national stature and a comprehensive if idiosyncratic vision. This increases the concerns many Japanese have about the dynamism of their political system. The lack of popular leaders other than Abe does not make people confident about the country's ability to resolve difficult political issues once he is off the stage. His successor could easily be the type of colorless bureaucrat who occupied too much of Japan's postwar history. Nor has the rump DPJ recovered any of its popularity or provided an even modestly compelling alternative vision for Japan that might lead to a real two-party system. To a disturbing degree in the mid-2010s, in Japan, *l'etat c'est Abe*.

As committed to democracy as the Japanese are, their pessimism suggests a future in which ever-larger segments of the population give up on political participation. That may ensure decades of continued rule by the LDP, but it means that the give-and-take of democratic governance will be weaker, as will the robust sense of choice among competing political alternatives.[55] Already, Japanese voters have not shown a preference for a stable, two-party parliamentary order, but seem content with one party or another having a dominant position. This will make it even harder for future governments to hold the types of national discussions needed to come up with and implement difficult policies designed to care for the country's aging population or keep it competitive. In all this, however, Japan is not unique but simply ahead of some of its neighbors.

Gyeongbokgung Palace sits majestically at the head of one of Seoul's widest boulevards, a testament to Korea's past tragedies. First built in the late fourteenth century, it was abandoned for hundreds of years and then rebuilt in 1895 before being largely destroyed during the Japanese occupation of Korea. Recent decades have seen a large-scale restoration of the palace complex, but it remains a reminder of the bitter history between Korea and Japan, and Korea's repeated recovery from adversity.

Despite their fraught history, South Korea and Japan share numerous similarities. Both are democracies, and South Korea has appeared even more politically stable and dynamic than Japan in recent years, thanks in part to its presidential system that ensures a six-year period of political continuity for each administration. The world watched transfixed in the late 1980s as widespread student protests forced the country's authoritarian military rulers to agree to hold democratic elections and to free political prisoners.[56] Since then, South Korea has been a model of liberal democracy and has grown far more integrated into regional and global politics. Yet amid these successes, it struggles politically to balance the older generation's strong liberal tendencies with its children's political apathy.[57]

While its democracy is now deeply rooted, South Korea faces challenges that could lead to greater political discord and threaten its future. Perhaps the biggest risk is corruption, an endemic problem in a society still based in part on familial links. Corruption is well known in the corporate world, but it remains a major issue in public life, and scandals regularly consume politicians. The most spectacular recent example was the scandal that ensnared former president Roh Moo-hyun, who served from 2003 to 2008. Roh was a populist who emerged from the left-wing student movements of the 1960s. He pursued a controversial foreign policy of reaching out to North Korea while rhetorically distancing himself from the United States. After being investigated for presidential bribery after leaving office, Roh committed suicide by jumping off a cliff near his home in May 2009, shocking the nation.

Roh's successor, Lee Myung-bak, roared into office in 2008 based on his success as CEO of Hyundai Engineering and Construction, and later as mayor of Seoul. Though nicknamed "the bulldozer" for his ability to get things done, he, too, found running a national government far more difficult than ruling a boardroom. He managed a generally positive economic record and made efforts to raise South Korea's international profile but left office in 2012 with approval ratings under 20 percent—in no small part because he, too, became enmeshed in corruption scandals involving family members and political allies.[58] The stain on Korea's politicians has spread far and wide, raising cynicism across society.

Another challenge to South Korean democracy is ensuring limits on government power. This is a sensitive subject in a country that is barely one generation removed from authoritarian rule. South Koreans skeptical of the enduring strength of the democratic process had their fears confirmed by the mid-2014 conviction of the country's former spy chief for interfering in the 2012 election. The official was found guilty of directing intelligence officers to post online criticisms of liberal politicians.[59] What made the episode worry liberals was that the eventual winner of the 2012 election, and beneficiary of the dirty tricks, was Park Geun-hye, the daughter of former South Korean president Park Chung-hee, who ruled as a military strongman after taking power in a coup in 1961. Park, a committed democrat, is nonetheless a link to a dark period in South Korea's past, when democracy seemed unattainable and the government all but unconstrained. Recent reports that under both Presidents Lee and Park, South Koreans' privacy was breached by telecommunications companies has only added to fears of creeping authoritarianism.[60]

As in all democracies, governing competence ranks highly with South Korea's citizens. President Park has made a series of missteps that have raised doubts about her ability. Confidence in her government declined sharply after the sinking of a ferry in April 2014 that claimed three hundred lives, many of them students. Her prime minister resigned to take responsibility for the botched government response to the tragedy, but Park was unable to find a replacement, with two candidates withdrawing their nominations. This debacle cemented the image of a politician unable to deal with crises. Worse, in April 2015, her second premier resigned after just two months in office, after being accused of illegally accepting cash from a businessman.

By the end of 2015, South Korean activists had had enough. Tens of thousands jammed downtown Seoul in December to protest increasing government control over labor laws and history textbooks, among other issues.[61] After a court found a South Korean author guilty of defamation and the government indicted her for writing a book questioning the official explanation of World War II–era "comfort women" as sex slaves, fears about freedom of expression under Park were openly expressed.[62] Combined with suggestions that she has intimidated political opponents, these fiascos have depressed Park's approval rating, which barely broke 40 percent for most of the second year of her term.[63]

Perhaps most dangerously, South Korean politicians face a deeply dissatisfied society, deriving in part from persistent social hierarchies and the pressure to maintain high living standards. In one poll, over 85 percent of respondents said that they struggled with their sense of purpose.[64] Social divisions are growing, as economic and political structures privilege those from influential families. Young South Koreans not from the elite often despair of their future, citing low wages, high prices, long working hours, and lack of upward mobility. They openly call their country a living "hell."[65] Distrust that the government has their best interests at heart contributes to this malaise and even exceeds similar laments from their peers in Japan.

Yet unlike Japan, South Korea confronts one of the most dangerous security challenges in the entire region, a risk that dominates its domestic political discussions. The six-decade-long division of the Korean peninsula has made it one of the world's hotspots. The secretive and absolute rule of the Kim family in North Korea has surprised decades of observers who long ago assumed that Pyongyang's totalitarian system would collapse under its own weight.[66] And it might have, if not for support first from the Soviet Union and then from China. With that help, the Kim regime has maintained its hold on power, positioned itself as a constant menace to regional stability, and remained an unsolvable irritant to its neighbors and the United States. The death of North Korea's second dictator, Kim Jong-il, in December 2011, led many to hope for a "Pyongyang Spring."[67] Instead, his successor, the young Kim Jong-un, rapidly consolidated his hold on power, bloodily purged some of his father's closest supporters including his own uncle, and conducted nuclear and ballistic missile tests that unnerved the region.

The question of unification thus dominates South Korean politics and divides its citizens. Older Koreans, who remember life before the division or who personally know those living under the North's control, are far more likely to support unification than the younger generation. By some estimates, overall support for unification has dropped below 60 percent, with support by youth registering under 40 percent.[68]

Ask a Korean student in her twenties what she thinks of unification, and the answer is likely to resemble one I received a few years ago. "The North Koreans are too different from us, and it will cost too much money. I don't want to be paying for North Korea for the rest of my life," a political science major at Seoul National University told me, a comment echoed by a number of her peers listening to us. What this portends for domestic politics is unclear, but as the older generation dies out, the government's constant support for unification may falter as younger politicians with different views rise to more powerful positions. A sudden collapse of North Korea or moves by Seoul to push unification could result in serious domestic political tension.

The possibility of North Korea precipitating a political crisis in the South also is an ever-present fear. President Park is particularly sensitive to this possibility, given that her mother was murdered in 1974 in an assassination attempt on her father by a Japanese-born Korean sympathetic to the North. In 1983, North Korean agents tried to assassinate President Chun Doo-hwan during a state visit to Rangoon, Burma. The bomb they set missed Chun but killed twenty-one people, including three senior South Korean cabinet ministers and over a dozen presidential advisers and journalists. This sordid history is one reason current President Park tried to imprison an opposition politician for supposed treason in support of the North and disband his small, pro-unification party.[69] As events like these show, North Korea's long shadow is far from disappearing. As long as the current regime remains in Pyongyang, the stability of South Korean politics can never be taken for granted.

Struggling to Stay on Track: Southeast Asia

Americans get a bad rap for being ignorant of the world. Some of that criticism is probably warranted. For example, ask a group of Americans what they think of when they hear the word "Asia," and they'll more likely than not reply, "China, Japan, and Korea." Most news coverage of the region reinforces such perceptions.

The rest of the Indo-Pacific seems to occupy a space in Western minds that derives from the exotic fantasies of Joseph Conrad or James Michener. Yet the countries of Southeast Asia constitute one of the most vibrant parts of entire world. Southeast Asia's ten nations are a collection of peninsular and archipelagic states, with a combined population of 620 million and GDP of $2.2 trillion.[70] The region replicates all the diversity of the Indo-Pacific: democracies and autocracies, modernized and developing nations, giant nations and tiny states. Liberalism has made great strides here since the end of World War II, but today, democracy seems to be faltering. In Thailand and Malaysia it is in clear retreat.[71] Other countries, like Vietnam or Laos, show few signs of meaningful liberalization. Recent moves in Burma toward democracy offer hope, but the road forward will be difficult.

Throughout Southeast Asia, political stability and development remain the overriding concerns. The region's greatest risk factors are at home, in the domestic politics of countries still making the transition to democracy and modernization, where de facto one-party democracies are the dominant form of government. Our discussion will focus on these quasi-liberalized nations and largely leave untouched those of the Mekong Valley.

As globalization has reached into Southeast Asia, its people have shown themselves to desire the same things as their counterparts in the rest of the Indo-Pacific—or the world. These desires include political participation, social stability, and economic opportunity. Except for Singapore and Malaysia, the nations of Southeast Asia remain largely relegated to providing raw materials or producing at the lower end of the value chain. Their political systems are often overwhelmed by the need to improve poor infrastructure. Most of them are decades behind richer Asian countries in the use of computers and the Internet, and they lack sufficient transportation routes, research facilities, higher educational systems, and smoothly working capital markets. What Southeast Asian nations do have

going for them is their relative youth, with barely 5 percent of their collective populations over sixty-five years of age.[72]

This struggle to balance development with democracy is easily seen in
Indonesia. Just as China naturally draws attention as Asia's dominant
power, on the smaller stage of Southeast Asia, Indonesia casts the biggest
shadow. It is the largest country in Southeast Asia, an archipelago of over
sixteen thousand islands whose 250 million citizens range from Jakarta
high-tech workers to neolithic Borneo tribesmen. This diversity has meant
fraught political unity in Indonesia, and Jakarta has struggled to stabilize
political power after the thirty-year authoritarian reign of Suharto, which
ended in 1998.[73]

The political story of Indonesia is one of constant effort to control a
sprawling land. Its democratic process began with the domestic protests
and popular uprising that forced Suharto out amid the Asian financial crisis of 1997–98, leading to the first direct presidential election, in 2004.[74]
Until then, much of Jakarta's political energy since the mid-1970s had
been spent on keeping the country united. Its nearly quarter-century brutal occupation of East Timor became an international cause until Jakarta
surrendered control in 1999. A thirty-year insurgency in the eastern province of Aceh was settled in 2005, after the massive Christmas tsunami of
the previous year. Human rights abuses perpetrated by the Indonesian
military during the occupation of East Timor and the Aceh insurgency
led to global isolation until the armed forces underwent reforms under
former president S. B. Yudhonyo, a former army general who was elected
in 2004. Some groups, like Amnesty International, continue to charge
that the government is not fulfilling its commitments under the Aceh
peace treaty.[75]

With a quarter of a billion people and an average age of twenty-six, Indonesia should be poised for explosive economic growth over the next
generation. Yet the economic reform program of Yudhonyo lost steam
during his second term, in part because of endemic protectionist feelings
at home. From a development perspective, the country remains plagued
by inefficient infrastructure and political tension caused by uneven modernization throughout the archipelago. In 2009 the government embarked
on a plan to dramatically increase or upgrade the country's roads, rail lines,
ports, and airports, but by 2013, fewer than half of the goals had been

met.[76] A funding gap of over $5 billion hampered Jakarta's ambitious plans and undercut Yudhonyo's popularity.

The lack of domestic development was the driving issue in the 2014 national elections, which saw the victory of former Jakarta governor Joko Widodo. "Jokowi," as he is known, campaigned as a charismatic populist reformer unconnected to Indonesia's elites. He presented himself as a new-style politician, not wedded to traditional business or military interests. Jokowi promised a corruption-free administration in which the influence of the military would be reduced. His background as a furniture businessman and mayor of a medium-sized city added to the perception that he represented a generational break in Indonesian politics.[77]

Jokowi's impressive 53 percent of the vote underscored ordinary Indonesians' desire for a government that they can feel close to, yet his party only won enough parliamentary seats to form a minority coalition. Even before he took office, Jokowi faced opposition to his plans for broader democratization when the Indonesian parliament voted to end direct elections for local offices, such as mayors and governors. Instead, it returned this power to regional legislatures that are often corrupt and influenced by local powerbrokers.[78] This is a perfect example of Asia's unfinished political revolutions, as the push for more democracy clashes with forces of elite control—and often loses. Partly in response to the obstacles Jokowi has faced, his attempts to be seen as a strong leader have led to both domestic unease and international condemnation. In particular, his refusal to grant clemency to nine convicted death row drug smugglers in April 2015, eight of whom were foreign, was decried for its callousness.[79]

Indonesians have traditionally had little trust in their government, largely because of human rights abuses by the military and the brutality with which separatist movements were put down. Widodo's election was thus a symbolic moment for Indonesia as it tries to move beyond its first, hesitant years of democracy and escape the lingering shadow of the military in politics. Perhaps not surprisingly, his first year in office proved rocky, as vested interests opposed his economic reforms and the new president struggled to master the intricacies of parliamentary governing and crafting coherent policies. As a result, his popularity ebbed and flowed throughout the year.[80] In the end, Widodo's success will ultimately depend on reducing the influence of big business in government, eliminating corruption, and promoting balanced economic development. In a country as complex as Indonesia, such success is far from a sure bet.

Unlike Indonesia, which has struggled with insurgencies, domestic terrorism, and its past record of authoritarian rule, both Malaysia and Singapore are stable one-party states with little overt social unrest. Despite their small size, the two nations play an outsized role in the region. Singapore and Kuala Lumpur are filled with gleaming skyscrapers, evidence of the wealth they have built through tightly controlled politics and state-sponsored development. The top-down direction provided by Singapore's legendary leader Lee Kuan Yew and Malaysia's United Malay National Organization have led to high rates of development in both countries compared with their Southeast Asian neighbors. Visitors to Singapore cannot but remark on how clean and efficiently organized the island state appears to be. Foreign corporations rave over the ease of doing business there, accolades that are increasingly applied to Malaysia as well. Yet dissatisfaction with decades of one-party rule has led to protests in Malaysia and concerns in Singapore. The main risk to both is that their political systems will fail to become more inclusive, raising the possibility that as domestic dissent rises, government will become more authoritarian.

If you want to understand the purity of purpose that animates Singaporean policy, you need only to sit on a hotel balcony and watch the hundreds of cargo, oil, and cruise ships crowding the waters around the island. Singapore has always been and will remain an entrepôt in one of the world's most strategic spots. Its perfect location at the terminus of the Malacca Strait into the South China Sea led the Englishman Stanford Raffles to found it as a trading post in 1819. Today, it is a city-state of 5.5 million people, a small spot of land in the vast Indo-Pacific that has turned itself into a logistics and financial hub for the entire region. After Singapore's independence from Malaysia in 1965, leader Lee Kuan Yew, who died in March 2015, expanded Singapore's trading role, making its port one of the world's five largest, and built up its financial sector to compete with those of Hong Kong and Tokyo.[81]

Lee's People's Action Party (PAP) has dominated politics since Singapore became self-governing in 1959. Unlike many other multiethnic states, Singapore has assiduously integrated the nation's Chinese, Indians, and Malays into a homogenous whole. A professional yet strict legal system helps make Singapore one of the safest and least corrupt countries in all of Asia, encouraging thousands of foreign firms to open offices there. Its leading ministers are paid enormous salaries, in the millions of dollars, to discourage corruption.[82]

While remaining one of Asia's most globalized cities and having an unemployment rate that has not topped 4 percent for a decade, Singapore nonetheless faces numerous problems. These include an aging population as a result of the world's lowest birthrate, an influx of unskilled workers, growing income inequality, and limits to the expansion of its financial and logistics sectors.[83] Whether Singapore can harness its human capital to become a "smart nation," as some of its government officials want it to do, is another question. As a logistics hub it is unparalleled, but as a place for research institutes, world-class universities, R&D labs, and the like, it will face stiff competition, both inside the region and out.

Singapore's greatest risk comes from a government that finds itself bogged down by demands for greater democracy and economic equality when it also must prepare the next generation of development plans, continue competing with Hong Kong as a site for regional finance, and deal with a general economic slowdown in the region. At the same time, some social strains are also becoming evident, as long-settled ethnically Indian residents complain about illiterate workers from the subcontinent coming to Singapore for cheap jobs, driving down wages. In response, the government in recent years has set immigration limits on low-skilled labor.

Concern over these challenges has sparked criticism of the PAP's stranglehold on politics. In the 2011 parliamentary elections, the opposition picked up the most seats in its history, albeit only six out of eighty-seven; by 2015, the opposition had dropped in half, to just three seats out of eighty-seven. Yet as the independence generation of Singapore fades from the scene, many observers expect opposition parties to gain support, though they may adopt the same economic and social policies that have made Singapore a unique case in Asian development.

Here is where the government's restrictions on free speech, enabled by constitutional powers, pose a threat to the future. Already, Singapore is criticized by groups including Amnesty International for its Official Secrets and Sedition Acts, which limit freedom of expression, as well as restraints on the media and in the educational sphere. If frustration builds at the lack of opportunity for political diversity, society will need ways to express displeasure and release communal frustration. Without providing such means of sociopolitical evolution, the government will face perhaps its most severe test since independence itself. For now, however, Singapore continues its unique path, leading in economic trends in the region while continuing to evolve in political ones.

Just north of Singapore stretches Malaysia, which also includes territory on the island of Borneo. The Federated Malay States separated from Great Britain in the late 1950s and banded together in 1963. Malaysia occupies a unique geographic position between Indonesia to the south and the rest of Southeast Asia to its north, as well as straddling the eastern and western boundaries of the South China Sea. Like Indonesia and Thailand, it fronts the critical Strait of Malacca, which connects the Indian Ocean to the South China Sea.

Malaysia's struggle with democracy has had many difficult periods and now seems to be entering another. The nearly quarter-century rule of Premier Mahathir Mohamad, from 1980 to 2003, saw the imposition of internal security laws that restricted civil liberties and curbed judicial independence. At the same time, Mahathir became controversial abroad for spouting anti-Western sentiments and for making anti-Semitic statements. Yet his main concern was to modernize Malaysia and build up its infrastructure. His success helped attract foreign investment and raised the country's standard of living far beyond that of its neighbors. Gross domestic product (based on a purchasing power parity calculation) stood at $25,600 per capita in 2014.[84]

Run since independence by the United Malay National Organization (UMNO), Malaysia has been inching toward fully free elections, but it has yet to show that it will unreservedly embrace democracy. Nor are opposition groups assured of the government's willingness to give them access to the political arena. Malaysia made some strides under Prime Minister Najib Razak since he came to office in 2009, as he gradually opened up domestic political competition, at least for national elections. Spurning Mahathir's frequent anti-Americanism, Najib formed a close relationship with U.S. president Barack Obama and raised Malaysia's global profile.

Yet democracy watchers in Malaysia have grown increasingly worried as Najib's government seemed to reverse course, and began pressuring, even harassing, opposition parties. Since 2000, the government has repeatedly targeted opposition leader and former deputy prime minister Anwar Ibrahim, who was jailed in March 2014 under sodomy laws after his original acquittal was overturned.[85] Najib's reputation as a reformer was further tarnished by the government's harassment of democracy activists and after he instituted a major crackdown on public demonstrations in 2012. Worse, allegations that Najib illegally pocketed $700 million from the state government fund plunged Malaysia into political turmoil in 2015, and his being cleared of legal suspicion did not undo the political damage. Not only has his popularity plummeted in response, but former leader Mahathir publicly criticized his former protégé in the spring of 2015. Mahathir in turn has been accused of trying to wrest control of UMNO back from Najib, raising fears of a political crisis.[86]

Corruption and party infighting are not the only political problems Malaysia faces. The country has come under criticism as well for not protecting the rights of religious minorities such as Christians and Hindus, and it is generally considered more religiously conservative than its southern neighbor Indonesia. This points out another political risk in the Indo-Pacific, and one particular to Malaysia and Indonesia (and India, as we shall see later in this chapter): the potential for sectarian unrest. Indonesia is the world's largest Muslim country, with over two hundred million mostly Sunni adherents. For the most part, Islam in Indonesia is tolerant and comparatively liberal, supporting religious pluralism despite some radical sects that have committed rare atrocities in recent years.[87] Yet as the 2002 terrorist bombing in Bali and the January 2016 Islamic State attack in Jakarta showed, the tendrils of jihadism remain a threat to Indonesia's future.

Malaysia presents a more complicated picture. Sixty percent of its nearly thirty million people are Muslim, and they seem to be slipping into a more fundamentalist attitude. Many observers note the spread of sharia law in Malaysia despite official religious freedom.[88] Further, Prime Minister Najib has abandoned plans to scrap the country's colonial-era Sedition Act, instead buttressing it to protect the sanctity of Islam, a move supported by the country's Islamist opposition party.[89] When asked about the country's supposed liberalization and turn to the West, numerous political leaders shrug their shoulders and say, "That's Najib," indicating that support for the premier's policies is wide but shallow. Few Malaysians I talked with say that they would be surprised to see Malaysia's inherent conservatism take on a larger, and possibly antidemocratic, role. Najib himself seems to be moving toward this position.

Yet Islam is not the only source of democratic challenges to Asia's political regimes. To support a claim that the Indo-Pacific remains in the midst of unfinished revolutions, we need only briefly to look at the United States' ally Thailand. Thailand has a rare history, being one of only a handful of Asian nations never colonized by Europeans (Japan was another).[90] Its independence is fiercely guarded and its monarch is the glue that holds the political system together. Yet Thailand's revered King Bhumibol, who has ruled since 1946 and is the world's longest-reigning monarch, is in his late eighties. His son and likely successor is widely disliked and mocked for his lifestyle, raising fears that the next generation will be unable to command the same respect and act as a source of national stability. However, Thailand's strict lèse-majesté laws prevent any meaningful social discussion of the country's monarchy or its connection to politics.

Thailand has struggled to ensure both stability and democracy, and currently both are losing. Decades of military rule gave way to an unstable democracy in 1973, and the military took power again briefly in 1991. Fifteen years later, in 2006, Thailand was destabilized once more when the military intervened to oust President Thaksin Shinawatra, who had been accused of corruption.[91] Democracy was restored the following year, but the country was then rocked from 2008 through 2010 by protests between antigovernment and pro-Thaksin factions, in which major public sites in Bangkok were occupied and taken over. The demonstrations and riots, which also shut down the capital's international airport for a time, revealed deep splits between Thailand's rural and urban populations. These divisions were a reminder that modernization often exacerbates sociopolitical tensions and is by no means assured of resolving them.[92]

While the world waited to see if full-scale civil unrest would break out, in 2011, the ousted Thaksin's younger sister, Yingluck, formed a majority government after general elections and became the youngest prime minister in Thailand's modern history. Three years later, in May 2014, Yingluck too was removed in a military coup. The country's new leader, coup leader and former general Prayuth Chan-ocha, has made it clear that the military will not relinquish power in the near future, though his junta offered to resume elections if Thais accepted a constitution that curtailed some governmental independence.[93] The military again has shown that democracy in Thailand can never be taken for granted. When, or if, it will be restored is far from assured, and politics in Thailand remains in stasis.

Stability and liberalization hang in the balance in Southeast Asia, represented on the one side by fragile Thailand and on the other by Indonesia and Malaysia. It may be too much to say that elections in Jakarta or Kuala Lumpur have served as a moral challenge to authoritarianism, but an important indicator of democracy's appeal is provided by the events unfolding in Myanmar (Burma). At the end of 2015, Burma provided a spark of hope in a region where democracy seemed either stagnant or in retreat. In elections that November, former dissident and Nobel Peace Prize winner Aung San Suu Kyi's National League for Democracy (NLD) party won a smashing victory in the country's first election in a quarter-century. The NLD won 86 percent of the contested seats, relegating the military junta's party to a rump minority. Asia's democracies, along with those in the West, had watched developments in the "Burmese spring" since 2010, long hoping for an easing of fifty years of authoritarian rule.[94]

When President Thein Sein lifted the two-decade house confinement of Aung San Suu Kyi in November 2010 and allowed her to be elected to the national parliament two years later, many compared it to the release of Nelson Mandela in South Africa in 1990. Optimists hailed Aung's freedom as a sign that Myanmar's military junta was responding to international sanctions and had decided on a path of gradual democratization. There was hope that a more democratic bloc in Southeast Asia could develop if Myanmar kept to the path of gradual liberalization. A few years later, the regime slowed its liberalization policy and instead continued to harass pro-democracy activists, repress religious minorities, and imprison journalists. Even more worrisome, despite touting a free and fair election in 2015, the junta refused to change the constitution to allow Suu Kyi to run for president.[95]

Yet the NLD's victory does not mean that democracy has triumphed in Burma. To begin with, the NLD will share power with the military, as fully a quarter of the parliamentary seats are reserved for the serving officers. In addition, the ministers of Home Affairs, Defense, and Border Area Affairs will be appointed by the head of the armed forces. Perhaps most important, the military controls a majority of seats on the National Defense and Security Council, which can declare a state of emergency and appoint the head of the armed forces. The military thus remains a potent threat in the coming years, and missteps by the new NLD government could lead to instability that the military could use to grab more power.

Similarly, statements by Aung San Suu Kyi that she will be "above" the president and control power in any government were turned into reality when the new government created a position expressly for her. As "state counselor," she will be the country's de facto leader, raising questions about democratic governance in Myanmar. As in any democracy, a failure to live up to expectations or signs of overreaching could weaken support for the NLD, giving the military-backed opposition new credibility. In short, Myanmar's democratic battle has only begun.

Repeated backsliding in places like Thailand, Myanmar, and Malaysia is a warning sign of greater risks ahead for political stability and democratization in this subregion. Southeast Asia may have all the makings for a vibrant future, but democracy has by no means won out. It is an open question whether these nations can follow the path blazed by South Korea, Taiwan, and others.

India: The Risk of Complexity

China may impress observers with its immensity, Japan and South Korea with their modern societies, but India is an assault on the senses. First-time visitors are overwhelmed by the sights, sounds, and colors of a society in perpetual motion. The contrasts of immense wealth and unimaginable poverty, refined art and street hawkers, profound philosophy and raucous democracy all combine to make India unlike any other place on earth.

Yet the triumph and the mystery of India are one and the same: how can this behemoth of 1.2 billion people, with hundreds of languages, ethnicities, cultures, and levels of development, remain a thriving democracy within a united country? How can any government possibly be effective in such a sprawling, challenged civilization? For that is what India is: not just a society but an entire civilization, with thousands of years of history.[96]

"We are a dream, you know," a senior Indian politician told me in the cool of his official, whitewashed villa in New Delhi's government sector. "Think about it: we have 800 million voters and twice as many opinions. Democracy is a dream, but also a miracle, because we have done it."

Such pride, bordering on arrogance, is not misplaced. India's tragic birth out of British colonialism and the bloody partition from Pakistan in 1948 remain the defining events of its modern history.[97] Waging wars with Pakistan and surviving long-serving prime minister Indira Gandhi's centralization of power and rule by decree, Indian democracy has never failed, yet it seems constantly fragile. At moments, that risk has become palpably physical. The assassinations of both Indira Gandhi in 1984, while prime minister, and her son Rajiv Gandhi in 1991, while campaigning for a return to the premiership, underscored the ever-present danger of religious fanaticism and insurgent groups. One of the greatest threats to continued domestic stability in India is the dangerous genii of religious radicalism, which remains at constant risk of exploding. India's 966 million Hindus, accounting for 80 percent of the population, coexist uneasily with its 172 million Muslims. Sectarian violence can be sudden and stunning in its intensity. Gujarat's deadly 2002 riots, in which nearly eight hundred Muslims and over two hundred fifty Hindus were killed, and the riot that killed over one thousand persons in Mumbai in 1993 are reminders that Indian society is balanced on a knife's edge.

Religion is not the only powder keg. Like Indonesia, India has struggled with regional separatist campaigns. Decades-old rebellions, such as the Naxalite-Maoist movement that began in the country's northeast in 1967, continue to emerge. Naxalite insurgents attacked a convoy of Indian Congress Party leaders in May 2013, killing close to thirty politicians, one of numerous reminders that democracy in India is sometimes paid for in blood. Attacks on local officials and farmers keep the northeast, in particular, in a state of heightened security.

Such violent dangers are the ones that make headlines. But reviewing India's history or talking to its many impressive officials reveals a more mundane yet significant risk: its repeated tendency to turn inward. For four decades after independence, Indian voters were satisfied to live under a one-party democracy, giving the Gandhi's Congress Party a dominance hardly matched elsewhere.[98] India's traditional nonalignment policy was also a result of this inwardness. As in Asia's other major democracy, Japan, the lack of robust political competition at the national level let the country avoid the bitter medicine needed for social and economic development and reform.[99]

The lack of political alternatives left India often lagging behind the main streams of global development, ultimately making governance more difficult at home. The Congress Party's dominance from independence through the late 1980s effectively cut the country off from much of the world. Dead-end economic policies and a sclerotic governing party ultimately left it nearly bankrupt and lagging behind other states that had already embraced liberalization. By the time New Delhi was forced to fly its remaining gold reserves to London to underwrite an emergency loan in 1991, even the Congress Party was forced to accept globalization as the price of economic survival.[100]

As a democracy, India should not have needed a crisis in order to change; voters could have chosen a different course at any time. Yet inertia has played as strong a role here as in other democracies, leaving mounting problems that eventually bring a democratic backlash. In India's case, the repeated failures of different administrations and the perception of rising incompetence finally pushed voters to embrace a two-party system in 1998. That year, they gave a parliamentary majority to a coalition led by the Hindu nationalist Bharatiya Janata Party (BJP). In 2004, power turned back to the Congress Party, whose leadership under Prime Minister Manmohan Singh built on BJP ideas. Singh, the father of Indian economic reform in the 1990s, pursued policies in his first term that brought nearly a decade of high growth and allowed India to emerge onto the global political scene. For a while, it seemed as though the world's most populous democracy was finally poised to enter a new era of domestic development.

These great hopes slowly dissipated, however, underscoring the risks still plaguing India's political revolution. The always-present threat of religious terrorism and war with Pakistan reared its head again during the 2000s, wrenching domestic political attention back to India's northwest border. After bombings in Mumbai in 1993 and 2006, the city again was targeted in November 2008. A daring and horrific terrorist attack by ten armed gunmen murdered 174 people, including women, children, and Western tourists, and kept the nation transfixed for the four days that it played out on live television. The subcontinent seemed close to war when it was revealed that the terrorists were a cell trained in Pakistan and supported by Pakistani security services.[101] Indian officials attempted for months to punish those responsible while preventing a new Indo-Pakistan war. The "11/26" attack, as it became known, haunted Indian society in the years after the carnage, dashing the hopes of many that the country could focus on domestic development.

Just as worries about terrorism consumed the public imagination as the 2010s began, concerns also intensified over New Delhi's ability to maintain economic growth. Prime Minister Singh, who became the first Indian premier since Jawaharlal Nehru to win a consecutive second term in office, lost much of the reformist momentum and diplomatic vision that made his first term such a success. An economic slowdown after 2011, tied to the global recession, brought sobriety to foreign observers who thought they had found the next China.[102] Repeated electoral failures by the Congress Party put Singh's government on the defensive and raised questions about its basic competence.[103]

Corruption also hangs heavily over domestic politics. Possibly the greatest failing of India's domestic political system is its inability or unwillingness to curb widespread corruption. Singh was no more successful at this than his predecessors. The risk to sitting governments, as well as to trust in democracy as a whole, has become one of India's major electoral issues.[104] Everything from the granting of state licenses to the distribution of food and oil to the poor is wracked by incredible inefficiency, waste, and graft. Examples are legion, but a few give the flavor of how massive and endemic the problem has become.

One of the most publicized stains on Singh's tenure was a multiyear scandal surrounding the sale of telecommunications licenses, in which up to $37 billion of public monies was stolen. "We had to pay in order to pay!" a Western businessman involved in the scandal told me, punning on the usual saw about corruption. "We were expected to bribe our way into the precompetition to decide who would actually be in the final competition for the contracts. That means they wanted us to offer bribes in order to make the serious bribes later on. It was unlike anything I'd ever seen." The Indian Supreme Court later invalidated more than two hundred licenses.[105] Similarly, what was supposed to be a triumph for New Delhi turned into a national scandal when the chief organizer and other officials of the 2010 Commonwealth Games were arrested a year after the event for accepting bribes to favor certain construction and equipment companies. Delays and fraud made the Games cost thirty-five times what was initially projected.[106]

Indian governments of any party seem unable to limit corruption, and society is permeated by it. According to the watchdog group Transparency International, 54 percent of Indians claimed to have paid a bribe of some kind in 2013.[107] The group ranked India ninety-fourth out of 183 nations for corruption.[108] One newspaper calculated that bribery and kickbacks in India totaled nearly $6 billion in 2011–12 alone.[109]

Such backroom dealing not only undermined support for Singh's government but also tarnished New Delhi's globalization policies, as many Western firms were driven away by the perception that competition for development contracts was not honest. Nor were the most competent Indian companies winning the bidding competition, which raised concerns about how well projects would be managed. Just as important, the extent of corruption cast doubt on the political system's ability to enforce existing laws, craft new ones to deal with uncovered areas, and restore confidence in officials' impartiality.[110]

Largely as a result of its governing incompetency and inability to prevent seemingly endless scandal, the Congress Party lost in a landslide in May 2014, despite turning back to the Gandhi dynasty and tapping young political scion Rahul Gandhi as its next leader.[111] Gandhi's lackluster campaign led to a dominating victory for the Hindu nationalist BJP, bringing former Gujarat chief minister Narendra Modi into office as prime minister.

Modi's inauguration marked yet another peaceful transfer of power between parties in India, and he took power with a burst of energy unseen in recent years. Like his close friend Shinzo Abe in Japan, Modi campaigned on bringing major reform to India and unleashing market forces to fight lingering autarkic policies. He also promised tough measures against the endemic corruption. Yet he so far has given little indication of any firm plan for delivering on these promises.[112] Sometimes he has run into political opposition, such as with his plan to institute a reformed, nationwide sales tax, which the parliament refused to enact. At other times, Modi himself has quietly buried his reform policies, including ones to modernize land acquisition laws or privatize many state enterprises. A failure to embrace reform could have a political effect in India like what happened in Japan: political stasis as power passes from party to party with little change. That voters already doubt Modi's abilities was shown in November 2015, when his BJP lost important state elections to the opposition.

Modi has yet to end the sense of drift in Indian politics and assure the voters he is not ignoring long-term problems. A bold claim to have solutions is what propelled him to power, yet he has just begun the journey of making politics not merely responsive to the desires of the voters, but actually focused on how to position the country for balanced and widespread development. There are many types of political risk, and compared with the chronic instability of Thailand or the looming dissent in China, Indian democracy is undoubtedly on solid ground. But while the foundations of Indian democracy are strong, the political dangers facing New Delhi are unique and should not be underestimated.

The most visible political risk to India's future is sectarianism, an area where Modi's past makes him vulnerable to attack. Modi has been shadowed by his inflammatory statements as chief minister of Gujarat, and his critics continue to question his culpability for the massacre of nearly eight hundred Muslims in riots while he was in charge there. These doubts weaken his ability to speak as a true national leader, despite his attempts to put the past behind him and call for religious unity in the face of attacks on Muslims. Being seen as unconcerned with religious violence could unleash massive protests and riots in a country always on edge over sectarian differences.

Outside of the religious divide, perhaps the biggest political risk is simply that India's unfinished revolution will continue to underperform. Perhaps its democracy cannot create the opportunities for work, education, and a better life that hundreds of millions of its citizens want and deserve. For all its success, India has miles to go in ensuring stability and creating the conditions for growth throughout the country. The risk is therefore nothing as dramatic as revolution or political collapse, but rather the persistence of corruption, incompetence, and the lack of political courage to take on special interests. All of these conspire to keep India forever the country of the future, as the wags once described Argentina. Perhaps this is what my acquaintance meant when he described India and its democracy as a dream.

The question of political control and the effectiveness of government in Asia has never been more important than today. The spread of democracy means that tens of millions of more Asians demand accountable and effective government, and are willing to swing between parties to find it. At the same time, authoritarian governments have long provided both security and economic rewards in return for political passivity by their citizens. As their ability to continue to do so is called into question, the fragility of their political power is put on display. For governments of all stripes, moreover, the spread of the Internet and other communications technologies means that scandals and failures cannot be hidden, and the digital voices of the people are increasingly united.

Equally important, the struggle between democracy and authoritarianism continues throughout the Indo-Pacific, at both the domestic and regional levels. Because the region is more tightly integrated today than at any time in its past, what happens inside one country's borders can spill over to affect its neighbors. Moreover, the reverse also applies: what happens in the region can have a disproportionate impact on domestic politics. The inner and the outer are now intertwined, yet as we will explore next, without an effective regional community to deal with increasingly common problems.

5

WHY CAN'T WE ALL JUST GET ALONG?

"Where is Asia's NATO?" casual observers of the region often ask, or almost as often, "Why isn't there an 'Asian Union?'" Surely, they think, Tokyo or Singapore, possibly Beijing, will have an impressive United Nations– or European Union–style regional headquarters with legions of diplomats and important meetings. When they discover that nothing like it exists, they start to wonder why Asia isn't a *real* region like Europe, meaning, why isn't it united?

The answer is pretty simple. The Indo-Pacific may be the world's most economically dynamic area, but as we have seen, it is also the most politically diverse region imaginable. This diversity has so far prevented the nations of Asia from uniting the way Europe has. Moreover, the regional political organizations that do exist are less ambitious, more like the Organization of American States or the Arab League than NATO.[1]

More than any other region except perhaps the Middle East, the Asia-Pacific remains fettered by centuries of history. Its largest and most powerful nations—China, Japan, and India—were also its major imperial powers through millennia of history. Today, these giants have no formal allies among their neighbors, and few close partnerships. In part because of this, Asia lacks long-standing, tested, respected political mechanisms for cooperation between states. This is a problem for a region with both major security tensions and a need for continued economic integration. Given the stakes, all countries in the region should be striving to create and maintain a political community that contributes to both growth and political stability. Yet such an achievement is far off on the horizon.

Why has Asia been unable to create its own Asian Union or NATO? One answer appears to be its inability to end the distrust stemming from its history of colonialism and war.[2] We might also propose other answers more related to today's political environment. The key to NATO's success during the Cold War was the shared interests of its members, all of which were democracies. Recent history seems to show that the more democracies a region has, the more likely it is to develop effective multilateral political institutions, and to remain politically stable.[3] By contrast, a lack of democracies and the absence of a viable regional political community tend to increase the risk of competition, distrust, and instability. All this can be seen in the Indo-Pacific.

Traditionally in Asia, China's size often allowed it to dominate and conquer smaller nations, and at the same time to act as a brake on warfare between smaller states. India played the same role on the western edge of the region. For much of its history, Asia was disturbed by battles around the Chinese periphery but witnessed less conflict in the interior, except during and after the collapse of Chinese dynasties. This balance broke down only between 1894 and 1945, when Imperial Japan set out to destroy the Chinese system and reconstitute the Asian political order around itself.[4]

This history points to yet another reason why political cooperation is so elusive in the Asia-Pacific. Whereas Europe has had at least five centuries of experimentation with the nation-state model and the development of modern diplomatic methods, much of Asia has been free from colonialism only for a half-century or so—within living memory. National founders such as Singapore's Lee Kuan Yew, who died only in 2015, cast a long shadow over the postindependence lives of their countries.

Independence and sovereignty are thus relatively new concepts in Asia's historical consciousness. For centuries, the Indo-Pacific was dominated by a hierarchical conception of political order centered on the Chinese emperor, or by the completely separate political cycles of the Indian dynasties. Then, during the late nineteenth and early twentieth centuries, a century or so of modern colonization by Europeans and the Japanese instituted a new concept of political hierarchy and control. Recently, in just a few decades, this vast geographic area has made another abrupt switch, from domination by European and Asian colonizers to sovereign independence for all of its member states. The remnants of formerly dominant Indo-Pacific powers today in Tokyo, Beijing, and New Delhi skew what might be a smoother transition toward equal political community, and often fuel resentful historical memories.

Why Asia's Democracies Don't Lead the Way

Let's return to our conceptual risk map. A survey of Asia's political structures quickly reveals a gap in the map: there is little liberal leadership able to create a stable Western-style political community. Even America's key allies in the region, democratic nations that are part of a global alliance structure, are unable to jointly provide political leadership. Why is this so? The best way to begin is by looking at Asia's most developed democracy.

If one joins the hundreds of joggers who daily run around the outer grounds of the Imperial Palace in downtown Tokyo, a slight detour off the path and up a hill on the north side of the palace brings one to Yasukuni Shrine. Founded in 1869, at the beginning of Japan's modern era, it became the main place to worship the souls of all Japanese who gave their lives in the country's wars.

Yasukuni is no Arlington National Cemetery, and it holds no official position. Approached through its massive, orange Shinto *torii* gate, it seems little different from other large shrines in Tokyo. For decades after World War II, it garnered no attention. Even after the spirits of fourteen Class A war criminals, including Prime Minister Tojo Hideki, were enshrined there in October 1978, there was little outcry, though Emperor Hirohito refused to visit the shrine in person afterward. Only in the mid-1980s, when conservative prime minister Yasuhiro Nakasone paid his respects at the shrine, did Japan's neighbors start paying attention. In the early 2000s, Yasukuni suddenly became a major issue, and Japanese leaders or officials who visited the shrine were denounced by China and South Korea, among others, for glorifying Japan's imperial aggression. The continuing appeal of Japan's so-called peace constitution, written by the

Americans at the outset of the postwar occupation, did little to dampen more fervent critics, who darkly warned that Japan had not learned from its tragic history. That the Japanese economic miracle also had come to a crashing halt, while China's star was ascendant, only seemed to make it easier to criticize Asia's once-most-powerful nation.

While it may be hard now to remember, for much of the post–World War II–era China was eclipsed by the rise of Japan. Japan's spectacular economic recovery from total defeat in the Pacific War led to widespread expectations that it would become the dominant political actor in Asia, especially given its unique alliance with the United States. These expectations were dashed by Japan's economic slowdown in the 1990s, which coincided with a leadership unable to put forward a compelling vision for the country's role in Asia.[5] Instead of emerging as a new global leader, Tokyo became seen as Washington's permanent junior partner. Perhaps the nadir of its political influence came during the 1991 Gulf War, when the world's then second-largest economy failed to provide any material support to the thirty-three-nation coalition that ousted Iraq from Kuwait. Even tiny Senegal sent troops, but Tokyo ultimately provided only a few billion dollars of financial support, which was derided as "checkbook diplomacy."[6]

Tokyo seemed to have learned the lessons of the Gulf War after the terror attacks of September 11, 2001, when it rushed to support the United States in Afghanistan and the Indian Ocean. Yet because of its constitutional restrictions on the use of force and widespread public opposition to the dispatch of troops overseas, Japan's contribution was much less than that of Great Britain, Australia, or a host of other countries. The relatively little that Tokyo did was driven almost entirely by Prime Minister Junichiro Koizumi,[7] whose close personal relationship with U.S. president George W. Bush led to policies that seemed to herald the beginnings of a new Japanese global activism as well as affirm a truly global alliance between Washington and Tokyo.[8] Though hampered by constitutional limits, Koizumi did as much as was legally and politically possible to send Japanese troops overseas for logistics and reconstruction efforts. Many supporters of the alliance in both Washington and Tokyo thought that this presaged a new era in which Japan would finally live up to the missed opportunities of the 1980s and become the most powerful nation in East Asia.[9]

For half a decade after Koizumi left office, in mid-2006, however, no Japanese premier lasted for more than a year. Shinzo Abe's return for a second term as prime minister in December 2012 seemed to promise both much sought-after stability and a shift in Japan's foreign policy priorities. Returning to many of the themes he espoused during his first term in office, from 2006 to 2007, Abe adopted a policy that in essence offered Japan as a democratic, liberal partner for Asian nations growing wary of China's increasing power and influence. Though often couched in security terms, Abe's vision as he has developed it over the years is ultimately a political one, contrasting destabilizing authoritarianism with cooperative liberalism.[10]

Yet Tokyo's desire to overturn China's predominance and shape Asia's regional political architecture has so far fallen short of its hopes. Though it will take years for the full impact of Abe's foreign policy reforms to be known, among the reasons why Japan has not yet been successful is the intertwined nature of politics, economics, and security in the Indo-Pacific. Perhaps the most important reason for Japan's inability to be Asia's political leader is quite simply that Japan no longer has the region's largest or fastest-growing economy. Even as the region's largest democratic economy, its political influence is reduced to the extent that China is seen as Asia's strongest nation. Second, Japan's bid for regional leadership is regularly frustrated by the resolve of Asia's smaller nations not to be drawn into a Sino-Japanese struggle for dominance. As a senior Malaysian diplomat tells me, "We do not have the problems with China that [America] or Japan has, and we don't want to get caught in the middle of fighting giants."

One might assume that the likeliest source of regional support for a Japanese leadership role would be other democratic nations, but few are yet willing to throw their support behind Tokyo. This is despite Japan's efforts to maintain a steady focus on Southeast Asia, a policy dating back to the 1970s that includes supporting countries like Vietnam and the Philippines in their opposition to China's growing influence.[11]

Even with growing concerns about China's power, Tokyo remains unable to capitalize on these fears to establish itself as an alternative power center that does not threaten those around it. Given the smaller nations' economic dependence on China and their weak defensive capabilities, they

are wary of being perceived as anti-Beijing. At best, these nations negoti
ate a middle ground between Beijing and Tokyo, sometimes playing the
one off against the other for aid or political support. Such a transactional
approach makes sense when neither Japan nor China can claim outright
hegemony in Asia.

As the outcry over Yasukuni Shrine showed, no small part of Tokyo's
difficulties is tied to Japan's wartime atrocities in Asia in the 1930s and
1940s and the resulting mistrust of Japanese intentions. Seven decades
after its unconditional surrender, Japan has not shaken off the ghosts of
World War II.[12] In particular, Japan's relationship with South Korea, a
country that should be its most natural democratic ally in Asia, is continually haunted by ghosts of the past. Despite a historic apology in
December 2015 for Japan's use of Korean "comfort women" during World
War II, other ambiguous statements by Abe or those close to him about
sexual slavery and Japan's war guilt have cast doubt on his sincerity. The
visits by Abe and other Japanese leaders to Yasukuni continue to strain
relations abroad, especially in South Korea. Similarly, the long-running
dispute over public school textbooks that appear to whitewash Japan's imperial past continue to poison foreign relations.

"Until Japan fully accepts its war responsibility," a Korean politician told
me, "it cannot be a leader in Asia." This attitude is reflected in the comments of senior Korean leaders, including President Park Geun-hye, who
has called for Tokyo to make a "courageous decision" to fully acknowledge its responsibility for past actions.[13] This lingering anger makes it difficult for Asia's most developed democracy to exert leadership in a rapidly
changing environment.

In the game of great power competition in Asia, Beijing is only too
happy to continue to stoke anti-Japanese resentment both at home and
abroad. Some of its actions are blatantly provocative. For example, in 2014,
it built a shrine and a museum honoring a Korean student activist who
assassinated Japan's first prime minister and later colonial governor of
Korea, Ito Hirobumi, in 1909. Seven decades after the end of World War II,
Chinese president Xi Jinping also introduced two new national holidays in China commemorating the 1937 Nanjing Massacre and the 1945
defeat of Japan. While these holidays are primarily meant for Chinese domestic consumption, they also serve as reminders to the rest of the region

about Japan's imperial past. With actions like these, Beijing and Tokyo are unable to develop better ties, thus keeping the region's two major powers at loggerheads.

Such schemes not only isolate Tokyo but also keep it diplomatically off-balance. For their part, Japanese express frustration with the lack of acceptance of their repentance, and Abe himself has stated that the time of endless apologies is over. Japan's diplomatic standoff with China and South Korea, along with other nations, leaves Asia adrift, unable to coalesce around a natural center that could guide the way to a more durable regional community.

Asia's other democracies, and U.S. allies, do not have the same baggage as Japan, but they fare even worse as regional leaders. One of the Asia-Pacific's greatest success stories is South Korea, yet that half-peninsular nation also finds itself trapped by its tragic history. Sundered from its northern half since the end of World War II, South Korea has lived for generations in a political twilight, even as it made a stunning move from authoritarianism to democracy in the 1980s and leapt from third-world to first-world status among global economies.[14]

Yet the continuing threat of attack or terrorism from North Korea has long limited Seoul's ability to assume a larger role on the regional stage. The division of the peninsula, now reaching into its third generation, is an existential crisis that dominates every discussion of South Korean security and foreign relations. Relations with the North are an endless gray zone of waiting for some change in the governance of Pyongyang, combined with fear that accident or miscalculation, or simply the native aggressiveness of the Kim regime, will plunge the peninsula back into fratricidal war. South Korea's diplomatic efforts for the most part are centered on either putting pressure on Pyongyang or attempting some type of engagement with the mercurial regime. Seoul will remain primarily inwardly focused as long as the peninsula is divided and its citizens remain at risk of attack.

In part to assure continued close relations with its ally the United States but also out of a strong sense of national pride, South Korea has struggled not to be defined solely by the stalemate with the North. Yet that desire is tempered by a realistic understanding that it is a "minnow among whales," as one South Korean politician describes it. A medium-sized nation of fifty million people, it remains a close ally of the United States, sending troops to support UN and U.S. military operations and taking a seat at all major international organizations. Under former president Lee Myung-bak, who served from 2008 to 2013 and forged a close relationship with Barack Obama, Seoul branded itself "Global Korea," trying to take on leadership roles in the region and around the world.[15] Examples of this policy included hosting the G-20 meeting in 2011 and the Nuclear Nonproliferation Summit in 2012.

Given Japan's inability to overcome the past and India's continued adherence to a nonaligned approach, some thought that Seoul, perhaps along with Jakarta and Kuala Lumpur, might offer a new locus of leadership and give Washington new partners that might redraw Asia's political map. As the most developed of the "new Asia" nations, Seoul eagerly accepted this role.

Yet South Korea seems to have bumped up against the natural limits of its political influence. Above all, its tragic history with Japan continues to impede it from reaching out to the neighbor that, having the most similar values, should be its natural partner.[16] Moreover, the two sides have a simmering diplomatic dispute over the Liancourt Rocks, located in the Sea of Japan, which the Japanese call the Takeshima Islands and the Koreans the Dokdo Islands. This territorial argument, which we will discuss more in chapter 6, continues to poison relations and feed nationalist fervor on both sides.

What about other democracies? Australia also occupies ambiguous political territory. While no self-imposed security or political restrictions inhibit its role in the Indo-Pacific, it has sat uneasily between its European roots and its Asian future.[17] "We're a big land, but a small people," an Australian official tells me, alluding to its twenty-four million citizens' ever-present awareness of giant China and Indonesia.

A continent unto itself, Australia brings forth images of sandy beaches and the desolate Outback. If it has had one enduring strength in regional political gamesmanship, it is as a standard bearer of liberal values. This has long helped Canberra to punch above its weight, playing a leading role in regional forums while maintaining the closest of bonds with the United States.[18]

Yet the tension is growing between Australia's political role and its export-heavy economy's dependence on external trade. China has become the dominant outside figure in Australia's economy and its major trade partner, accounting for over $155 billion of Australia's exports and foreign direct investment in 2014. As a result, Australian leaders, particularly two-time prime minister Kevin Rudd, who served from 2007 to 2010 and again in 2013, have trod a fine line, trying to put Sino-Australian relations on a firmer footing while attempting to limit the country's vulnerability to Chinese economic pressure. A June 2015 free trade agreement between the two presaged even tighter interdependence, and possibly tighter political relations.[19]

Not unlike their Asian counterparts, Australian policymakers and thinkers have grown increasingly worried about the long-term risk of being caught between China and the United States. Some argue that Canberra should acknowledge the inevitability of China's rise and seek a closer relationship with Beijing.[20] Others worry that the United States may begin to take a smaller role in the Indo-Pacific, thus weakening liberal nations throughout the region.[21] Given its relatively small armed forces, Canberra focuses primarily on diplomacy and on promoting democratic values among potential partners in Southeast Asia and elsewhere. This was the impetus behind then Prime Minister Rudd's 2009 call for an "Asia Pacific Community" that would go beyond the East Asia Summit and the limited initiatives of the Association of Southeast Asian Nations (ASEAN).[22] This ambitious yet vague plan never gained traction, in part because of the difficulty of creating a common vision among nations with such different political and social systems.

Despite the tepid reception given to Rudd's proposal, Australia remains a central part of Asia's liberal community. It has continuously deepened ties with Japan, holding trilateral meetings with Washington and Tokyo, and begun defense cooperation. Canberra also promotes good governance and development in Asia, as it did in Fiji after the 2006 military coup or in postindependence East Timor.[23] Its largely liberal refugee policy makes it a leader on human rights in the region, though a surge in illegal boat people reaching its shores starting in 2013 has led to tougher enforcement of immigration laws. Lingering problems at home with its indigenous Aboriginal population also raise questions of institutional racism.[24] Yet for all its willingness to lead in promoting liberal values in the region and to be a major partner of the United States, Australia's leaders understand that it can play but a limited role compared with China, Japan, or India. "We know we can't compete with the big players," a seasoned Australian diplomat tells me, "so we don't try to. We look for niche opportunities." That has served Australia well, but it does little to fill the gap in Asia's political risk map.

India's Ambiguity

The temperature hovers around 100°F, and the heat radiating off the stone sculptures only intensifies the suffocating air. I am captivated by the fantastical rock carvings of numerous sanctuaries, bursting with gods and creatures from Indian mythology.

I have come to Mahabalipuram, now a UNESCO World Heritage site, an hour south of Chennai on India's Coromandel Coast. For nearly a millennium, starting in the first century CE, Mahabalipuram was one of India's most important ports and political sites, eventually becoming absorbed into one of the several kingdoms that dominated southeastern Asia. These kingdoms spread Indian political influence and religion overseas, and colonized areas in today's Indonesia, Burma, Thailand, and Malaysia.[25] Standing in the shadow of the magnificent Shore Temple, I can look east past a new seawall to the Indian Ocean. Across the vast expanse of water lies Southeast Asia, a region to which India's gaze has again returned after centuries of neglect.

One of the great foreign policy questions for India today is how, and how far, to return to Asia, and how to leverage its size and potential power into a larger diplomatic role. Yet much as New Delhi is drawn to its ancient area of influence, its attention is always pulled to the ever-present threat of conflict with Pakistan. "We can't escape our history," a senior Indian diplomat says over coffee in his spartan office, "but we know that the future lies in Asia. The question is how to shift our focus there when our security is still in question."

When Japan failed to leverage its democratic credentials into regional political leadership during the 2000s, some cast their eyes to the other end of the Indo-Pacific, wondering if another democratic leader might emerge.[26] To do so, however, India would have to cross both geographic and historical boundaries. The nation is often discussed in terms that imply a degree of separation from the rest of Asia. Surrounded by ocean on its eastern and western coasts and by towering mountain ranges in the north, the Indian subcontinent is in many ways its own ecosystem.

Until recent times, India's links with Japan and Korea, as well as with the Chinese heartland, were tenuous. They focused largely on cultural transmission, for example, of Hinduism and Buddhism. Since partition in 1947, India's smaller neighbors to the north and east, including Bangladesh, Myanmar, Nepal, and Bhutan, have had to deal with Indian policies that were seen as overbearing, especially on border issues.[27] In recent years, however, India has been drawn into the region's collective consciousness, helping to redefine the contours of "Asia" to include the wider framework of the "Indo-Pacific." In this new construct, India is naturally seen as an integral part of the region. This was amplified by New Delhi's increased activity in eastern Asia, after it took advantage of economic liberalization at home to begin reorienting its foreign policy.[28]

It is convenient to date the beginning of India's reengagement with Asia with the "Look East" policy, which was rolled out in the early 1990s by Prime Minister P. V. Narasimha Rao of the Congress Party.[29] The policy was never intended to supplant New Delhi's traditional focus on Pakistan and the northwest, but it was continued by his successors in both the Congress Party and the Hindu nationalist Bharatiya Janata Party (BJP). The Look East policy was guided by two assumptions: first, that deeper ties with the nations of the Indo-Pacific region could offer needed economic opportunities, and second, that India and China were competing for regional influence. The policy was thus a departure from the traditional stance of nonalignment that defined New Delhi's foreign policy after independence and during the Cold War.[30]

China played no small role in India's reengagement with Asia. Visiting New Delhi, I ask various officials whether China is a security challenge or an economic boon, or both. "We have no problems with China that we can't deal with," a senior Indian diplomat assures me. "We know how to deal with Beijing." His confidence is impressive, but Sino-Indian political relations have always been tense. They were bad enough to boil over into a short war in 1962 that saw some contested border territory fall into Chinese hands. New Delhi has also considered Beijing's political and military ties to Pakistan a constant threat, one that has the potential of encircling India, further straining relations between the two.[31]

As China became more powerful in the early 2000s, New Delhi decided to slowly engage more deeply with Beijing, as well as the rest of Asia, in particular with Japan. Indian officials would never admit they were engaging in a tacit balancing strategy against China, but at regular high-level Indo-Japanese political and military meetings, the future of the Indo-Pacific was frequently discussed. Japanese prime ministers Junichiro Koizumi and Shinzo Abe placed strong emphasis on improving ties with India, including economic ones, and trade between India and Japan increased by more than 50 percent from 2009 to 2014, reaching $16.3 billion.[32] Emblematic of this new relationship was the December 2006 "Joint Statement towards Japan-India Strategic and Global Partnership," signed by Manmohan Singh and Shinzo Abe, which "affirm[ed] that Japan and India are natural partners as the largest and most developed democracies of Asia."[33]

Unfortunately, a deeper democratic alignment that could have filled in the vacuum of political leadership in Asia has so far failed to define its goals. At the beginning of their rapprochement with India, Japan's leaders pushed too far too quickly. Prime Minister Abe, during his first brief tenure in office in 2006–7, alarmed New Delhi with his call for a de facto quadrilateral alignment of Japan, the United States, Australia, and India. This was quickly seen as an attempt to encircle China, and Indian leaders recoiled from such a radical idea.[34] After Abe resigned the premiership, Indo-Japanese ties began to wane, only to be revived with his return to power in late 2012. A further deepening between New Delhi and Tokyo commenced with the election of Narendra Modi in mid-2014. Since then, the two sides have grown increasingly close, with Abe serving as the chief guest at India's National Day celebrations in 2014 and the conclusion of deals to export Japanese defense equipment to India. Yet neither Tokyo nor New Delhi is ready to declare anything like a functional alliance or propose a new democracy-only organization in Asia, highlighting the limits that democratic cooperation still faces.

Policymakers in New Delhi have cast their diplomatic net wider than just at Japan. Another goal of the Look East policy was to bring India closer to Southeast Asian nations, particularly through enhanced dialogue and cooperation with ASEAN. Given the Indian diaspora populations in Singapore and Malaysia, as well as thriving business communities in Japan and elsewhere in the region, it was natural for India to begin thinking about a larger political role in Asia. Less than ten years after joining the security-oriented ASEAN Regional Forum, in 1996, India became one of the founding members of a new initiative, the East Asia Summit. Its inclusion was in part a result of Japanese insistence that more democratic nations be added.[35] Narendra Modi continued the process of improving relations between India and its smaller neighbors, for example, by agreeing in June 2015 to the dissolution of more than two hundred archaic eighteenth-century territorial enclaves dotting both sides of the border with Bangladesh.[36]

While it may seem that India has come down on the side of internationalism, it has at times frustrated officials in Washington and Tokyo who hoped to enroll it firmly in the liberal camp. Former prime minister Singh carefully balanced the tinderbox relationship with Pakistan, and made some moves to ease India's strained relations with neighbors such as Bangladesh. But those who were disappointed by Singh's lack of enthusiasm for turning India into an effective counterweight to China find his successor Modi far more eager to expand India's political role. Trying to underscore his new emphasis on Asia, Modi announced at the November 2014 ASEAN Summit that India's "Look East" policy had become "Act East."[37] That will not, he assured his audience, mean a clash between India and China but rather the continued evolution of Indian regional diplomacy.

From the perspective of regional politics, however, India seems to remain close to its traditionally nonaligned status. "We want friendly relations with all our neighbors," my diplomat friend assures me, but in this case, such admirable ecumenism means a policy that keeps India uncommitted to one grouping or the other, and therefore oddly on the sidelines. Its political role in the Indo-Pacific remains under construction. Having chosen not to cast its lot solely with the democracies, New Delhi finds itself instead floating in a vacuum. Like its giant neighbor China, it will remain in the center of the Indo-Pacific's unsettled political equilibrium simply because of its size, but it will not fill the gap in the map of regional democratic leadership.

Before moving on to the other major actors in this risk region, we should stop and ask whether it matters that Asia's democratic nations, and those allied with the United States, have not succeeded in becoming (or have tried to become) political leaders in the Indo-Pacific. To ask such a question is to make a presumption that the expansion of democracy and liberalism is a good thing, for individual countries and the region alike.

One reason for concern is that an ad hoc approach to promoting liberal political values is limited by its very nature. Even given democracy's impressive advance throughout much of Asia during the 1980s and 1990s, as discussed in chapter 4, how much more might have been achieved with a more cohesive liberal community? For most of the Cold War, the United States did not try to build an integrated regional alliance system based on democratic norms. While this could have changed as the Cold War ended, the lingering distrust between Japan and its neighbors made it politically infeasible. Washington simply lacked a broader strategic vision for American policy in the Indo-Pacific that could have inspired an alternative to its long-standing bilateral approach. If policymakers had focused on the ongoing struggle in Asia between liberalism and authoritarianism, then a broader multilateral political alliance might have helped spread democracy even further, overcome some of the historical legacies, and promoted greater regional integration and stability.

One can never know exactly what would have happened, but unlike in Europe, where democratic nations have banded together to form durable political links and thereby helped ensure democracy's survival and increased regional stability, Asia's democratic leaders have so far failed to show similar boldness. The absence of such a democratic community is one reason Asia faces so much risk today, but it is not the only one.

The Risk of Doing Too Little

The taxicab speeds past our stop and the driver swears in Indonesian (I assume) as he is forced to drive blocks out of his way in dense traffic

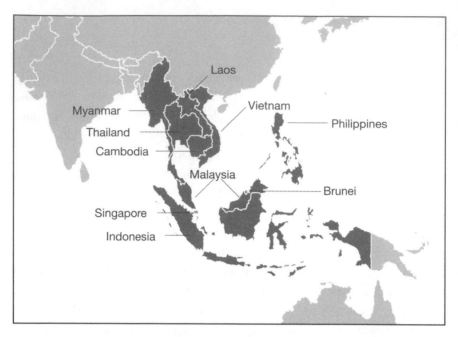

ASEAN Member States. Artwork by Claude Aubert.

before he can turn around. I can't blame him for missing our turn, since my destination is hard to find geographically, and sometimes politically.

Tucked behind thick foliage and a wrought iron fence on the traffic-congested main boulevard of Jakarta sits the headquarters of ASEAN. Often mistaken for an Asian version of NATO or the European Community, ASEAN is far more modest. Its secretary-general, all but unknown to outsiders, draws none of the publicity that the heads of the European Union or United Nations receive. The ASEAN secretariat numbers around sixty persons, just one-tenth the size of the European Commission's, despite covering a region of 630 million people.[38]

The invisibility of ASEAN's headquarters ironically mirrors the group's ambiguous role in Asia. It is ever present yet often ineffectual, respected but often ignored. ASEAN and its headquarters are a perfect symbol of Asia's lack of political community. What ASEAN represents is the germ of a community, an attempt to create order from the multitude of political systems in the Indo-Pacific. Yet it might never evolve beyond its self-imposed limitations.

While the United States was building up its alliance structure in the Pacific in the 1950s and 1960s, some Asian nations began slowly and hesitantly to form a political community among themselves. In 1967, Indonesia, Malaysia, the Philippines, Singapore, and Thailand formed ASEAN, the region's first indigenous multilateral organization. In succeeding decades, membership was extended to Brunei, Myanmar, Cambodia, Laos, and Vietnam, for a total of ten countries.[39]

Forming ASEAN was a calculation born out of a realistic view of the Indo-Pacific. Asia's smaller nations could not hope to compete economically or militarily with giants like China, India, and Japan. Banding together was a rational way to pool their strengths and leverage common policies so as to gain greater influence. Yet the ASEAN nations were themselves hardly united. They had no shared political values or anything resembling Europe's common market. Despite being neighbors, they had as much mistrust of each other as of the looming Asian giants on their borders or across the waters. Even within ASEAN, moreover, there was a hierarchy. Having the headquarters in Jakarta raised questions—which have never been fully settled—about the relative strength of the group's larger nations, such as Indonesia, compared with smaller ones. These difficulties have combined to make ASEAN less than the sum of its parts.

Since the association consisted of smaller nations without high-profile diplomatic policies, economic power, or much military capacity, ASEAN's initial efforts were focused on the modest goal of simply gaining acceptance for the existence of any permanent Asian regional organization. Since the collapse of Japan's wartime empire in 1945, there had been no attempt to re-create any type of regional order. Rather, the region was loosely divided into the bloc of Soviet allies, which included Vietnam, Cambodia, and Laos (but not China, after 1964) and a bloc of America's allies, which included both liberal and autocratic countries.

That Southeast Asia would tread its own path was made clear in 1955, when Indonesian leader Sukarno hosted the Bandung Conference, gathering nations opposed to either side in the Cold War. This evolved into the Non-Aligned Movement (NAM), established in 1961.[40] The NAM had a global membership, and almost all Asian nations eventually joined, including founding ASEAN members Indonesia, Malaysia, and Singapore as well as Vietnam, Cambodia, Laos, and Myanmar. Clearly, one could be a Soviet ally yet also be a member in good standing of the ostensibly nonaligned nations. In 1993, after the Cold War ended, American allies the Philippines and Thailand also joined the NAM, as did Mongolia. Yet the NAM did little more than occasionally gather, and failed to become any type of formal organization that functioned as an effective counterpart to the superpowers.

Nor did ASEAN hold ambitious goals. Its members did not envision their association becoming anything like the European Community. Nor could it ever be a replacement for the last stable political order in Asia, the Qing Empire. The association realistically refrained from seeking to be an alternative political pole to the Soviet Union, China, or the United States. But as an expression of the idea that the Indo-Pacific region should move beyond the fragmented political environment of the postcolonial era, ASEAN picked up the baton from Asia's leading nations, particularly China and Japan, which were unable to envision or pursue such a multilateral initiative. Although the scope of ASEAN's activities was at first limited to its neighborhood of Southeast Asia, it provided a vision of a much broader community.[41]

A constant criticism of ASEAN has been that it is basically a talk shop, where showing up was more than 90 percent of success. Because it is officially devoted to the ideal of a community of equals, it has been forced to operate at the level of its lowest common denominator. This means requiring consensus among members and avoiding legally binding agreements so as to ensure unanimity. ASEAN operates a bit like the eighteenth-century Polish diet, where one member could veto any legislation or disband the parliament. This has made adopting or carrying out any meaningful agenda problematic. Such structural weakness was one reason other countries had trouble determining how important the association was, or deciding how to deal with it while maintaining bilateral relations with its members. Not until 2008, four decades after the group's founding, did the United States finally name an ambassador to ASEAN, shortly after Japan did.

Nor was unanimity within ASEAN easily achieved, given the outsized influence of Indonesia and the high international profile of Singapore. "Look," a Western nongovernmental organization (NGO) official told me in Jakarta, "it's still an achievement that they keep meeting in regular summits. Talking is better than the alternative." A former high-ranking Indonesian official frankly admitted to me, "We [Indonesia] are committed to the 'ASEAN way,'" a shorthand for that expected consensus, "but there is a tension, in that Jakarta unconsciously expects its voice to be given more weight, due to its size." The realities of political gamesmanship affect ASEAN as much as any other organization.

One insurance for ostensible equality also limits the organization's effectiveness. Every year the ASEAN chairmanship rotates. While egalitarian in theory, this arrangement often brings rapid changes in approach, and precludes keeping the same priorities for more than one year, as democracies like the Philippines give way to authoritarian states like Myanmar or Laos, and vice versa. Sacrificing effectiveness for community has meant that progress on actual policies is often excruciatingly slow. In the second decade of the twenty-first century, the organization is an established voice in the Indo-Pacific, but questions about its importance and future continue to surround it.

ASEAN's primary goal has always been to forge closer ties among its own members. From the beginning, it embraced the principle of nonintervention in member states' affairs.[42] It has focused on promoting cooperation on issues ranging from humanitarian aid and disaster relief to human trafficking.[43] Yet even here the organization has had modest impact, and sometimes been an utter failure. Its shortcomings were manifest during 2015 when the crisis of the Rohingyan boat people came to international attention.

The Rohingyans claimed to be a distinct Muslim ethnic minority fleeing persecution in Myanmar, though many were also Bangladeshi. For months, no ASEAN nation would recognize them as refugees or legally take them in.[44] Thousands of desperate Rohingyans crowded onto rickety boats and floated for days in the Indian Ocean without adequate food or medical supplies. Others were smuggled into Malaysia or Thailand, which turned a blind eye to their illegal presence but offered no overt help. Only when mass graves of Rohingyans were publicized, along with pictures of packed boats adrift at sea, did ASEAN finally begin to offer aid and accept a few asylum seekers. The fact that this humanitarian crisis was all but ignored by ASEAN's members, who could tout forty years of cooperation among themselves, tragically showed how national interests continue to triumph over regional needs.

Just as important, the limited capabilities of ASEAN's member states mean that major humanitarian aid or disaster relief for the region must come from outside. This was made clear after the massive 2004 Indonesian tsunami, which killed an estimated 250,000 people, making it one of Asia's worst natural disasters in recent history. The United States, Japan, and Australia provided the bulk of the initial disaster relief, medical supplies, and drinking water to hundreds of thousands of affected civilians while ASEAN's leading states largely looked on.[45]

For all these reasons, ASEAN's goals remain modest. Collectively, the association is committed to a long-term, three-stage process of building a "security community, by focusing on confidence building, crisis management, and preventive diplomacy."[46] These benchmarks were designed to address the lack of working relationships among ASEAN's members by building political ties and by identifying common challenges and considering how to address them. The easiest to tackle was confidence building, which was achieved largely through regular meetings and annual high-level summits. Effective crisis management and preventive diplomacy have been far harder, and ASEAN even has failed to prevent military clashes between its members. In 2011, for example, Thai and Cambodian forces fired on each other during a dispute over control of several ancient temples on their shared border. The skirmishes killed several soldiers on both sides despite attempts by Indonesian troops to act as peacekeepers.[47]

Yet if there is one area where ASEAN has carved out a niche role for itself, it is in becoming the de facto center of multilateral initiatives in the Indo-Pacific. Starting in the 1990s, ASEAN's diplomatic outreach filled a vacuum left by the region's larger powers, and the association became a driver of Asian community building. In the wake of the end of the Cold War, it organized an ASEAN Regional Forum (ARF) in 1994 to discuss pan-Asian security and political issues. Almost the entire Indo-Pacific participates in the ARF: in addition to the ten ASEAN members, the group includes Australia, Bangladesh, Canada, mainland China, the European Union, India, Japan, North Korea, South Korea, Mongolia, New Zealand, Pakistan, Papua New Guinea, Russia, East Timor, the United States, and Sri Lanka. The ARF's goals, like those of its parent organization, are to foster dialogue and consultation and promote confidence building and preventive diplomacy in the region.[48]

While the ARF has in no way become a collective security organization or a standing political mechanism, it may be the leading venue in the Indo-Pacific for discussing region-wide security concerns, though not without sometimes causing controversy itself. It was at the 2010 ARF in Hanoi, for example, that U.S. secretary of state Hillary Clinton first proclaimed that the peaceful resolution of South China Sea territorial disputes was a "national interest" of the United States (which will be discussed fully in chapter 6).[49] The statement, aimed squarely at China, became the basis of the Obama administration's "pivot" to Asia.

As an Asian organization, ASEAN is most concerned with protecting the regional interests of its members. It was natural that, starting in 1996, ASEAN directly addressed the elephant(s) in the room: how to ensure the peaceful integration of Asia's giants with the rest of the region. In what was billed as the "ASEAN+3" process, the organization hosted regular summit meetings with China, Japan, and South Korea.[50] While hampered as usual by the lack of a firm agenda, the very act of holding high-level regular meetings among all the countries of East Asia represented a significant break with the past.

As with other initiatives, there was no presumption that ASEAN+3 would become more than a diplomatic gathering or that it would supplant traditional diplomatic ties, let alone bring about the dismantling of the bilateral alliance system the United States had set up in Asia. It seemed merely another layer in the structure of Indo-Pacific political relations. The fact that it was the smaller nations of Southeast Asia that banded together and finally brought the large powers to the discussion table simply highlighted the gap in the political map of Asia. It was a stark reminder of the difficulties Beijing, Tokyo, and Seoul continue to have in translating their power and influence into a more formal political expression.

ASEAN continues to dream big. Its latest initiative builds on both the ARF and the ASEAN+3 process. Starting in 2005, the association has hosted the East Asia Summit (EAS), which brings together the ASEAN+3 group along with Australia, New Zealand, and India. The sixth meeting, held in Bali in November 2011, included the United States and Russia as

East Asian Summit Member States. Artwork by Claude Aubert.

well and was the most "pan-Asian" multinational initiative yet attempted in the region.[51]

It would be a mistake, of course, to see the EAS as Asia's answer to the European Union. The EAS grew from political jockeying for influence between Japan and China with their Southeast Asian neighbors. As China's influence in the ASEAN+3 process group grew with its economic power, Japan and some Southeast Asian nations called for the group's expansion. Tokyo lobbied hard for three democratic nations to be added, thereby creating a nascent ASEAN+6. This soon morphed into the EAS, which quickly attracted Washington and Moscow.

Once the United States joined, the liberal tilt of the meeting became unmistakable, but the political gamesmanship also increased. What was intended as a forum for collaborative endeavor came increasingly to be seen as a zero-sum political game. For example, President Barack Obama attended the EAS in 2011–12 and 2014, further raising the summit's profile; but when he skipped the meeting in 2013 because of a domestic budget showdown, international media portrayed it as a "win" for Chinese president Xi Jinping.[52]

Despite the attention it has drawn, the EAS, like ASEAN itself, has been hampered by unambitious agendas and a lack of agreement among members.[53] For now, the summit has focused on uncontroversial issues such as trade and energy security or eliminating malaria, while human rights, rule of law, and traditional security questions have been far less prominent. Still, the EAS is important precisely because it is so highly valued by Asian nations, which are aware of the gap in their political relations. Many now find it inconceivable that the region's nations would not hold an annual summit gathering, and while not sufficient, that alone is to be welcomed.

Bigger hopes are tempered by the understanding that the process is just beginning. With Russian and American participation, some have called the EAS "ASEAN+8," but no matter how prestigious, it will remain largely a talking shop for some time. As with all things ASEAN, the EAS speaks more to hopes of real cooperation and the development of community than to any specific accomplishments.

For all the criticism leveled at ASEAN about its inability to turn itself into a more robust multinational organization, it has nonetheless made itself central to the Indo-Pacific environment. As the only indigenous multilateral political mechanism, it has become an important broker for bringing larger nations into regular regional discussions. Still, the limitations of its model are ever more apparent, and not always under the ASEAN nations' control. Political community in Asia depends on the actions and attitudes of the region's giants, yet China in particular remains ambivalent and often antagonistic to greater cooperation.

Influence without Friends: China's Challenge

It was the diplomatic shot heard round the world. At the ASEAN Regional Forum in July 2010, China found itself ganged up on, perhaps for the first time on the global stage. When then-secretary of state Hillary

Clinton made a widely reported comment that America considered it a U.S. national interest to have Southeast Asia's territorial disputes settled peacefully, Chinese foreign minister Yang Jiechi fired back with words that could have come straight from Thucydides's Melian Dialogue. Glaring across the table at Singapore's foreign minister, he said, "China is a big country and other countries are small countries, and that's just a fact."[54]

If size were all that mattered, China would be the political leader of the Indo-Pacific. Yet just as Japan ran into roadblocks on its way to predominance in the 1980s, so too has the Middle Kingdom traveled a rocky road. If China's leadership wants to understand why it is having so much trouble translating its economic strength into political influence, it needs only to look in the mirror.

In ways both obvious and not, a country's influence abroad is connected to deeper questions of domestic political philosophy. It seems evident that how a government acts at home influences how it conducts itself abroad. Autocratic regimes, when they turn to the international arena, rarely become paragons of liberal behavior. States that deny their citizens fundamental rights are not surprisingly distrusted by their neighbors. Not only are they suspect precisely because of how they treat their own people, but outsiders intuitively understand that the spirit informing a country's actions at home will be similar beyond its borders.

From one perspective, modern China's relations with its neighbors began on the back foot. The reasons were not only its relative underdevelopment and oppressive Communist regime but also the long history of Chinese dominance that continues to shape the identities of nations such as Vietnam, Korea, and Japan.[55] In this region, where history is rarely forgotten, victories and defeats in battles from a millennium ago are still celebrated or mourned in popular culture. China's path since 1949, which isolated it from many of its neighbors and limited the political role it could play, is only another chapter in this history.

The struggle between liberalism and communism in Asia was not as dramatic as that in Europe during the Cold War, when the Iron Curtain drew a line down the middle of the continent, but the shifting battlefronts of the Indo-Pacific were no less contested and often bloodier. Though the greatest shock was the victory of Mao Zedong's rebels against Chinese Nationalist forces in 1949, Communist movements subsequently won victories in Vietnam, Laos, and Cambodia and mounted long-term insurgencies in the Philippines and Malaysia. After the 1964 Sino-Soviet split, however, it was not Beijing that initially became the most powerful member of Asia's illiberal bloc; that position was taken by the Soviet Union, while China was viewed warily even by its authoritarian neighbors.[56]

Even when China supported regional communist movements, its efforts did not necessarily translate into closer political relations with its ideologically compatible neighbors. In the case of Beijing and Hanoi, mutual antipathy burst into a brief war in 1979.[57] The well-publicized excesses of Mao's China made other Asian nations wary of the destructive energies and passions roiling the world's largest country. As for the nations allied with the United States, such as Japan, Thailand, and South Korea, they felt deeply threatened by China's ideology, and firmly repressed indigenous communist parties even while trying to maintain peaceful relations with Beijing.[58]

China gained little political trust in the region after the Cold War as well. In the past two decades, nations throughout the Asia-Pacific have developed a new ambivalence toward Beijing's political role, despite its explosive economic growth. On one hand, China is the major trading partner for all Asian nations and the productive center of the global economy. On the other hand, in recent years Beijing has attempted to recapture its traditional regional dominance and has chafed against what it sees as Western-inspired restraints on its ability to influence its smaller neighbors. The Chinese Communist Party's steps toward regaining what it sees as China's rightful position have included not only a major military buildup but also a new political assertiveness over contentious issues such as disputed territory.

For a while in the 1990s, it seemed that China would indeed reemerge as the most powerful political actor in the region, and many observers wonder why it has not yet done so. The confidence that Chinese leaders gained from their unparalleled economic growth after Deng Xiaoping's reforms of the 1980s led to a more energetic and assertive foreign policy. Their diplomacy also became more sophisticated, and China's discussions of its "peaceful rise" and role as a good neighbor were designed to win over states traditionally wary of its outsized influence.[59]

What we might call China's "political globalization" was expressed in a flurry of initiatives in the 1990s and early 2000s that became known as "smile diplomacy," an attempt to pull its neighbors ever closer through political support and generous trade deals.[60] For example, Beijing concluded a free trade agreement (FTA) with ASEAN that came into effect in 2010.[61] Not only is this the largest FTA in the region (at least until the Trans-Pacific Partnership comes into force), it has given China enormous influence in ASEAN's multilateral deliberations, and for years helped to dampen resistance to China's territorial claims in the South China Sea. Beijing has used foreign aid and trade relations to garner support. This explains (at least in part) Cambodia and Laos's ongoing alignment with China, and against most of ASEAN, on such issues as South China Sea territorial disputes and maritime codes of conduct.[62]

China's leaders have also taken advantage of specific diplomatic mechanisms to increase their political influence. Perhaps the best example of this is the Six-Party Talks, the failed attempt that ran from 2003 through 2012 to prevent North Korea from becoming a nuclear power. Prodded by Washington, Beijing positioned itself as the broker between Pyongyang and the United States. In many quarters it was suddenly seen as a major diplomatic player and the only power with the ability to change the Kim regime's behavior.[63] Every time North Korean provoked or attacked its neighbors, commentators and diplomats worldwide averred that Beijing held the magic keys to controlling Pyongyang, despite mounting evidence that Beijing either had no intention of doing so or far less influence than was thought. In the same way, many in Asia argue that the EAS and other multilateral initiatives are meaningless without Beijing's participation.

So why didn't these trends result in a stable, enduring political leadership role for China? Part of the reason is that China has failed to develop any real partners that it can count on, work with, or trust. As the 2010 ARF altercation in Hanoi showed, Beijing has at times let its natural sense of superiority turn into an overbearing attitude toward its neighbors.

Much of the goodwill China gained from its smile diplomacy has been squandered by Beijing's assertive stance on regional territorial disputes (which will be discussed fully in chapter 6). In addition, it began to be seen as obstructionist in dealing with North Korea, for example, by repeatedly watering down proposed UN sanctions against Pyongyang. When the United States subtly criticized Chinese actions, Beijing pushed back even more, alternating its outbursts with periods of quiescence but never moderating its positions. These actions undid years of diplomacy that had raised China's stature and correspondingly lowered those of Japan and even the United States.[64]

A crucial element of China's difficulties is that it invites suspicion by consistently supporting countries—most notably North Korea, Iran, Sudan, and until recently Myanmar—that threaten their neighbors, oppress their people, or seek to destabilize the international order. Those that China has favored, being often isolated from the larger world, have become millstones around Beijing's neck rather than the building blocks of a successful community of interests. North Korea, for example, has if anything become more unpredictable and threatening under its new leader, Kim Jong-un, than it was in the past. Similarly, Myanmar also was an international pariah until its recent steps toward democracy and away from China.

Beijing rarely has wavered in its support for these disruptive regional actors or others elsewhere the world. It finds itself continually at odds with liberal nations over issues like UN sanctions of North Korea and Iran. It is not only "China hawks" in Japan and the United States who now believe that Beijing's policies indicate a clear desire to reshape or undermine the global political order. At a minimum, the impression is now widespread that China seeks to frustrate efforts of the United States and its partners to resolve regional and international crises caused by rogue states.[65]

China has drawn suspicion even from supposedly cooperative initiatives. In 2014, for example, it announced its intention to establish a new financial lending institution for the Indo-Pacific region, to be called the Asian Infrastructure Investment Bank (AIIB). That October it established the bank with twenty-one cofounders and a proposed $100 billion in capitalization. But Washington and Tokyo soon came to see the AIIB as an economic tool to reshape Asia's political architecture by reducing the influence of the World Bank and the Asian Development Bank. The World Bank, headquartered in Washington, D.C., and headed by an American, and the Asian Development Bank, located in Manila but run largely by Japanese officials, had traditionally represented the dominance of a Western, liberal financial order in Asia. Beijing touted the AIIB as a more effective and responsive organization that would have Asia's interests at heart.

Yet global support for the AIIB did not implicitly mean trust in Beijing. Many nations feared missing out on the financial benefits of membership, while they also perceived a decline in Washington's role in Asia. And the Obama administration's response to the gambit, a confused and ineffective attempt to prevent its allies and major Asian economies from joining the AIIB, achieved just the opposite result. By March 2015, every Asian country except Japan had signed on.[66] Adding insult to injury, leading American allies in Europe, including Great Britain and France, also joined. In response, the Obama administration publicly criticized Great Britain, its closest global ally, for "constant accommodation" of Beijing.[67] Yet if Beijing's success in establishing the bank with a global membership led many to view it as a more powerful political player in the Asia-Pacific, it was not seen as more trustworthy, as continuing Western and Asian criticism of its actions in the South China Sea or in its civil society crackdown showed.

China remains largely friendless in the Indo-Pacific, an ironic state of affairs given its economic stature and high diplomatic profile. While no nation, large or small, can afford to ignore China economically, and many fear it militarily, few feel close to it politically. Perhaps because of these difficulties in maintaining its diplomatic momentum in Asia, Beijing has sought to expand its political influence outside of the Indo-Pacific, in Central Asia, Latin America, and sub-Saharan Africa.[68] This was a revolutionary step for a country that had always focused on domestic issues and only secondarily on foreign ones, and then only in its near abroad. This apparent expansionism also raised fears in America and other parts of the world that a wealthier China was willing to get involved in areas far from its traditional backyard. Yet all this activity outside the Asia-Pacific simply reflects the poor state of China's relations with its neighbors and its inability to work closely with any of them.

This lack of true friends or allies is perhaps the Chinese leadership's most troublesome diplomatic issue. Despite engaging in multilateral negotiations, China often acts as though regional politics were a zero-sum game. This is certainly its attitude toward Japan. China's size and economic power appear to impede it from treating most other nations in the region as equals. When bringing up old questions of history or confidently predicting long-term trends of Chinese growth, officials in Beijing often end up intimidating and sometimes insulting other nations' diplomats.

Ever sensitive to diplomatic resistance, Beijing is apt to respond with aggressive language. In a clever yet ominous pop culture reference, it described Japan as a "Voldemort" over Yasukuni Shrine visits by Japanese politicians. More worrisome, it has consistently refused to disavow saber-rattling statements by military officers, government-connected academics, and party-run media, such as the claim that war with America is "inevitable" unless Washington accepts Chinese territorial claims in the South China Sea.[69]

Beijing's isolation is thus explainable in terms of both history and current trends. From this perspective, its foreign policy, while impressive on the surface, is just as fragile as its internal politics and does little to fill in the gap in Indo-Pacific political leadership.

Is the lack of a strong regional political mechanism actually a risk factor to be worried about? After all, Asian nations have not fought each other since the 1979 Sino-Vietnamese border war, their regional trade has exploded over the past two decades, and they all meet peacefully to discuss important regional questions. Tourists and travelers are not harassed at borders, and goods and services are peacefully exchanged throughout the region every day. Why would we want to impose the suffocating bureaucracy of the European Union or the sometimes corrupt inefficiency of the United Nations on vibrant Asia?

Asia does not need either a mini–United Nations or a European Union. Yet the vacuum created by the absence of a time-tested, successful, regional political organization has been filled by the type of jockeying among major states that often heightens diplomatic tensions. Smaller nations feel pressured to pick sides when their greatest desire is to antagonize neither, as witnessed by Cambodia and Laos's constant support for China and the Philippines' desire for U.S. backing. Even worse, the lack of real regional mechanisms for dealing with disputes and security threats means that potential conflict is left largely unaddressed. Unfortunately, these security threats are slowly getting worse.

6

HIC SUNT DRACONES: THE CLOUDS OF WAR

In August 2014, in a scene out of *Top Gun*, one of China's most advanced fighter jets buzzed a U.S. Navy surveillance plane in international airspace off the Chinese coast. Approaching at six hundred miles per hour, the Su-27 jet flashed its underside to show its weapons and then did a barrel roll over the lumbering U.S. aircraft, flying as close as twenty feet from the Americans.[1] The midair gymnastics undoubtedly made pilots from both sides think about a similar incident in April 2001, when a hot dog Chinese fighter pilot collided with a similar U.S. plane, killing himself and forcing the Americans to make an emergency landing on Chinese territory.[2]

Such face-offs are not as rare as one might think. In late November 2013, high above the East China Sea, two U.S. Air Force B-52 bombers found themselves shadowed by Chinese fighter aircraft. The Americans were flying through a new air defense zone declared by Beijing that overlapped Japanese territorial airspace, and the Chinese government had issued orders that all aircraft flying in the zone identify themselves or risk being shot down. At the same time, Japanese coast guard vessels were confronting Chinese maritime patrol ships in waters around a set of hotly disputed islands in the East China Sea.

As dynamic as Asia's political picture is, so too is its security environment. Given the growing trade and wealth in the region, a casual visitor to Asia could be excused for assuming that Indo-Pacific nations are too busy getting rich to waste time on territorial disputes and make shows of military strength. In fact, modernization and economic growth have led to a new era of insecurity and a growing threat of armed conflict.

When I began the research for this book, few serious observers of Asia worried about military conflict, except for the perennial danger of North Korea. By the time I wrote these words, one of the most anticipated novels of 2015 was a techno-thriller about a Sino-American conflict.[3] Yet even if popular culture is beginning to sense a new market, to most observers, war in the Indo-Pacific still seems very remote.

Perhaps because much of Asia has been peaceful for a few decades, many outside the region—and inside it as well—seem to take for granted that it will always be so, despite the recent tension.[4] As their European counterparts did in the first decade of the twentieth century, many observers today argue that the great volume of trade, the unhindered movement of people, and the bevy of regional political organizations have made war in Asia impossible. And like their predecessors in the pre–World War I "proud tower" of Europe, they ignore the trends that point toward increasing conflict.[5] Some might think we are dealing with a chicken-and-egg question: Has Asia become stable and peaceful because of economic growth, or has economic growth been made possible by Asia's stability?

As a historian, I am largely influenced by a "realist" view of international relations, believing that states above all seek to assure their security in an anarchic world.[6] They may do so cooperatively or by seeking advantage over others, but since states almost always act in pursuit of their own interests, there is always the danger of conflict. Since the 1940s, Asia, like much of the rest of the world, has been living in a historically abnormal period of relative peace, making us forget that competition and conflict are endemic to human nature.

Asia's "Great Game"

While it is not yet seeing military clashes like those in Eastern Europe or the Middle East, the Indo-Pacific contains its own "great game" between large and small powers. Some of this competition is simply for greater influence, but some is for concrete gain such as wrestling away territory or gaining de facto client states. At the highest level, that between China and its neighbors, it is for determining the basic structure of the region and the rules and norms that guide it. It is a contest in which no nation, not even China, feels assured of its own strength. Asia's simmering military competition, standoffs, mini-confrontations, and saber rattling have until recently been ignored in good-news discussions of the Indo-Pacific.

In some ways, our entire journey through Asia's risk map has been aiming us toward this final region, whose features can be seen far more clearly than complex economic issues or slowly evolving demographic trends. In medieval maps, the border of this region would have carried the legend *Hic sunt dracones* ("Here be dragons") to indicate unknown dangers and warn travelers to be wary. Wariness over the future stability and security of Asia is more than warranted. Among the realms of our risk map, the question of security is by definition the most dangerous. Its borders directly abut the regional political challenges discussed in chapter 5, but its contours also are defined by demographics, domestic political pressures, and slowing economic growth.

Investors, traders, policymakers, defense planners, and scholars should not take Asia's stability for granted. The Asia-Pacific today is the most militarized region in the world. Some of the world's largest armed forces, such as the Chinese People's Liberation Army and the North Korean military, jostle against some of the most technologically advanced, like the Japanese Self-Defense Forces, and combat ready, like the South Koreans. The United States bases 360,000 military and civilian personnel in the Pacific along with nearly one hundred ships and hundreds of airplanes, from fighter jets to bombers. Six of the world's most powerful militaries are located at least partly in the Indo-Pacific: the United States, China, Russia, Japan, South Korea, and India. Four of those countries are official nuclear powers, and North Korea is an undeclared nuclear state. Warfare both old and new is practiced in the region, as China and North Korea have been accused of repeated cyberattacks on their neighbors and on other nations. Given this environment, conflict appears just as likely an outcome as is continued stability.

This assertion may sound alarmist. After all, the Indo-Pacific has not seen a region-wide total war since 1945. After Hiroshima and Nagasaki, the last major clash between Asian nations was the 1962 Sino-Indian War, and there has been no extended conflict between Asian nations since the

1979 Sino-Vietnamese border war. The 1960s-era Vietnam War is properly seen not as a conflict between nations but as an anticolonial revolt that turned into a civil war followed by U.S. intervention.

While it is true that great power–style wars have not occurred in Asia since 1945, the rarity of clashes between neighbors is fully made up for by costs of decolonization and the frequency and devastation of civil war. The bloody partition of India and Pakistan in 1947 caused between two hundred thousand and one million casualties while displacing fourteen million people, and it led to decades of enmity and low-intensity conflict between New Delhi and Islamabad.[7] The Khmer Rouge wrought havoc on Cambodia in the 1970s, filling the Killing Fields with one million corpses, just a few years after the Vietnam War led to the deaths of an estimated one million Vietnamese. Two decades earlier, the division of the Korean Peninsula led to a major war in the 1950s, the deaths of perhaps a million people, and an armed standoff that has continued now for sixty years.[8]

The Philippines and Indonesia, while avoiding full-scale civil war, have fought Muslim insurgencies for much of their history, leading them to an almost exclusive focus on their own problems.[9] Decolonization and the overthrow of European-run governments caused massive disruptions throughout the region after World War II, starting of course with the Indian subcontinent but also affecting Malaysia, Singapore, and Indonesia, as well as much of Indochina.[10]

Still, the region has avoided the widespread devastation of a major international conflict. Since the 1960s, this regional peace has allowed most Asian countries to focus on economic growth and political stability. It has also created the conditions whereby intraregional trade and political links could be built over time.[11] The nations of Asia that were free from civil conflict could focus on peaceful pursuits because they had little fear of their external environment and did not have to spend massive amounts of national treasure on defense or reconstruction.[12]

Today, however, the rapid transformation of Asia's security environment threatens to undo the work of decades. China's rise is upsetting the political and military equilibrium and causing other nations to build their own military power. In addition, North Korea has moved from bizarre annoyance to deadly threat, while numerous territorial disputes between

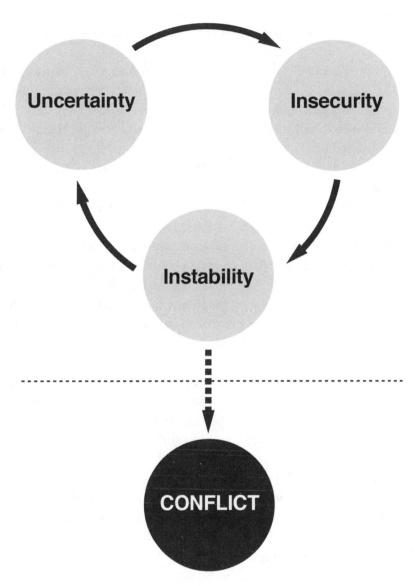

The Risk Cycle. Artwork by Olivier Ballou.

countries both large and small are helping fuel the arms race. The rules that have long governed international relations in Asia appear to be breaking down.

One way to understand what is happening is to imagine a security "risk cycle." The risk cycle begins with growing *uncertainty* derived from trends like China's dramatic military modernization, North Korea's nuclear program, and unresolved border disputes. Worry over how far these trends will worsen and perceptions that they are intensifying add to the general unease. Asia passed this part of the risk cycle more than a decade ago.

The next turn of the cycle leads to greater feelings of *insecurity*. With no extranational power that can compel nations to act peacefully, every nation must look out for its own interests. Thus the perception that things are getting worse leads to a concrete sense of threat. For example, smaller countries that border assertive or aggressive nations, or countries with nagging territorial disputes, begin to believe that their security and safety are directly threatened, and they question whether they can defend their national interests. Some begin to modestly build up their militaries, hoping to improve their chances of protecting their interests, or at least send a signal to the nations they perceive as threatening them.

This sense of insecurity can spread throughout the region. Other nations, watching the actions of states that feel insecure, may themselves respond in destabilizing ways, by doubling down on disputed claims or else building up their own militaries as a precaution. These moves and countermoves lead to a downward spiral in which actions taken for defensive reasons are seen by others as aggressive.[13] Nations both big and small, including Japan, South Korea, Taiwan, Vietnam, and the Philippines, have felt dramatically less secure in recent years, and their attempts to restore their sense of safety have led in turn to increased tension with China or further worry by their neighbors.

The final turn of the risk cycle brings actual *instability*. States ultimately feel forced to act to protect their interests. Instability may emerge through aggressive actions like confronting another nation's military or attempting to secure control over contested territory. It is not surprising that a long-term sense of insecurity can lead a state to take actions that destabilize its environment. As disputes deepen and military budgets grow, conflict becomes more likely, whether through accident or choice.[14]

Several moments mark Asia's movement through the risk cycle into an environment of instability. One may have been 2006, when North Korea conducted its first nuclear test; that event cranked the insecurity meter as high as it could go.[15] Another moment might have been in August of 2012, when Japan, insecure over Chinese probing around a set of disputed islands in the East China Sea, chose to nationalize several of them. The result has been a paramilitary face-off that shows no signs of receding.[16] A third was the 2012 Scarborough Shoal incident between China and the Philippines, in which Chinese maritime patrol ships essentially wrested away contested territory, thus confirming many small Asian nations' fears about China's growing strength.[17]

The Asia-Pacific has been disturbed by constant confrontations and small skirmishes but no outbreak of general hostilities. Even when states pull back from armed confrontation, temporarily reducing instability, the specter of uncertainty soon returns, and the cycle begins again. The region has failed to reverse its risk cycle, in part because of the absence of strong diplomatic mechanisms, as discussed in chapter 5. War is not preordained, but once the risk cycle reaches this last stage, instability, the immediate question is how bad it will become and whether minor flare-ups will turn into serious clashes. The long-term goal must be to extinguish the causes of instability and restore a sense of security. Asia has not begun that process, in part because of its bloody history.

The legacy of World War II, civil war, decolonization, and the Cold War lives on. The Asia-Pacific is a region where power politics lies just beneath the surface and a lack of trust pervades regional relations. The suspicion and worry have increased as China has begun flexing its muscles. Even without an ongoing war, the region now spends more than Europe on military budgets, paying out $287 billion in 2013 for weaponry.[18] What is it that Asians fear so much?

Lines of Dispute: Asia's Unsettled Borders

Just like Korea's hidden "tunnel of aggression" down which I crawled, until recently most of Asia's security risks have been largely out of sight. The most immediate danger in Asia today comes from numerous territorial disputes, on both land and sea. To Westerners, the idea of border quarrels seems like a remnant from nineteenth-century Europe, but in Asia, feuds over both land borders and numerous island groups continue to threaten long-term stability. In the absence of both mutual trust and established mechanisms for settling competing claims, these disagreements are a series of ticking time bombs that have the potential to dramatically upset Asia's equilibrium. Each is inextricably linked to nationalist impulses in all the claimant countries, making them even harder to resolve.

If we are charting the trend lines of risk, we should be worried that these disputes, instead of slowly subsiding and being resolved amicably, seem to be growing more intractable. Risk that should be falling is instead rising. As Asia's nations become wealthier and have more resources to devote to their militaries, they seem less interested in avoiding confrontation. And as nations grapple with domestic political and economic pressures, the tide of nationalism rises higher, forcing governments into ever-more-assertive positions. Mapping Asia's major territorial quarrels will reveal their complexity, uniqueness, and danger.

In making a risk map, it is natural to rank dangers by their intensity. Which border dispute, then, most imperils security in Asia? Few would disagree that the region's most dangerous confrontation is on the divided Korean peninsula, where two large and highly trained militaries have faced each other since 1953 across a no-man's-land separated by barbed wire.

One might think that antipathies would attenuate over the decades, but in the case of Korea, they would be mistaken. To ring in 2016, the North Korean government shocked the world by announcing it had detonated a hydrogen bomb, its fourth nuclear test. Lauding what it called the "H-bomb of justice," Pyongyang claimed it had perfected the technology to miniaturize a fusion device. South Korea measured the seismic activity of the explosion and U.S. spy planes sniffed the air over North Korea, searching for traces of radiation. Though nuclear experts around the world soon raised doubts that it was indeed a hydrogen bomb detonation, there was little doubt that Pyongyang had conducted another nuclear test, thus starkly reaffirming the existential threat that it desires to pose to its neighbors.[19]

For six decades, the totalitarian Kim family regime has turned North Korea into a prison state and launched numerous attacks against its neighbors.[20] A list of Pyongyang's erratic aggressions could fill pages, like a rap sheet of a repeat offender. It includes the kidnapping of South Korean and Japanese nationals from their homelands during the 1970s and 1980s, sophisticated counterfeiting and smuggling operations, paramilitary incursions into neighboring countries, threats of war, and low-level attacks on South Korea, such as the 2010 sinking of a South Korean naval vessel at sea and the bombing of a South Korean island.[21]

The cycle of outreach, negotiation, and disillusionment by which the United States and its allies have dealt with North Korea throughout the 1990s and 2000s was interrupted by the death of longtime dictator Kim Jong-Il in December 2011 and the accession of Kim Jong-un, his third and youngest son. In a sign of just how fanatically secretive the North is, the world was unaware of the younger Kim's existence until shortly before he took power, and there was much speculation on whether his elder half-brothers would accept his rule or would plunge the country into civil war. Almost comically, there were hopes abroad for a "Pyongyang Spring," thanks to a brief moment of "glasnost" with the news of Kim's marriage to a young former North Korean pop star, a few photo opportunities with Mickey Mouse, and an inexplicable friendship with the former pro basketball star Dennis Rodman.[22]

Several years into his rule, such hopes have been dashed. Kim Jong-un appears to be firmly in control of North Korea and as ruthless as his father. In 2013 he ordered the execution of his uncle Jang Sung Taek, the power behind the throne for the younger Kim's father and reportedly China's man in Pyongyang.[23] Since then, Kim Jong-un has at least equaled his father in cult of personality, bloody purges, disruptive behavior, and regional saber rattling.

Whether through traditional or nontraditional means, this hermit regime has steadily grown to pose a threat outside its borders. North Korea maintains a military of approximately 1.2 million troops, including the world's largest number of Special Forces units, though much of its equipment is outdated and of unknown quality.[24] Many of North Korea's 13,000 artillery pieces are within range of Seoul, as is much of its arsenal of short- and medium-range ballistic missiles. Together, these weapons could kill thousands of civilians in Seoul and destroy much of South Korea's government in the first hours of a war.[25] Seoul, in turn, is just as armed, though with more modern weapons.

Visiting the Demilitarized Zone separating North and South drives home the fragility of peace on the Korean peninsula. Miles of barbed wire punctuated by guard houses dominate a landscape dotted with half-century-old land mines. The emptiness in the South's "Area of Civilian Control" along the border reinforces the belief that as long as the Kim regime remains in power, there can be no normality on this peninsula.

Keenly aware that its survival depends on being "bulletproof," and also of its weakness in conventional arms compared with South Korea, in the 1990s Pyongyang started pursuing a nuclear weapons program and focused on building long-range ballistic missiles. Breaking the so-called Agreed Framework it signed with the Clinton administration in 1994, it pursued a two-track approach to developing a nuclear capability, utilizing both plutonium and highly enriched uranium processes. Despite ongoing negotiations with the United States, it succeeded in conducting nuclear tests in 2006, 2009, 2013, and 2016. These were paralleled by long-range ballistic missile launches that, in late 2012, appeared to succeed.[26] After years of downplaying North Korea's capabilities, senior U.S. officials now consider it a danger to Japan and U.S. territories. In April 2015, the American admiral in charge of NORAD (the North American Aerospace Defense command) declared North Korea's road-mobile intercontinental ballistic missiles as an "operational threat" and stated that Pyongyang could mount nuclear weapons on them, a judgment he followed the next year with the statement that the missiles likely could reach the U.S. homeland.[27]

Pyongyang's repeated violations of denuclearization agreements and its attempts to proliferate weapons of mass destruction (WMD) underscore the danger it poses and make diplomacy a leap of faith at best.[28] Nor has the regime limited itself to pursuing weapons of mass destruction (WMD). In December 2014, Pyongyang opened a new chapter in its aggression by launching cyberattacks against Sony Pictures in America, destroying the company's computer systems, stealing intellectual property, and publicly releasing private emails and business details.[29]

The inability of the United States and its allies to prevent Pyongyang's successful nuclear and missile tests or cyberattacks has not been lost on other rogue regimes around the world, particularly Iran. Frustratingly for Washington, China continues to act as the Kim family's protector, providing crucial aid and trade and looking the other way when the North proliferates WMDs or banned technology.[30] Beijing appears to have long ago decided that the risks of supporting North Korea outweighed the benefit it gets from the North's constant menace to the United States and U.S. allies.

Officials in Asia and the West often express exasperation that there is no simple answer when dealing with North Korea. Many privately call it the "land of bad options." Halfhearted pressure on the regime has had no effect, nor has diplomacy. The Six-Party Talks, which linked the United States, South Korea, China, Japan, and Russia, have failed because Pyongyang has broken each agreement. Numerous sanctions on the North have been watered down by China and Russia, Pyongyang's allies in the United Nations; others, North Korea has simply evaded. The only effective sanctions, which targeted the personal wealth of the Kim family, were pre-emptively surrendered by the George W. Bush administration in exchange for yet more promises soon broken by the North.[31] Yet Washington, Seoul, and their partners continue to hope that one day, negotiations will succeed where all previous attempts have failed, and that North Korea will denuclearize and stop threatening its neighbors.

North Korea's intractability, along with its regular military probes to test South Korean and American resolve, keeps Northeast Asia on the precipice of conflict. Pyongyang is for all intents and purposes a nuclear power, though the rest of the world will not yet admit it. The mercurial regime instills a sense of permanent instability and stokes fears that one day it will miscalculate and plunge the peninsula into war. There can be no relaxation of vigilance and no hope of denuclearization as long as the Kim regime survives, and the longer that it does, the more the chance of armed conflict increases.

Few other border disputes in Asia have as high a level of risk. They nonetheless hold their own dangers and add to the region's instability. Ranking just behind the Koreas in order of risk potential is the status of Taiwan, the Republic of China.

As I stand on the observation deck of Taipei 101, one of the world's tallest buildings, an older Taiwanese gentleman turns to me and sweeps his hand over the vista. "You can see almost all of our island from here, but do you really see it as a nation?" he asks. While for all practical purposes an independent country, Taiwan occupies a unique limbo in international law. Walking the streets of Taipei or Kaohsiung, one senses pride that this country of twenty-three million people is the world's only ethnically Chinese democracy. Indeed, it is one of the world's most robust democracies, having thrown off nearly forty years of authoritarian rule by its founder, Chiang Kai-shek, and his son in 1987.[32]

But the shadow hanging over Taiwan cannot be easily dismissed. Since 1949, the People's Republic of China has claimed the island as one of its provinces and has successfully coerced or persuaded much of the rest of the world not to acknowledge it as a sovereign state. Beijing showed its seriousness about asserting control over Taiwan in 1955, when it shelled small islands off the coast; only President Dwight Eisenhower's order to send U.S. aircraft carriers into the Taiwan Strait stopped the Chinese from upping the ante.[33] In the succeeding decades, Chinese pressure has gradually increased, even though war has not broken out.

American support for Taiwan took a step backward when President Jimmy Carter, following the lead of the Nixon administration, made the decision in 1978 to derecognize Taiwan as the price of normalization of relations with China.[34] Since then, the U.S. government has maintained in Taipei an office called the American Institute of Taiwan, which serves as a nonofficial diplomatic mission. The number of nations maintaining diplomatic relations with Taiwan continues to shrink, thanks to Beijing's offers of aid in exchange for diplomatic recognition of the mainland; today, just twenty-two states have formal relations with Taiwan.

Beijing's goal has long been to isolate Taiwan, cutting it off from the world. Mainland China continues to put pressure on the island, denying it access to most regional or international organizations and above all maintaining an overwhelming military presence across the Taiwan Strait. Beijing has emplaced over 1,100 short-range ballistic missiles facing Taiwan and has built up its airborne attack and amphibious capabilities for a threatened invasion should the people of Taiwan vote to declare their independence.[35]

As we saw in chapter 4, the Chinese Communist Party's overriding security goal is to prevent any province or region from breaking free of Beijing's grip. Preventing any declaration of independence by Taiwan thus remains China's single most important security issue, to which Beijing is sufficiently dedicated so that it has not hesitated to threaten hostilities during uncertain times. Few in the region have forgotten that during Taiwan's first free elections, in 1996, China launched ballistic missiles into Taiwanese waters. In response, U.S. president Bill Clinton copied Eisenhower's lead in ordering American aircraft carriers into the strait.[36] While Beijing made no further attempts to interfere with the election, its message had been sent, and China's military modernization since then has only made its threat more credible.

Beijing has not been able to prevent democracy in Taiwan, but it continues to regard formal independence as nonnegotiable. In March 2005, concerned that the Democratic Progressive Party (DPP), then holding power in Taipei, might call for a referendum on sovereignty, Beijing passed an "antisecession" law that bluntly stated that even the mere declaration by Taiwan of its independence would justify an armed response.[37] The DPP's repeated hints that it might nonetheless call for an independence referendum threatened the so-called One China policy, a long-standing agreement in which both Taipei and Beijing assert that that there is only one China, but which each government claims. Such ambiguity marks much of cross-strait relations, giving it an Alice in Wonderland feel.

Washington has danced a fine line over Taiwan since the 1970s. It adheres to a position of acknowledging neither Taiwan's sovereignty nor China's sovereignty over Taiwan and equally ambiguously does not dispute the One China policy. Yet Beijing's willingness in 2005 to punish feared Taiwanese moves toward independence underscored that a rising China felt comfortable enough to threaten military action despite continued U.S. demands that neither side unbalance the status quo. Unlike Clinton, however, then President George W. Bush offered a muted response, raising concerns in Taiwan that Washington was more worried about its relations with Beijing than about Taiwan's freedom. Locked in by a fear of damaging relations with Beijing, Washington policymakers have described their strategy as one of "strategic ambiguity," designed to keep Beijing uncertain about how the United States would respond to aggressive Chinese moves.[38]

Tensions across the strait were eased with the return to power in 2008 of the less nationalist Kuomintang (KMT) Party under President

Ma Ying-jeou. Taipei and Beijing signed a broad range of agreements designed to liberalize relations, increase trade, and draw the two sides closer. Direct flights between Taiwan and China started in 2008, while an Economic Cooperation Framework Agreement allowed for greater cross-strait investment and exchange. In November 2015, President Ma met with President Xi in Singapore—the first meeting of cross-strait leaders in over six decades.[39] Yet many observers worry that Beijing is trying to accomplish through close economic ties the de facto absorption it cannot gain militarily.[40] These skeptics ask why, if relations are now so friendly, Beijing has not reduced its military buildup or dropped its opposition to Taiwan's attempts to modernize its military.

After eight years of relative calm across the strait, the DPP returned to power in the January 2016 presidential elections. Fueled by worries over Ma's closeness to China and growing opposition to reunification with the mainland, voters sent a message against continuing too far on the path to rapprochement. Given the election results, observers worried that new president Tsai Ing-wen, Taiwan's first female leader, would move the island back toward independence, thereby risking a cross-strait crisis. While Tsai reassured those who feared a new war of words between Beijing and Taipei, the independence question could yet again lead to a more coercive Chinese policy toward Taiwan. Taiwan's self-identity is far from settled, meaning that its survival is also not assured. Perhaps nowhere else is domestic politics so intimately intertwined with foreign politics.

How can twenty-three million people defend themselves against a country of 1.3 billion? For Taiwan, it has been by having a powerful friend across the Pacific. Ask any Taiwanese defense official over drinks what worries him the most, and he will answer that Washington seems to be slowly backing away from its commitment to help the island defend itself against the mainland. When President Carter severed formal diplomatic ties with Taiwan and let it lose its seat at the United Nations in the late 1970s, the U.S. Congress jumped in to ensure support of the island by passing the Taiwan Relations Act (TRA).[41] While not a formal defensive alliance, the TRA committed the United States to supply Taipei with military hardware so as to maintain a credible defense against the Chinese threat. Ronald Reagan formalized this with a presidential understanding that

Taiwan's military would be kept at par with the mainland's, despite the antagonists difference in size.[42]

Such promises were easy to keep when China's military was an outdated home defense force and its economy a minor part of the global picture. But for the past twenty years, the Chinese defense budget has grown by double digits nearly every year, and the country now boasts one of the most modern militaries in Asia. Its military and economic strength has altered the balance of power between Washington and Beijing, making recent American administrations far more cautious in their support for Taiwan. Both the George W. Bush and the Obama administrations decided not to sell newer F-16s to Taipei, in what appeared to be a validation of the belief that Washington is no longer willing to let Taiwan remain an obstacle to closer Sino-U.S. relations. Taiwan's decaying ability to defend itself may perversely reduce the chance of military conflict with the mainland. Yet a cross-strait war could start at any time should the people of Taiwan decide they want to declare themselves a sovereign nation.

It sounds like the cynical height of realpolitik, but this bedeviling, intractable dispute remains a concern only so long as Taiwan continues to act as a nation-state. Should it give up that pretense, one of the leading potential causes of war in Asia would be removed. The cost, however, would be enormous, given that stability will have been bought at the price of freedom for twenty-three million people. Moreover, such a capitulation might make Asia less secure, as the surrender of Taiwan could embolden China to assert control over other contested territories. Whether the Chinese leadership will embark on a riskier course of action fueled by national pride and perhaps hubris remains the great security question of our time.

Asia's other border disputes are on a smaller scale, but they still keep the region on edge, especially when they involve some of the world's biggest nations. India's biggest border conflict is with Pakistan, over Jammu and Kashmir, but no one in New Delhi forgets that it also has unresolved disputes with China over control of two areas. The province of Aksai Chin, located in the Himalayas on the border of India and Tibet, taken by the Chinese in the brief border war of 1962, is part of an estimated ninety-two thousand square kilometers of contested territory claimed by China.[43] China, meanwhile, still claims the Indian state of Arunachal Pradesh, which its troops occupied during the 1962 war but from which it retreated at the end of the war. Despite a 1996 agreement to settle the issue of Arunachal Pradesh and establish a "Line of Actual Control," the Chinese began reasserting their claims in the mid-2000s, leading New Delhi to station more troops in the region. A February 2015 visit to the state by Indian prime minister Narendra Modi further strained relations with China.[44]

Although largely quiescent for over half a century, the Sino-Indian border regions have lately seen repeated brief incursions of Chinese troops into Indian territory. A three-week face-off between thousands of troops from both sides in 2013 raised alarm bells in capitals across the region. Since then, both sides have continued to deploy troops high in the mountains, with India having as many as seventy thousand in the area, though China has done far more to improve military positions on its side of the border.[45]

Though both capitals play down the border dispute, it reflects the larger geopolitical competition between India and China.[46] Despite some common positions, such as their shared opposition to global climate change regulation, New Delhi and Beijing increasingly consider each other strategic competitors and security threats. India feels this all the more strongly given Beijing's close ties with Pakistan and the de facto crescent of Sino-Pakistani control arcing from west to north over India.[47] The likelihood of a clash between the world's two most populous nations can never be ruled out, given their distrust and geopolitical jostling, and the specter of conflict is a reminder that Asia's land borders are as contested as its maritime ones.

It is not just the region's larger countries that are embroiled in disputes. Even small Asian nations have border spats that cause ongoing distrust and prevent closer diplomatic relations. Decades of confidence building and interaction among the members of the Association of Southeast Asian Nations (ASEAN) have not yet enabled them to avoid occasional dangerous encounters.

Between 2008 and 2011, for example, Thailand and Cambodia fought multiple armed skirmishes, sparked by a dispute over a contested Buddhist temple on their shared border. The battles killed dozens of soldiers as well as civilians as fighting raged around disputed villages along the border. After a particularly fierce clash in February 2011, Cambodia's long-serving prime minister Hun Sen claimed that the two nations were engaged in a "real war."[48] In April 2011, after three years of intermittent battles and the confirmed deaths of over thirty soldiers from both sides, Cambodia turned to the International Court of Justice. The court mandated a de-militarized zone on the border, and ignoring Thailand's request to have the case dismissed, ultimately ruled in Cambodia's favor in November of 2013, a verdict that Thailand's military government appeared to accept after its coup in 2014.[49]

These clashes were a stark reminder of just how far ASEAN has to go in forging an effective community, and of how minor disagreements can flare up into armed hostilities. The constant fighting led Indonesia to try to mediate, and its lack of success underscored the inability of even Southeast Asia's largest nation to resolve neighboring security crises.[50] The incident raised concerns that instability within ASEAN's community could cause its larger nations to feel compelled to intervene, violating the association's core concept of sovereign equality.

Land disputes are easy for Westerners to understand, given the history of warfare in Europe and the Americas. The same cannot be said for perhaps Asia's most rapidly growing risk factor: the numerous maritime territorial disputes that pockmark the Asia-Pacific. These involve multiple claimants and lie along the crucial shared waterways that link the Indo-Pacific to Europe and the Western Hemisphere, and thus make global trade possible. Any disruption in the free flow of goods from the region to the rest of the world would have a significant impact on the global economy and could even cause outside powers to consider intervening.

Because these disputes entangle all the region's major players, they hinder the development of deeper relations of trust. Having settled their own border disputes decades ago (except, it appears, in Ukraine), few Western observers believe Asia's nations would actually fight over isolated rocks in the middle of the sea. But to dismiss the possibility would be a dangerous mistake. The island disputes are the most flammable element in an unstable system.

There are contested islands throughout the region. In the extreme northeast lies the Kurile Islands chain, stretching between Russia's Kamchatka Peninsula and Japan's northern home island of Hokkaido. An object of dispute for over a century, the four southernmost Kuriles were captured by Soviet Russia in 1945, at the end of World War II. Tokyo still refuses to accept Russia's control, and repeated Russian arrests of Japanese fishermen in the waters around the islands have kept the issue alive for decades.

Given their strategically important position controlling Russia's access to the northern Pacific, the Kuriles are the main stumbling block to closer Russo-Japanese ties. Moscow, under Vladimir Putin, has made clear its intention to rebuild its military strength in the Pacific, including boosting air defenses and naval vessels on or near the Kuriles. Both Putin and his predecessor, Dmitry Medvedev, visited the islands, underscoring Moscow's resistance to negotiating their future. Given the growth of China's navy, Beijing's stated interest in future Arctic trade routes, and the increasing militarization of the Arctic, Moscow is keeping a wary eye on both China and Japan. Russia's new interest in regaining great power status in the Pacific means the islands will continue to disrupt the triangle of Russo-Sino-Japanese relations.[51]

Other territorial disputes have shaded into the seriocomic. In the mid-2000s, New Yorkers picking up their dry cleaning undoubtedly tried to puzzle out the meaning of the message emblazoned on the plastic bags that wrapped their clothes: "Dokdo Is Korean Territory."[52] Several hundred miles south of the Kuriles in the Sea of Japan, the Liancourt Rocks, known in Korean as the Dokdo Islands and in Japanese as the Takeshima Islands, remain a major irritant between Tokyo and Seoul. They are presently controlled by South Korea, but Japanese groups from nearby coastal areas continue to assert Japan's sovereignty, leading to regular anti-Japanese demonstrations in South Korea. The visit of South Korean president Lee Myung-bak to the islands in 2012, the first by a sitting Korean leader, hardened Seoul's position and made diplomatic outreach to Japan over the issue all but impossible.

The islands are the only major security issue between Tokyo and Seoul, but disagreement over them flares up repeatedly. They are a major source of anti-Japanese nationalism in South Korea, mixing with the highly contentious issue of World War II "comfort women." The level of passion connected to the issue was revealed by a 2005 incident in which a Korean man set himself on fire in protest against Japan's claims. Later that year, a mother and son publicly cut a finger off each hand for the same reason.[53] The two neighbors' inability to resolve the Liancourt Rocks issue is a major reason they cannot work more closely on broader security initiatives. The unresolved status of the islands also means that the two sides remain at risk of an accidental clash that would send bilateral relations cratering further.

Despite the passions they ignite, the Kurile Islands and Liancourt Rocks disputes are unlikely to lead to outright war. The same cannot be said for two other island quarrels in the region. The object of perhaps the most dangerous dispute is found in the southernmost waters of the East China Sea, a small grouping of islands that pits Japan against China and Taiwan. The strategically located Senkakus (known as the Diaoyu in Chinese and as the Pinnacle Islands to European explorers) form the end of a chain of island groups that begins with the southern home island of Japan and terminates just northeast of Taiwan. These tiny islands separate the East China Sea from the western Pacific Ocean, and could be used by Japan to cut off China's access to the western Pacific. They also sit astride potentially rich undersea oil and gas reserves, which both China and Japan have been exploring and feuding over in recent years.[54]

Japan's control over the Senkakus began after its victory in the 1895 Sino-Japanese War. The islands, owned by a private family, were returned to Tokyo's administrative control in 1972, when the United States reverted postwar sovereignty of Okinawa to Japan. Since 2010, the Senkakus have been an object of paramilitary competition between Japan and China. Both sides claim sovereignty, and Beijing has tried to undermine Tokyo's claims of sole administrative control. Groups of Chinese fishermen have regularly intruded into the waters around the islands, leading the Japanese coast guard to confront them. This, in turn, has led to the repeated dispatch of Chinese patrol vessels to intimidate the Japanese. When Japan arrested the crew of a fishing boat that had rammed one of its coast guard vessels in September 2010, diplomatic relations between Beijing and Tokyo almost collapsed.[55] Ties were stabilized only after Japan released the boat and its captain.

The situation deteriorated again in August 2012, when the Japanese government announced it was buying several of the disputed islands from their owner, in essence nationalizing them. Beijing interpreted this as a violation of the status quo, and responded by increasing its paramilitary pressure.[56] Pictures of Chinese and Japanese fishing boats and maritime vessels prow-to-prow or shadowing each other, sometimes with both countries' military planes in nearby skies, underscore how close to armed conflict the two sides have come. Both refuse to negotiate over the islands, and Tokyo relies on its alliance with Washington as the ultimate guarantor of its ability to control the Senkakus. President Obama publicly reaffirmed in April 2014 that the Senkakus fall under the mutual defense treaty between Washington and Tokyo, thus making it a trilateral issue that could draw America into any conflict.[57] The longer the issue festers, the more likely it becomes that an accident or miscalculation could cause a military clash between Asia's two great powers.

A separate, equally dangerous set of disputes pits China against a number of its smaller neighbors in the South China Sea. Here the squabble is even more complicated. The first disagreement concerns control of the Spratly Islands, which are contested by China, Taiwan, Vietnam, the Philippines, Malaysia, and Brunei. Another dispute is over the Paracel Islands, pitting China, Taiwan, and Vietnam against each other.

Once again, fishing access is a trigger for confrontation, but larger strategic issues drive the disputes. The regular incursion of largely Chinese fishing trawlers in contested waters draws in the other nations' coast guards and maritime patrol vessels. Chinese patrol boats almost always back up their fishermen, threatening the other nations' smaller vessels, which usually back off, ceding effective control to China. Asia's smaller nations thus find themselves largely powerless to fend off Beijing's advances. This is what happened at the Scarborough Shoal, an isolated area in the Spratly Islands long claimed by the Philippines but effectively controlled by Chinese ships since a standoff in 2012 between both nations' maritime vessels. A few months later, a Chinese patrol vessel rammed and sank a Vietnamese fishing boat that was part of a small flotilla harassing a Chinese oil-drilling platform in Vietnamese waters.[58]

In response to condemnation of its actions, Beijing claims Vietnam and the Philippines are the aggressors, seeking to deny China access to its own waters. China rattled the region when it used a 1930s claim, called the "9-dash line," by the former Nationalist Government to assert control over all the islands in the South China Sea, and even the waters themselves.[59] Following these claims, Beijing has expanded its naval exercises in the region, reaching down to the southern end of the South China Sea, a thousand miles from the Chinese mainland. It also upgraded its military and civilian administrative structures in the South China Sea.

Most dramatically, starting in earnest in 2014, the Chinese government began a large-scale land-reclamation program in both the Spratlys and Paracels. Dredging up vast amounts of seabed sand, Beijing turned simple reefs into large islands capable of hosting airfields, harbors, and barracks. The U.S. government estimated that by May 2015, over two thousand acres of land had been created. Washington also revealed that China was building nine-thousand-foot (3,000-meter) runways on three of the new islands and installing radar, a possible prelude to antiaircraft missiles, and then perhaps deploying fighter jets and ships.[60] The Chinese began airplane landings on Fiery Cross Reef in January 2016, the largest of its newly created islands, confirming regional fears that the islands were intended for military purposes. Meanwhile, it based fighter jets and emplaced antiaircraft missiles on Woody Island, its largest possession in the Paracels, where Chinese claims are opposed by Vietnam and Taiwan.

This militarization of territory old and new serves a dual purpose. It both gives the Chinese navy and air force bases from which to project power throughout the South China Sea, and it bolsters Beijing's legal claims of territorial control. Beijing, contrary to international law, has demanded that regional powers recognize a twelve-mile territorial limit around its new islands. In effect, China is trying to colonize the South China Sea by physically making territory and then demanding legal protection for it.

Belatedly sensing the shift in the balance of power in the South China Sea, the Obama administration publicly laid down a redline in June 2015, when Secretary of Defense Ashton Carter asserted that U.S. naval ships would ignore the twelve-mile limit and American military planes would continue to fly over the ersatz islands. After months of warnings, the U.S. Navy sailed a destroyer, the USS *Lassen*, in waters near Subi Reef, another of China's new islands. However, questions about whether the United

States claimed freedom of navigation rights or the less provocative right of "innocent passage" diluted the strong statement the Obama administration hoped to make, even when it followed up with another transit in January 2016. Worse for Washington, its actions had little impact on Chinese military activities in the area, and Beijing ignored repeated U.S. demands to stop the reclamation process, while publicly warning U.S. surveillance flights away from the islands. Tensions rose sufficiently that a Chinese state-run newspaper declared war between China and the United States "inevitable" if Washington did not back down.[61] The world's two strongest powers thus find themselves face-to-face over reefs and rocks.

The issue over the Spratlys is equally one of power and strategy. From a political angle, China is attempting to rewrite the rules of international behavior, insisting that it can ignore competing claims, build islands, and assert control over common seas. It is a classic example of "might makes right" thinking against which smaller nations have little defense. From a strategic perspective, risk in the South China Sea is high because of its crucial location, which affects not just Asia but the entire world. The Spratlys in particular are close to the world's most strategic waterways, such as the Malacca Strait, through which more than seventy thousand ships per year carry 40 percent of the world's trade.[62] Any nation that gained the ability to control the sea or its crucial littoral waterways would thus present a threat to freedom of navigation and to the global economy.[63]

There is also an economic component to the struggle in the South China Sea. Valuable resources are part of the equation. There are an estimated trillions of cubic feet of oil and natural gas under the seabed, and the fishing grounds in some of the reefs are teeming with sea turtles and other exotic species. The Philippines and other nations charge China with massive environmental destruction, as it strips coral reefs and destroys delicate ecosystems, leading to what many marine biologists are calling irreversible damage.[64] Beijing for its part complains that Vietnam and the Philippines have repeatedly violated agreements on oil exploration in the South China Sea. Chinese patrol ships have harassed Vietnamese exploration vessels and cut the moorings of Philippine fishing boats and drilling platforms.[65] In 2014, the temporary emplacement of a floating Chinese oil-drilling platform in waters claimed by Vietnam led to dozens of small boats from each side confronting each other and ultimately to the sinking of a Vietnamese fishing vessel. If such an incident led to the loss of life, then an armed response by the aggrieved side is by no means out of the question.

It is easy to see China as the aggressor in Asia's territorial disputes, given its size and power. In fact, there are many nations willing to use force to back up their claims. For example, within a year of taking office, Indonesia's new president Joko Widodo made good on a promise to protect his nation's fishing grounds by sinking or destroying dozens of captured fishing boats from China, Vietnam, Thailand, and the Philippines. On one day in May 2015, he drew international attention by blowing up forty-one boats.[66] Jakarta claims that more than five thousand foreign boats illegally fish in its waters every year. It is the lack of effective legal restraints that is leading even nations committed to multilateral diplomacy to protect their waters by force.

Disputants in Asia find increasingly creative ways to pursue their security goals. For example, they seize on the framework of international law, such as the Convention on the Law of the Sea, to promote their claims ever more rigidly.[67] Each nation asserts control or sovereignty based on a different definition of territorial rights, referring to competing interpretations in the treaties themselves. In the South China Sea, Beijing has refused repeated calls for a multilateral solution to the problem, insisting that all negotiations be bilateral. This, of course, benefits the Chinese position, as few smaller nations feel able to stand up to Beijing's pressure. Some, like Japan and the Philippines, have explicitly called on U.S. support, hoping that Washington's formidable naval strength in Asia will deter China from pressing its claims.

While China is not at the center of all of Asia's security disputes, it is nonetheless the most important factor in the region's growing instability. Justified or not, fears of Beijing's intentions are exacerbating tension and creating a security dilemma throughout the region. Having mapped security risk in Asia, it is now time to explore more carefully the driver of much of the risk cycle, and the region's responses to it.

Asia's Changing Military Balance of Power

Nearly a century before Christopher Columbus dared to cross the Atlantic Ocean, the seas belonged to China. During the first three decades of the fifteenth century, in the days when Henry V urged on his "band of brothers" before the Battle of Agincourt and Joan of Arc was burned at the stake, the great Chinese eunuch admiral Zheng He took fleets of over three hundred ships as far as the Red Sea and the east coast of Africa.[68] A figure once again revered in Chinese culture, Zheng He is for many Chinese a symbol of their country's traditional role as the strongest military power in Asia.

As it has done in economics and politics, China is changing the face of security in Asia in the twenty-first century. But intentionally or not, it is doing so in ways that are profoundly destabilizing. Throughout the Cold War, despite Soviet attempts to build a regional navy, the balance of power in Asia favored the United States and its partners. With no major threat to regional stability, the region's countries focused inwardly on civil war or on domestic development and decolonization.

Even in the waning years of the Cold War, however, the People's Republic of China had begun to follow a path that disturbed regional stability. It fought a bloody skirmish with Vietnamese troops in the Spratlys' Johnson Reef in 1988, in which seventy-four Vietnamese died and China forcibly took six reefs and atolls.[69] The Philippines surrendered the Mischief Reef to China in 1995 rather than suffer the fate of the Vietnamese.[70] The 1996 Taiwan Missile Crisis, in which Beijing fired ballistic missiles into Taiwanese waters during the island nation's first free presidential election, resulted in the Clinton administration dispatching two aircraft carrier strike groups to the Taiwan Strait. The decade ended with a 1999 U.S. congressional report highlighting how China had stolen classified information from American sources to develop its ballistic missile capabilities, which included the ability to target U.S. soil.[71]

Beijing chose this path because it considers the U.S. military presence and alliance system in the western Pacific a threat. This is despite Washington's ongoing efforts to integrate China into the global economic and political order, and in the absence of any obvious external obstacles to China's growth.[72] Its traditional adversary Japan remained economically stagnant throughout the 1990s and beyond, and after the 9/11 terror attacks, Washington's attention turned almost entirely to the Middle East. Despite this benign geopolitical environment, Beijing nonetheless continued to rapidly modernize its military.[73]

Its long-term buildup indicates a decision by Chinese leadership to try and reshape the regional security environment, and the understanding that to do so will require an overwhelming military capability. Some might argue that by seeking to modernize its antiquated military and develop the capability to better protect its homeland and interests, China has been acting like any rising power.[74] Yet Beijing retains a sense of grievance toward the world that makes it unwilling to act cooperatively. Instead, China's actions have become steadily more coercive and threatening the stronger it has become.

Since it began to be recognized as a global power, China has exhibited increasingly provocative behavior.[75] In the fall of 2006, for example, disturbing reports began circulating in Washington that a Chinese attack submarine had stalked the aircraft carrier USS *Kitty Hawk* in the western Pacific, apparently undetected by the ship's protective screen of naval vessels until it surfaced within torpedo firing range.[76] A few months later, in January 2007, the Chinese showed that their power extended to space, as they used a modified ballistic missile to shoot down one of their aging weather satellites.[77] This test was repeated in 2013 and 2014, scattering thousands of pieces of space debris in the orbits used by satellites from around the globe. Two years later, video of Chinese ships harassing a U.S. Navy surveillance vessel brought to light dangerous games of chicken on the high seas. By the end of the 2000s, Beijing had more than one thousand ballistic missiles pointed across the strait at Taiwan, and just a few years later its fighter jets routinely crossed into Japan's air defense identification zone, as they had not done since the Cold War.[78] Suddenly, China seemed a far greater military threat than many had dreamed even a decade before.

How the Chinese Fight: A Look at China's Modern Military

China's military modernization has been perhaps the most dramatic in history next to that of the United States during World War II. Yet unlike the American buildup, China's has happened during peacetime. Beijing officially spent $145 billion on defense in its 2015 budget, but by some estimates, a more accurate exchange rate comparison reveals that it spends the equivalent of $500 billion on its military, more than three-quarters of the U.S. budget.[79] Even as its economic growth slowed, Beijing

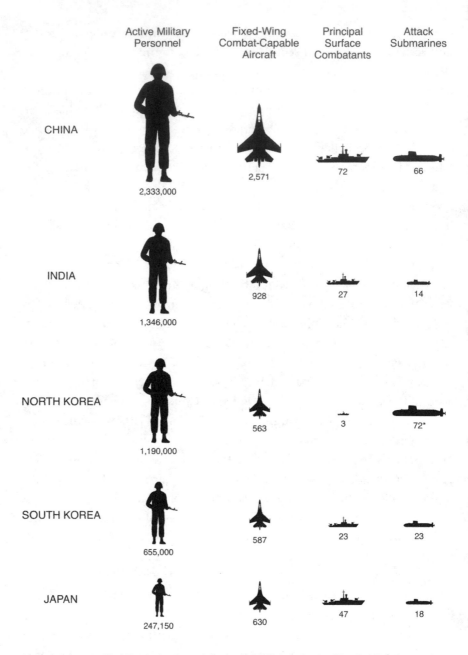

	Active Military Personnel	Fixed-Wing Combat-Capable Aircraft	Principal Surface Combatants	Attack Submarines
CHINA	2,333,000	2,571	72	66
INDIA	1,346,000	928	27	14
NORTH KOREA	1,190,000	563	3	72*
SOUTH KOREA	655,000	587	23	23
JAPAN	247,150	630	47	18

*Approximately twenty of North Korea's submarines are built using dated 1950s technology. In addition, North Korea has more than ten midget submarines, which do not possess the same range of operating capabilities as larger diesel attack submarines.

Indo-Pacific Military Force Comparison. Data from International Institute for Strategic Studies, *The Military Balance 2015*. Artwork by Olivier Ballou.

maintained 10 percent annual growth in its defense budget until 2016, when it announced the first drop in over a decade, to 7.5 percent.

The United States has not faced the possibility of such a military competitor since the collapse of the Soviet Union more than a quarter-century ago. When China's military modernization began, the soldiers, sailors, and airmen of the People's Liberation Army (PLA) were using technology and weapons from the 1950s.[80] China's navy was a coastal defense fleet, and its air force could hardly fly out of sight of land. Today, the PLA and its associated services are a dominant force in Asia and have begun operating around the globe, if on a small scale. But Beijing has also acquired advanced weapons with the intent of achieving military superiority over its neighbors and eliminating America's edge in the quality of its Pacific-based forces. All this activity is directed toward regaining China's traditional military dominance in Asia. China's security challenge in the Indo-Pacific is thus as much a political as it is a military one. And judging from the statements of Chinese leaders on down, they are prepared to wage this competition for dominance over the long haul.

The fifteenth-century admiral Zheng He is celebrated today in China because he fits the current national mood. In the past decade, during which it has reemerged as perhaps Asia's leading indigenous maritime power, China has made its most conspicuous military advances in the PLA Navy (PLAN), which has been transformed from a coastal patrol fleet into a sophisticated force capable of extended operation thousands of miles from China's coast.[81]

The PLAN, Asia's largest naval force, is increasingly adept at patrolling large swaths of the sea and undertaking joint operations. Its vessels now regularly steam through the East and South China Seas. In 2013, China launched its first aircraft carrier and announced plans to build at least two more, to add to its dozens of destroyers and frigates. It already operates more attack submarines than the U.S. Navy, and by 2020, according to the U.S. Congressional Research Service, the PLAN will have up to seventy-two modern subs.[82] Some of China's submarines already carry missiles that can travel 4,500 miles, able to hit the U.S. mainland, and the PLAN is working on both a more modern ballistic missile sub and a longer-range missile.

Japan and the Philippines in particular are worried about Chinese submarines' ability to target their shipping lanes and enforce blockades of vital raw materials. Of equal concern, especially given recent confrontations between Chinese and foreign vessels, is the PLAN's acquisition of advanced weapons, such as supersonic antiship cruise missiles and even an antiship ballistic missile, which U.S. Navy planners fear could target and destroy American aircraft carriers.[83]

Yet the growth of China's navy is not what the region's maritime states worry about the most. Beijing's first response in territorial disputes has been to send its maritime "police" forces—the more than two hundred patrol vessels of the China Maritime Safety Administration (MSA) and other agencies, such as the Fisheries Law Enforcement Command. Armed MSA ships regularly accompany private Chinese fishing vessels into contested waters and have been involved in numerous confrontations with the naval and coast guard forces of other nations, especially those of Japan, the Philippines, Indonesia, and Vietnam. For many Asian nations, these maritime patrols vessels are the face of today's China, staring down their own much smaller coast guards and navies. Even for Japan, which has a large, modern coast guard, the sheer number of Chinese patrol vessels is a concern, especially when Beijing is willing to send multiple vessels into Japanese-claimed waters off the Senkaku Islands on a regular basis.

How much of a threat is the Chinese navy in reality? Putting aside questions of government policy or national will, some doubt that it is really that formidable. "It's a paper tiger," one Western military attaché based in Beijing asserts confidentially, noting that it trains far less frequently than its competitors and isn't nearly as skilled in shipboard damage control and emergency response as the better-trained Asian navies. Without doubt, the PLAN is still qualitatively and operationally inferior to the U.S. Navy, and it stays largely in its home waters. Yet in assessing risk, the trend line is what is most important, and on this measure, the Chinese navy's ability to project power and sustain it over time is generally acknowledged to be growing and already far exceeds that of almost all its neighbors.

Despite the PLAN's continued limitations, Chinese naval thinking is evolving to take advantage of its new capabilities.[84] China's naval doctrine has shifted focus toward projecting naval power outside coastal zones into the "far seas" of the Pacific Ocean.[85] Much planning has gone into considering how to secure control of the "first island chain," which encompasses both the South and East China Seas as well as Japan's Ryukyu Island chain. Chinese control of this chain could be used to threaten most Asian nations' access through common waters to both the Pacific and Indian Oceans.

The PLAN is also ranging farther from home. In 2008, Beijing dispatched a small flotilla of two destroyers and a supply ship to the Arabian Sea to conduct antipiracy operations off the Horn of Africa, showing its capability to protect Chinese shipping halfway around the globe, while in May 2015, the PLAN joined the Russian navy for exercises in the Mediterranean, despite global condemnation of Russia's annexation of Crimea and invasion of eastern Ukraine. Such long-range operations illustrate China's growing competence and intent to hone its power projection capabilities.[86]

The rest of China's military is also developing, if not as quickly. The People's Liberation Army Air Force (PLAAF) has been modernizing its fleet of over 2,500 planes, buying "fourth-generation" fighters based on Russian models that some believe already are matches for the aging air forces of Japan and even the United States.[87] In early 2011, the PLAAF unveiled its first stealth prototype, the J-20, which most observers think is designed to go head-to-head with America's F-22 Raptor stealth fighter and may be ready as early as 2020.[88] This was followed in 2012 by another stealth fighter model, possibly designed to be launched from China's new aircraft carrier. The PLAAF is also acquiring remotely piloted drones and unmanned combat aerial vehicles based on U.S. models. So far, China's drones are fewer and of lesser quality than those of the U.S. military, but they already outnumber those of neighboring states.[89]

Like the Chinese navy, the PLAAF presents a growing challenge to nearby nations' air forces. While its primary mission remains defense of the Chinese homeland, planning for Taiwan Strait contingencies, including attacks on Taiwan, runs a close second. Recent reports suggest that Taiwan now would likely lose in a cross-strait air war.[90] Even more alarmingly for the rest of the region, the combat radius of China's more advanced jets can reach significant portions of the Japanese home islands, much of Indochina, and the northern reaches of Southeast Asia. They could provide an air umbrella for PLA forces invading contested islands such as the Senkakus, where they would outnumber both Japanese fighter jets and the few dozen American fighters based in Japan. Japan, the Philippines, and other nations worry that China's forces in the air are becoming as confident as those on the water. They interpret these trends as confirmation that the conventional military balance of power in Asia is shifting in China's favor.

Another layer of complexity in this already challenging environment is China's development of the ultimate weapon. When China mounted a huge military parade in September 2015 to mark the seventieth anniversary of the end of World War II, it prominently featured some of the country's most advanced ballistic missiles, nearly all of which are nuclear capable. After decades of keeping a low nuclear profile, Beijing is signaling the growing importance of its nuclear weapons capability to China's national power.

What really separates China from its neighbors, even those with strong defense forces, is its nuclear and ballistic missile program. China's rockets can reach most of the world; they range from short-range to intercontinental-range nuclear-tipped missiles, increasing numbers of which are road-mobile and thus almost impossible to track. China's missile forces today can target every country in the Indo-Pacific, as well as all major U.S. and allied bases in the region. Only the United States and Russia have more missiles, but some analysts suggest that China is not only continuing to field more long-range ballistic missiles than the U.S. government acknowledges but also giving them multiple warheads.[91] So far, Beijing refuses to discuss arms control, leaving it free to build as much as it wants. China's nuclear force may be quantitatively dwarfed by the number of U.S. nuclear weapons and missiles, but it is developing a robust and survivable nuclear capability. The question is how this will affect Beijing's broader foreign policies and its increased military activities in places like the South China Sea.

As with its other capabilities, China's nuclear strength has led officials to bully and threaten other nations, raising their sense of insecurity. Some senior Chinese military leaders have even threatened the United States. In one infamous case in 1995, a Chinese general warned an American observer that Washington should worry more about Los Angeles than Taipei, clearly implying a nuclear risk for the United States should it continue to support Taiwan. A decade later, another senior general said that "Americans will have to be prepared that hundreds of [U.S.] cities will be destroyed by the Chinese" in the case of a nuclear conflict over Taiwan.[92] Statements like these from top officials make Americans and Asians understandably nervous about China's intentions. Even more worrisome, there are indications that China's "no first use" policy has been reconsidered in recent years, indicating that nuclear warfighting may become more integrated into Chinese military planning.[93]

Given how little U.S. officials know about China's nuclear warfighting doctrine, the risk of miscommunication or miscalculation during a crisis is unacceptably high. Even the supposed "hotline" between Beijing and Washington is not a direct link between senior U.S. military officials and their Chinese counterparts.[94] Unlike the Cold War relationship between the United States and the USSR, there is almost no discussion between China and the United States regarding nuclear weapons or their use. Given the other stresses in the relationship, this can only be considered a growing risk factor.

A New Way of Fighting: The Cyberthreat

As Asians and Americans have begun to adjust their perception of China's military threat, a new and insidious danger has revealed itself. The area of China's military prowess that most worries American and Asian defense and economic experts today is the realm of cyberwar. Like their American counterparts, Chinese defense planners have adopted a doctrine of waging "local wars under informationalized conditions."[95] That means attempting to network their military operations on sea, on land, in the air, and in space using advanced electronic communications systems, much as U.S. forces do.

It is increasingly clear that China is actively exploring cyberwarfare as a separate warfighting discipline, either in support of other military operations or as an offensive means in its own right. This can be accomplished by utilizing computer network operations, electronic warfare, and kinetic strikes to "attack an enemy's networked information systems"—in other words, shut down their grid.[96] Targets would include intelligence, surveillance, and reconnaissance (ISR) systems, databases, satellites, and network architecture. The goal is to blind an enemy or disrupt their ability to achieve battlefield awareness and coordinate operations, thereby undermining the connectivity that underpins the U.S. way of fighting.[97]

The success of Russian cyberhackers in crashing Georgian government websites during their 2008 conflict showed that antinetwork operations are an increasingly viable means of causing disruption.[98] Not only military but economic systems, public service networks such as utilities, and governmental communications are at risk from an increased Chinese cyberwarfare capability. Cyberattacks would likely be used to sow domestic chaos that could force the withdrawal of opposing military forces.

Here is where two regions of our risk map overlap. Business leaders will tell you that China's cyberattacks are a grave economic threat. In ministries of defense or homeland security, meanwhile, cyberwar is seen as an unconventional national security threat. Both groups are right: the borders of our risk map cannot be drawn with unbroken lines. Some U.S. military officials would consider the cyber badlands an entirely separate risk region on my map of the Indo-Pacific.

The cyberthreat differs from other Chinese military capabilities in that it is already being used on a massive scale. Whether stealing business secrets or plans for advanced weapons, specialized units of the PLA (possibly in conjunction with the North Koreans) are conducting nonstop operations. For the past decade, thousands of sustained hacking attempts against Western and Asian businesses and governments have been traced to China. Beijing has rapidly developed a corps of advanced computer hackers. In early 2009, Canadian researchers exposed a Chinese electronic spy network targeting foreign computers, and in January 2013 a U.S. cybersecurity corporation released a report detailing massive operations by hacking groups controlled by the PLA.[99] Dozens of major U.S. and foreign corporations penetrated by Chinese hackers have lost terabytes of information and many trade secrets in perhaps the worst case of collective industrial espionage in history.

Just as damagingly, the Obama administration revealed in June 2015 that Chinese hackers had penetrated the computers of the Office of Personnel Management and gained access to the personnel files of every individual working for the U.S. government, including those holding top-secret security clearances. Subsequent investigations showed that as many as thirty-two million U.S. individuals may have had personal information compromised.[100] Some commentators called this a "cyber Pearl Harbor," noting that the Chinese not only might have gained leverage over millions of Americans holding security clearances but also showed their ability to operate undetected for months deep inside U.S. government computers.[101]

This is not just a domestic challenge. American and foreign defense contractors have been repeatedly attacked, and information about sensitive programs like the F-35 stealth fighter have been stolen in attacks traced back to China.[102] Official U.S. government reports claim that dozens of military development and research programs have been infiltrated and nearly every major U.S. weapons programs has been penetrated.[103] If this is true, then U.S. taxpayers have been unwittingly subsidizing the modernization of the Chinese military. In all, hundreds of millions of pages of trade secrets and government communications have been intercepted by Chinese sources.

For U.S. military and civil planners, this is the future face of warfare. U.S. military and commercial communications satellites could be targeted by Chinese missiles, destroying U.S. troops' ability to operate. Military computer systems could be hacked or crashed. Planes would be grounded and ships would have difficulty aiming their weapons. Logistics lines could be wrecked and communications with headquarters impeded. At home, utilities could be shut down, while banks, hospitals, and other necessary organizations could be thrown into chaos. It is the twenty-first-century version of strategic bombing during World War II.

Smaller Asian nations, which cannot sustain defensive cyber operations, would almost certainly be overwhelmed if such an attack were aimed at them. To critics who say that such fears are overblown, the record of China's actions and the trajectory of its military development strongly suggest that Beijing is preparing to fight in cyberspace, cripple enemies' domestic systems, and then use modern conventional weapons to dominate its region.

No serious observer would claim that China wants war, but Beijing is acting like a classic rising challenger to the status quo. It no longer appears content to let the United States remain the region's preeminent military power, or to let it work with allies to ensure that no Asian nation becomes powerful enough to dominate the Indo-Pacific. Beijing's stated goal is to reshape the military balance of power over the long run. In military terms, it is aiming to achieve "anti-access/area denial (A2/AD)" capability in its home waters, including the Taiwan Strait and into the South China Sea.[104] An A2/AD strategy aims at preventing other forces from entering the waters and skies around a particular point such as a contested island or even an entire sea. It then focuses on denying them the ability to operate freely in areas where they are already located. U.S. or Asian ships inside an A2/AD zone would be cut off from supplies or help and then attacked. Their bases would be destroyed by ballistic missiles, thus isolating ground-based troops, amphibious marines, and air forces.

Looking at the trend over the past decade, it is easy to conclude that the PLA and the Chinese leadership are probing to see how far they can push regional states and the United States into acquiescing to China's military activities in Asian waters. Success in making other nations accept Chinese territorial claims, especially without risking even a minor military confrontation, would be an enormous victory. For this reason, the way the region responds to China's military buildup holds great importance in determining whether Asia remains peaceful or is plunged into conflict.

A Porcupine Strategy

One reason the risk of armed conflict is growing is that China's neighbors have not stood idly by while Beijing has built the region's largest military. Almost all of Asia's states are maritime traders and thus deeply concerned about their access to the world's oceans. The nations that can afford to do so have built up their own military capabilities in an effort to protect against Chinese bullying. The entire region has seen a flood of spending on advanced naval and air weapons, with little deepening of political trust between them.

Given that most of these countries want assured access to Asia's common maritime areas, it is not surprising that they are rapidly building their navies. If war breaks out in Asia, it will almost certainly do so first on the seas. Almost every nation in the region is increasing its submarine fleet, and some industry sources expect over one hundred new submarines to be built for Asian navies over the next two decades, at a total cost of $57 billion.[105] Other nations are buying new fighter jets and fielding their own drones; some are upgrading or developing their antiship missiles in case of a confrontation with the Chinese navy. No other Asian country can match China's spending or strength, but each hopes to be able to respond to incursions by Chinese fishing boats in contested waters or have enough of a defense force to make the Chinese navy think twice about moving into their waters. Yet all know that they can only delay, not prevent, the shift in the region's balance of power.

Even a wealthy country like Japan does not pretend that it could stand alone against China. As an island nation, however, it faces an existential threat to its survival should it be cut off from the world's oceans. Under Prime Minister Shinzo Abe, Japan's defense budget has begun modestly climbing again after more than a decade of stagnation. His 2016 military budget reached $42.4 billion, making it the largest in the country's history.[106] Yet that record-breaking amount is less than one-third of what China publicly admits to spending on its military. What Japan lacks in quantity, it partly makes up in quality. Its military capabilities outstrip those of any of its neighbors, except for China, and it fields some of the region's most advanced ships, planes, and submarines. It has one of the world's most developed antiballistic missile programs, with plans to have six destroyers equipped with the Aegis ballistic missile defense system, and its antisubmarine capability is one of the few regional counterweights to China's growing submarine force.[107]

Japan's airspace covers some of the region's most vital shipping routes through the East China Sea and into the Pacific Ocean. Chinese and Russian fighters and bombers repeatedly cross into Japan's air defense identification zone or into the airspace around contested isles like the Senkakus, requiring Japan to scramble its air defenses hundreds of times each year. In 2014 its Air Self Defense Force scrambled nearly 950 times, a number not seen since the Cold War.[108] Japan is doing this with an aging fighter fleet composed mainly of approximately 375 F-15s and its domestic version of the F-16. The new level of air competition is the main reason Tokyo in 2012 chose the stealthy F-35 as its next-generation fighter. Yet even as it continues its broad-based modernization, Japan remains largely a defensive force, unable to project power in any meaningful way for any extended period.

The other great Asian power has a similar orientation. India's security policy is focused in three directions: toward the northwest and Pakistan, toward the northeast and China, and toward its maritime realm. Given its population and strategic position astride the Indian Ocean transit routes, as well as its long-standing tensions with China over land borders, India has abundant cause to try and become a significant military counterweight to China.

Despite focusing mainly on the security of its land borders, New Delhi is eager to increase its naval presence throughout the Indian Ocean. In part this is a response to the regular transit of Chinese naval vessels through these waters and Beijing's potential access to bases throughout the Indo-Pacific, especially in the countries encircling India, including ports in Pakistan, Myanmar, and Sri Lanka.[109] India's ownership of the strategically located Andaman and Nicobar Islands, on the eastern fringes of the Indian Ocean, gives it an important role in maintaining maritime security in the waterways that lead from the Indian Ocean through the Strait of Malacca and into the South China Sea, but the islands also are targets for any nation wishing to control the critical passage. In recent years, New Delhi has increased the presence of ships and the patrol of aircraft over its islands, especially as PLA navy ships pass through these waters on deployments to the Horn of Africa or on global voyages.[110]

Still, India remains decades away from challenging the Chinese military. While maintaining its long-standing nuclear deterrent, it has embarked on a major conventional building campaign, reflecting the overall militarization of the Indo-Pacific. New Delhi now deploys fifteen submarines, a handful of guided missile destroyers, and a few dozen smaller vessels, and it drew worldwide attention by purchasing a former Soviet aircraft carrier and also commissioning its own. It is aiming at building a nuclear submarine force and is constructing an indigenous ballistic missile submarine.[111] Some industry sources believe India will be the world's largest purchaser of naval equipment in coming years, spending over $46 billion over the next two decades.[112] In addition, while its air force has close to a thousand planes, it is planning on upgrading its aging and underpowered fighter fleet and is currently developing a purported fifth-generation stealth fighter, the PAK-FA, with Russia, to keep up in the stealth race pioneered by the United States.[113] This will make a powerful force, but not one that could defeat China in a war.

China's neighbors are aiming at what might be called a "porcupine" strategy.[114] Each aims at developing sufficient defenses to protect its home waters and skies against a larger and more capable power. None expects to mount much offensive capacity, but they hope that Beijing will hesitate to get pricked by their spines. Yet by taking this strategy, each state has chosen to forgo the potential of a larger, coordinated regional response to China's increasingly coercive actions. Each state is isolated and therefore increasingly nervous about the shifting balance of power and the increase in regional tensions. Whether in the East or South China Seas, or the mountain passes near the Himalayas, China's military presence is a constant reminder of the fragility of stability in the Indo-Pacific, and a warning against miscalculation or the expression of aggressive nationalism.

Among all of Asia's risk zones examined in this book, the region of security is perhaps the easiest to map. Its dangers are not hidden and can be discerned from the open disputes and heated rhetoric that mark festering disagreements. Its landmarks include contested borders, paramilitary confrontations, and increasingly sophisticated armed forces. Even its newer dangers, like cyberwarfare, are known if not always seen.

One aspect in particular stands out. While a rogue regime like North Korea remains a constant threat, the true changes in the security map are coming from China. Even in a cursory review like the one above, the large gulf growing between China and its neighbors is inescapable. While Japan and India maintain an almost exclusively defensive orientation, Beijing is concentrating on developing the region's predominant ability to project power, by sea, air, land, or cyberspace.[115] Much like the economic map, in the past two decades Asia's security map has been dramatically redrawn by China's growth. But whereas the widening of the economic region has been largely beneficial—though now riddled with hidden faults—the transformation of Asia's security balance has been entirely destabilizing.

We have now completed our mapping of the various risk regions that threaten to end the "Asian Century." Their borders are uneven, their size varies, and the level of risk that each holds is not constant. But this exercise has allowed us to move away from the news of the day and chart instead the key trends that are unfolding in economics, society, politics, and security.

Maps are useful only so far as they help us to reach our destination. It is time now to use our map to figure out how to navigate the risk regions of the Indo-Pacific. In doing so, we change from observers to participants, and our map becomes a tool for managing risk and reshaping the region so as to reduce the danger of catastrophe.

7

MANAGING RISK IN ASIA

As a graduate student decades ago, I would occasionally take a break from my studies by going into my university's map library. I would look at copies of Ptolemy's famous map of the Mediterranean world, scientific in spirit if based on limited knowledge. The medieval maps were rich in imagination, filled with beasts and fancies, yet a giant step backward from their classical predecessors. The message of Asian maps was clear: the world revolved around the court of the Chinese emperors or mythical Buddhist mountains at the center of creation.

For me, maps bring clarity, even when they are speculative or are more about concepts than about geography. Mapping risk in the Indo-Pacific is at once a mental exercise and the first step toward a useful plan of action. In this book we have mapped a series of risk regions in an effort to diagnose dangers that may spell the end of what many have come to call the "Asian Century." Our mapping has not been comprehensive, since no book can fully capture all of Asia's dynamism, opportunities, and challenges. Nor are the risk regions we have explored by any means the only ones that should engage our attention or that may someday play a major role in the region's politics and economics.

Our map traces five risk regions: the failure of economic reform, demographic pressure, unfinished political revolutions, the lack of regional political community, and the threat of conflict. The problems they illuminate are contributing to a growing level of risk that the world has ignored while celebrating Asia's successes. But now that we have a map, how do we and the countries involved navigate through the dangers of the Indo-Pacific?

Before seeking such answers, I must again stress that our cartographic exercise is not predictive. I make no claim that China's economy will crash or that the Korean peninsula will erupt in war. By its very nature, mapping risk can lead one to overestimate the possibility of serious disruption. It's easy to claim that the sky is falling, because if it doesn't, no one cares that you scared them, while if it does, the person who raised the alarm comes across as a genius and those who dismissed his warnings are derided as fools. Many books thus end with a set of future scenarios, essentially predicting the future without being explicit about it.[1]

The approach followed in this book is different. Charting risk in Asia provides an important critical approach to thinking about investing, policymaking, or simply reading the daily headlines. It is a way to avoid unpleasant surprises. Now that we have diagnosed Asia's dangers, however, it is natural to ask what we might reasonably expect. Our answers to this question will guide our responses.

As we navigate the risk regions, we should not be merely passive travelers. Instead, we can use our map not only to avoid threats but to manage and mitigate as many of the dangers as possible. Not everything lends itself to a solution, but we can act, at both the public and private levels, in ways that can preserve Asia's incredible successes and influence its subsequent development.

The idea of managing risk in such an enormous area can be overwhelming. How can so many different trends be addressed, or the myriad factors kept in mind? Asian nations must of course assure their own future by managing risk and avoiding war or stagnation. As politicians, business leaders, military officers, academics, journalists, and others in the United States think about the importance of the future of the Indo-Pacific, however, it should quickly become apparent that America can play an important, even unique role. For reasons of history, economics, and security, America is the most important external actor in Asia's destiny.

Yet most Americans have little interest in the dangers the Asia-Pacific faces. In a 2015 poll, Asia did not even make Americans' top twenty-three public policy priorities. The top spots went to terrorism, the economy, and jobs, respectively.[2] And yet America's future is increasingly dependent on a prosperous and stable Indo-Pacific. The question is how American gov ernment, business, academia, cultural exchange organizations, media, and the like can effectively engage with their Asian counterparts and play a constructive role in shaping the future of the Indo-Pacific. As they do so with their Asian partners, they must begin considering which risks seem most threatening, and create a plan for managing them based on their intensity.

How Close Is Asia to War?

After years of growing tensions in the East and South China Sea, citizens of ten Indo-Pacific nations were asked by the Pew Research Center in July 2014 if they feared that a war could break out between China and its neighbors. In all ten countries, half or more of respondents answered "yes," with 93 percent of Filipinos and 85 percent of Japanese predicting armed conflict.[3] People in Japan, the Philippines, and Vietnam all listed China as the greatest threat.

The Chinese too are warning that conflict is becoming more likely. The May 2015 article in the state-run *Global Times,* calling a U.S.-China war "inevitable" if Washington tries to curtail China's activities in the Spratly Islands, is only the most noteworthy of many such predictions.[4] Meanwhile, after years of downplaying the growing threat from North Korea, U.S. officials now admit that Pyongyang has intercontinental ballistic missiles that can reach the West Coast of the United States, and that the Kim regime most likely is able to put nuclear weapons on top of them.[5]

If one had to choose the region of Asia's risk map that presents the greatest near-term danger, it would be the area of security. None of Asia's players wants a military confrontation, of course, or fails to understand how a descent into major instability or outright war would harm their economies and societies.

As we saw in chapter 6, however, tensions in Asia seem to be growing with its wealth, not receding as they did in Europe after World War II. There are myriad spots in which an accident or a miscalculation by one side could force the other into an armed response and plunge Asia into some type of military confrontation. The most likely flashpoints are the

Korean peninsula and the East and South China Seas. The event might be an accident, like a North Korean missile launch gone awry, or something as simple as the sinking of a Chinese fishing boat by the Japanese coast guard. What should most worry us is that nearly all of the security risks we have charted involve one or more of the region's great powers, including the United States. That creates the potential for a larger confrontation. Given the lack of trust among Asia's states, there is no assurance that a conflict will be easily contained or localized.

How then can the nations of the Indo-Pacific navigate through this treacherous region? If simple economic integration were the answer, then an Asia that trades largely with itself and is highly interdependent should have no security risks at all. That is clearly not the case. Nor, clearly, do multilateral organizations by themselves provide a way out of military competition. Were this approach the key, then the existence of the Association of Southeast Asian Nations (ASEAN) or the East Asia Summit or a number of other groupings would end the threat of confrontation. That each security flashpoint is different, and therefore requires a different solution, goes without saying. Yet in the absence of any successful intra-Asian approach, we must consider the possibility that an outside actor can help redraw the map of security risk.

The United States is the most natural candidate for such a role. Although not an indigenous Asian power, it has a major military presence in the Indo-Pacific and has played a unique role over the past seven decades in maintaining stability with a variety of countries. No small part of Asia's general stability has been a result of the fact that for over sixty years, American ships and planes, soldiers, sailors, airmen, and Marines have helped keep the peace through the U.S. alliance system. Given the velocity of security change in Asia, however, America will have to come up with more innovative ways of working with its regional partners if it hopes to continue to provide stability.

Since 1945, U.S. strategy in Asia has been organized around a "hub-and-spoke" alliance arrangement, through which Washington has maintained formal bilateral security treaties with five nations: Australia (signed in 1951), the Philippines (1952), South Korea (1953), Thailand (1954), and Japan (1960).[6] Basing American troops in Japan, South Korea, and, until the 1990s, the Philippines provided strategic northern and southern

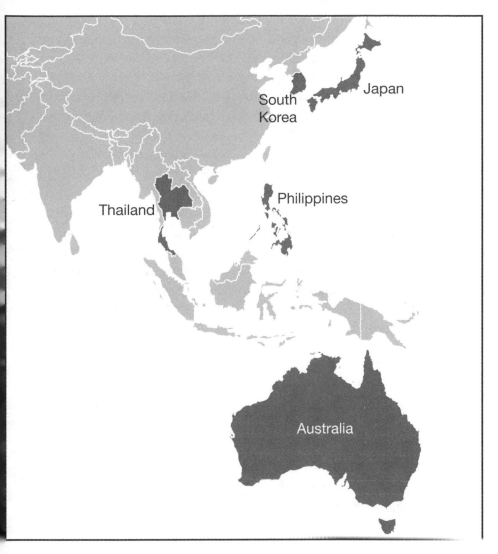

U.S. Treaty Allies in the Indo-Pacific. Artwork by Claude Aubert.

bases for U.S. forces. It is no exaggeration to say the United States is a
Pacific power because of its alliances.

Today, the American military presence in the Indo-Pacific falls under
the authority of U.S. Pacific Command (PACOM), one of America's global
combatant commands. A visitor to PACOM's headquarters at Camp Smith,
outside Honolulu, Hawaii, can be forgiven for imagining its commander

as a viceroy in control of nearly half the world. The command itself some-times seems like a semi-independent province, far from the imperial capital in Washington. Its "area of responsibility" reaches from the West Coast of the continental United States to the western Indian Ocean. The largest of America's global combatant commands, PACOM oversees a sphere of operations that contains nearly half the world's population and thirty-six countries.[7]

In normal times, PACOM's commander—always a four-star navy ad-miral—is the most powerful military officer on earth. In the mid-2010s, PACOM comprised over 300,000 U.S. servicemen and servicewomen in all branches of the armed forces, controlled about 1,500 aircraft, and fielded over one hundred ships and five aircraft carrier strike groups.[8] America's only permanently forward-based aircraft carrier is in Japan, and PACOM's commander can also use four other aircraft carrier strike groups based on the West Coast of the United States. Through the com-mander of Pacific Air Forces, PACOM controls F-22 stealth fighters, B-2 stealth bombers, B-52 strategic bombers, and other fighter squadrons.[9] Over fifty thousand U.S. military personnel are based in Japan and South Korea. U.S. forces have access to bases in Guam, Okinawa, Singapore, Australia, and (once again) the Philippines.[10]

These forces have helped keep stability in Asia for decades, but they have not prevented the ongoing shift in the balance of power. In response to China's growing assertiveness, President Barack Obama declared a "pivot" to the Asia-Pacific region in 2011 while on a visit to Australia.[11] He an-nounced a handful of initiatives, including basing both U.S. Marines and U.S. Air Force bombers in Australia, maintaining 60 percent of the navy's strength in Asia, and gaining access to more locations for temporary de-ployment of U.S. forces.[12] While many applauded these moves, doubts re-mained as to whether they added up to a real shift in Washington's global security posture given ongoing conflict in the Middle East and Ukraine.

Rebalancing is a good start, but Washington needs to ensure that its presence in the Indo-Pacific does not diminish. Even with ongoing bud-get restrictions and a shrinking U.S. military, America must remain the most credible military power in the Indo-Pacific to prevent the balance of power from shifting even more dramatically toward an increasingly as-sertive China and erratic North Korea.[13]

Although budget cuts are expected to result in potentially significant reductions in the number of active-duty ships and planes in the U.S. Navy and Air Force, the investment of keeping American forces in Asia is best thought of as an insurance policy. In times of trouble, moreover, extra insurance is often a prudent move. Given the growing security risks in Asia, future presidents should consider what would best provide that margin of safety. The permanent or regular deployment of a second aircraft carrier and strike group to the Pacific, as well as a greater percentage of U.S. submarines, is a good place to start, given their flexibility and often intimidating presence. Forward basing more U.S. fighter squadrons, preferably in Japan but with regular deployment to the Philippines, will help ensure that China cannot control the skies of Asia, especially over contested areas. While it may seem like a Cold War–era weapon, America's future next-generation bomber will play an important role as both a diplomatic instrument and a precision-strike weapon against increasingly sophisticated Chinese capabilities.[14] Above all, future U.S. presidents must remain committed to deploying America's most advanced military systems in Asia. This includes not only F-35s and Virginia-class attack submarines but new cyber capabilities that may be based in the continental United States but are employable abroad.[15] This will give American leaders both flexibility and political credibility, and give assurance to U.S. partners that they will not stand alone.

More ships and planes alone, however, is not enough. The hub-and-spoke alliance model organized around the U.S. PACOM is likely to remain the primary political and security arrangement between the United States and its allies. But given the worsening risk cycle in Asia deriving from China's military buildup, North Korea's nuclear and missile programs, and numerous territorial disputes, among other issues, it is time for the United States to pursue a new strategy. It has to link together both its close partners and other important nations that increasingly share common concerns.

A "Concentric Triangles" Strategy

Winston Churchill is reputed to have told his cabinet, "Gentlemen, we are out of money. Now we must think." The United States is not out of money, but after seven decades it must think anew about how to maintain stability in Asia. The goal has not changed; the United States remains committed to maintaining an open, rules-based security order in Asia and preventing war. But its means must change.

Washington does not need to uproot its current alliance structure, but it needs to update it. A new strategy should seek not only to draw America's current allies closer together but to encourage other Asian powers to forge deeper relations with the United States and Asia's leading liberal nations. Doing so will bring about greater cooperation and coordination among leading Asian states, based on a common set of shared interests, and can serve as a basis for engaging China and Russia in region-wide discussions.

This strategic approach can be thought of as a set of "concentric triangles." The outer triangle links Japan, South Korea, India, and Australia; the inner one connects Indonesia, Malaysia, the Philippines, and Singapore, with participation by Thailand and outreach to Vietnam. Among these states are Asia's largest and oldest democracies, some of its leading economies, and most strategically located nations. Washington's goal should not be an inflexible new alliance system, which is infeasible in the Indo-Pacific, but the construction of a community of interest based on a common set of rules, norms, behaviors, and coordination among the region's leading nations. The objective is to increase transparency, build trust, and make it easier to defend the maritime and aerospace commons.

While multilateralism and contemporary international law are based on the concept of equal sovereignty among nations, the United States should encourage larger nations to play a more significant role in helping protect the rules-based order. The outer triangle of Japan, South Korea, India, and Australia should serve as the anchor for political and security cooperation as well as for U.S. policy in the region. The political stability, liberal social system, and military capability of each nation in the outer triangle place them at the core of ensuring regional security.

Washington should also aim at enhancing its political and military cooperation with these pivotal nations. No matter how many troops, ships, and planes the United States places in Asia, they will always be comparatively few, operating at a great distance from their homeland, in countries where there may be significant public opposition to their presence. American

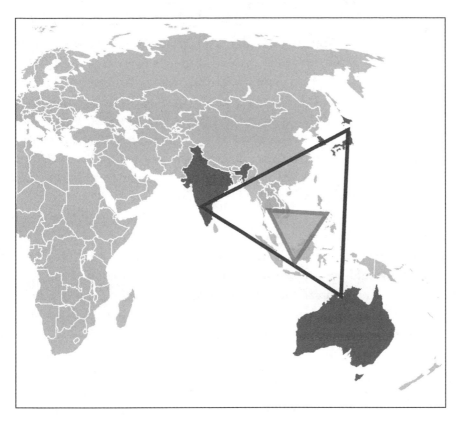

An American Concentric Triangles Strategy for Asia. Artwork by Claude Aubert.

military effectiveness thus depends on creating a community of security interests with Asia's major liberal nations.

Security cooperation does not begin with fighting side-by-side. Indeed, the goal of such cooperation is to avoid conflict by shaping the security environment. As a first step, then, Washington should organize regular security summits with Tokyo, Seoul, Canberra, and New Delhi, to address significant security issues and try to set regional standards and norms. Then, the nations should agree on a division of labor. Each country should agree to take the lead responsibility for providing the first response to problems in the geographic areas closest to them. These responses can include such things as disaster relief, combating piracy, attempting crisis mediation, and preventing proliferation of weapons of mass destruction.

Each outer triangle nation, moreover, has particular strengths that can be leveraged when needed. Japan, for example, has one of the world's best coast guard and disaster relief capabilities, as it showed during the Indonesia tsunami in 2004 and its own earthquake and tsunami disaster in 2011.[16] The Australian military is almost completely interoperable with American forces and has perhaps the highest level of combat capability and training, which it can use to work with regional states. South Korea's military is also one of the best-trained in the world and is a model for states moving from military authoritarianism to democracy and civilian control over the military.

India, not being a formal U.S. ally, occupies a different position from the three other outer triangle countries. But Prime Minister Modi wants to play a larger regional role, and Washington should give him the opportunity. It should push for greater political and security cooperation with New Delhi in the Indian Ocean and the Strait of Malacca, and in Southeast Asia generally. Expanding the scope of current military exchanges, such as the Malabar naval exercise, is a way for India to partner with the United States and other leading Asian nations, such as Japan, to create a security network.[17] The United States and Australia should seek to pool intelligence with India and Japan to gain a comprehensive awareness of threats and conditions from the Indian Ocean to the western Pacific.

So much for the larger players. Successfully implementing the other half of this strategy will require a more dramatic break with the past. The "inner triangle" of Indonesia, Malaysia, the Philippines, and Singapore—with the participation of Thailand and Vietnam when their domestic political situations have both stabilized and liberalized, respectively—needs a more localized set of responsibilities. Given their security concerns, it may be easier to engage these countries in enhancing maritime safety in the "inner commons" of the lower South China Sea, including the key waterways of the Malacca, Sunda, and Lombok Straits. All of these countries are concerned with instability engendered by territorial disputes with China, even if they have no direct disagreements with Beijing.

These states have cooperated through the ASEAN framework, but linking them with the larger powers of the outer triangle is a way to start building a new security architecture in the region. Such actions do not have to conflict with ASEAN's initiatives and should be seen as complementary. Washington should focus on building up the individual capabilities of each inner triangle nation, so that they can play a larger regional role in the future. When done in concert with political discussions, that can help them shape ASEAN's deliberations as well as form a nascent Southeast Asian community among themselves.

As with the outer triangle states, there should be regular security summits among U.S., Indonesian, Malaysian, Philippine, and Singaporean heads of state. The group should attempt to engage Vietnam in these discussions, the more so as Hanoi shows a commitment to gradual liberalization at home. Vietnam's strategic location and security differences with China, as well as its growing economic role, make it an important member of the inner triangle. Thailand, too, should be welcomed once its democratic political system is restored.

The inner triangle nations should be a particular target for upgraded exchanges of young military and police officers, joint military training, and capacity building. The 2015 Southeast Asia Maritime Security Initiative, a U.S. pilot program to provide funding for building up coast guards and establishing surveillance systems and exercises, is a good start. It should be funded, however, to the full $425 million originally proposed by the Senate Armed Services Committee, which was cut during congressional negotiations.[18] Adding in the resources of Japan, in particular, could increase the scope and impact of this type of program.

Reducing Asia's security risks can happen only if these two triangles are brought together. There are numerous ways to do this without threatening any nation's sense of security or making it feel it has to choose between the United States and China. Joint maritime patrols in sensitive waterways among both outer and inner triangle nations, with participation by the U.S. Navy, are a way to both build community and deter countries, like China, that seek to coerce other states over territorial disputes. Both Japan and the Philippines have broached the idea of joint patrols with the U.S. Navy in the South China Sea.[19] The same can be done with air patrols over contested or strategic territory. Sharing more maritime information, as well, will build confidence and trust.

There is an obvious objection to this approach: won't a concentric triangles strategy only increase the risk of conflict, since both China and North Korea will feel more threatened?

It is of little use to argue that the goal of this strategy is not to contain China. The worldview of Beijing's leaders has become increasingly rigid in recent years, as shown by their rhetoric, their continued development of offensive military systems, and their unwillingness to compromise on maritime territorial issues.[20] Yet Beijing is well aware that peace in the Indo-Pacific is what has allowed it to become a trading powerhouse and to build its own military without the need to use it. It is not naïve to appeal to China's rational self-interest.

At its best, the concentric triangles strategy will encourage Beijing to adapt its policies around accepted rules and norms. The coordinated patrols, information sharing, and other aspects of the strategy may make it clear to Beijing that its assertive behavior will cause it to be increasingly isolated in Asia and that its neighbors will act in concert to promote stability. Over time, we may hope that China's leaders will come to appreciate the benefits of constructive engagement that goes beyond trade or aid packages. If and when China's leadership chooses to help reduce the tensions it has done so much to create, it will find partners who already have created a community of interests.

As for North Korea, a firmer political community and a more cooperative set of security relationships will hardly change the Kim regime. But North Korean leaders, who have proven that they have a strong survival instinct, may be deterred from aggressive adventurism in a more robust security environment. At a minimum, the concentric triangles strategy may permit a common regional response to Pyongyang's provocations.

Most important, security risk in Asia will be lowered if a set of liberal actors in the region increasingly treat their neighborhood as an integrated community. For American policymakers, that means accepting that their strategy must be about the Indo-Pacific as a whole and not just China. The tendency of each new presidential administration to focus its Asia policy on China, sometimes to the exclusion of older relationships, is no longer appropriate when the Indo-Pacific is an increasingly integrated region of nations with common challenges and a growing sense of community.

It will of course take time to build the trust and working relationships necessary to make the concentric triangles strategy work. But it promises to redraw two regions of our risk map: security and political community. Washington and its partners should commit themselves steadily to move toward a more liberal Indo-Pacific that provides stability and opportunity for growth on a scale far beyond what today's common initiatives can provide.

Saving the Goose That Lays the Golden Egg

When most Americans think about Asia, they first think about economic growth. With good reason: it is Asia's economic strength that has helped transform trade and consumption over the past several decades. If an accidental military conflict is the major risk facing the Indo-Pacific in the short term, the biggest midterm risk is economic stagnation that infects the entire region.

Stagnation goes beyond mere slumps or slowdowns. It could start from a slump centered in one or more of the region's major economies, or one affecting many economies at once, like the 1998 Asian financial crisis.[21] Given Asia's vital role in global trade, economic stagnation in the region would have damaging worldwide effects. Just as important, severe economic troubles could spill over into other parts of our risk map. The most immediate result could be political instability in countries ranging from China to Indonesia. Economic dislocation could also bleed into security-related conflicts as governments dealing with social pressure at home turn to foreign adventurism to build popular support.

We already are likely seeing a major slowdown in China, whose growth rate has been declining for several years. The worry is how much China can recover; already some economists believe that China is in stagnation.[22] Worse, the region's mature economies, such as Japan and South Korea, seem unable to shake off continued sluggishness, their growth rates are being depressed by China's problems, and they no longer are strong enough to lift the rest of the region out of a prolonged slump. The effects on developing economies in Southeast Asia could be even more severe, short circuiting the region's modernization.

What if the region escapes stagnation, but is unable to recover its dynamism? Even moderate economic risk can have major effects. Neither Asians nor the rest of the world have asked how they will adjust to an Asia of predominantly mature economies, where no one is growing at 10 or even 7 percent a year, where inefficiencies retard innovation and modernization, and where entrepreneurship is hindered. That would not spell the end of economic opportunity, but it would challenge a fragile global economy.

So what can be done? Redrawing the map of economic risk must be done first by the nations themselves. So far their measures have had limited results, and there is a danger that halfhearted reform policies will only delay inevitable contractions and worsen inequality. Only a renewed commitment to serious reform will put Asia on a path to ensuring its future health. Government policies must realistically address problems, but businesses, too, must ensure that they are planning for the future, investing for long-term development, and contributing to socioeconomic development at home. All that is of course easier said than done, but there should be no doubt that economic health is what creates political and social stability. Self-interest in economic matters naturally lends itself to more rational action.

That said, however, we should once again consider what role an interested outsider can play. Just as with security risk, Asia's partners can nudge it in the direction of economic stability. Above all, the United States has a vested interest in reducing economic risk in Asia. America can play an important role by working with Asian trade partners, and some beyond the region, to continue pushing forward needed reform, and striving to create a culture of economic liberalization.

Does Trade with Asia Hurt or Help the United States?

Before I outline a proposed American role, it's worth reviewing just why the economic health of the Indo-Pacific is important to the United States, and why Americans should engage even more with Asia to reduce economic risk. Criticisms of free trade and its costs continue to roil the economic debate in the United States, as they do elsewhere.

Our consumer-oriented world is inconceivable without the role played by the nations of the Asia-Pacific. We all know that affordable and innovative Asian goods have benefited American households over the past four decades. Just as important, the growth of Asia's middle class has been a boon for American exporters. The American Chamber of Commerce estimates that eleven million American jobs are directly or indirectly dependent on trade with Asia.[23] Total trade in goods between America and Asia totaled $1.4 trillion in 2013. While Canada and Mexico are the

United States' largest export markets, exports to Asia totaled $475 billion in 2013 and accounted for 30 percent of all U.S. exports of goods. Asia accounted for just over one-third of all goods brought into the country, making it the largest source of goods from abroad.[24]

America's agricultural sector has become a net exporter of commodities like soy beans, beef, and rice to Asian nations, earning roughly $59 billion in 2011 (out of a total of $137 billion exported).[25] Companies like Boeing, Pfizer, and Dow sell billions of dollars in products each year in Asia, as aircraft, chemical, and medical instruments routinely top the list of U.S. exports to Asian countries.[26] While some traditional American industries like textiles have been hollowed out by Asian imports, successful U.S. exporters are increasingly high up the value chain, which translates into better-paying jobs. As a whole, Asia accounts for roughly 30 percent of America's total trade in goods and services. While most Americans may not know specific numbers, polls show that a majority understand the general benefits of trade. Fifty-eight percent of respondents in a recent poll indicated that free trade agreements are a "good thing for the U.S."[27]

American communities with direct investment from Asian countries have benefited enormously from those factories and tax bases. Japanese car manufacturers Toyota and Honda, for instance, have put down roots from California to Kentucky. More "Japanese" cars sold in America are made in the United States than in Japan. When you count direct employees, dealer employees, and supplier employees, Japanese carmakers account for over 1.3 million American jobs.[28] In 2013, Japan was the largest foreign direct investor in the United States, totaling a record $44.9 billion. It held a top spot in 2014 as well, though its investments slipped to $37.7 billion.[29] Much of that investment comes from mergers and acquisitions or from buying significant stakes in U.S. companies; one major example is the 2012 purchase by Japanese telecommunications giant Softbank of 70 percent of Sprint for $20 billion.[30] Such investment goes toward supporting U.S. jobs and products.

While few would quibble with Toyota opening a plant in Tennessee, many still ask whether it is wise to let foreign entities buy major American companies. Such investment is a major driver of financial exchange in today's global economy. In 2014, foreign firms invested $86 billion in the United States, much of it through mergers and acquisitions.[31] While such transactions always require a careful balancing of costs and benefits, some of the largest foreign investors also spark national security concerns. In 2008, the Chinese telecommunications giant Huawei was blocked from purchasing the U.S. telecommunications firm 3Com Corporation, and it later failed to win approval to acquire three more U.S. telecommunications companies, because of concerns over its ties to the Chinese military.[32]

Economic sectors that are not as sensitive as telecommunications can also cause concerns about foreign investment. The 2013 announcement of a Chinese company's purchase of Smithfield Foods, America's largest pork producer, for $4.7 billion caused speculation that the new owners would uproot the company and abandon domestic producers in favor of pork products imported from China.[33] The deal ultimately went through, and the pigs stayed Stateside. As much as local economies benefit from such investment, concerns over foreign ownership of U.S. companies remain high, sometimes with reason, other times without.

The biggest criticism of trade with Asia is America's massive current accounts deficit. Since China, Japan, South Korea, Vietnam, and Malaysia supply the majority of our cars, televisions, computers, clothing, and footwear, Americans pay out far more to Asian trade partners than U.S. companies take in. In 2014, the U.S. trade deficit with Asia was almost $537 billion.[34] Such an imbalance is sustainable in the short term in part through our trading partners' massive ongoing purchase of U.S. debt, primarily U.S. government Treasuries, to the tune of some $2 billion a day. By mid-2015, China and Japan had each accumulated some $1.2 trillion of Treasury bonds.[35]

Without this long-term holding of U.S. debt, American consumers would not be able to finance their purchases from Asia. Some see this as a virtuous cycle, but deficit hawks argue that it locks America and its closest economic partners into mutually assured destruction: any default by America would cripple our bondholders, while a change in their investment habits would cause America's interest rates to skyrocket and possibly crash the U.S. economy.

But the story of debt and trade deficits is not so simple. In a world where supply chains, capital flows, and intellectual property are all international, assessing value and profit is a tricky business. One of the best illustrations of globalization in action is the iPhone, and looking at its supply chain and profit distribution has become a popular pastime While the iPhone is owned and "made" by an American company, Apple, its parts come from America, Japan, Korea, Singapore, China, Germany, and the Netherlands. Japanese firms such as Toshiba, Murata, and Elpida supply crucial components, including the display, memory, and battery, while Korea's Samsung provides the semiconductor used as the applications processor.[36] American companies like Qualcomm and Sandisk supply other processors, flash memory, the camera, and power amplifiers. Those American and Japanese firms also have research and production centers located abroad, many of them in China or developing countries like Malaysia, where much of the designing and building of components is done.

Yet because the final product is assembled in China by Foxconn (a Taiwanese firm), the entire wholesale value of each iPhone (and iPad, too) is counted against the U.S. trade deficit with China. An increasing number of experts call this misleading. A 2010 study done in Japan concluded that Foxconn's final assembly adds just 1 percent of the value of a roughly $600 iPhone, while at least 60 percent of the profit goes to Apple and other American firms. The paper concluded that using a value-added approach, the iPhone actually produces a $48 million annual trade surplus for the United States, not the $2 billion deficit with China that is usually claimed.[37]

The economist Mark Perry has calculated that overall in 2010, the United States actually had a $32 billion "value-added" trade surplus with China, not a $133 billion deficit.[38] The U.S.-produced value of products imported from China, Perry estimated, represents about 55 percent of the items. By another calculation using similar reasoning, *The Economist* reported that America's reported $300 billion trade deficit with China in 2011 was actually only half that amount.[39]

Another issue, even more difficult to resolve, and far more politically sensitive, is the impact of free trade on jobs. One of the main critiques of free trade is that it causes the loss of American jobs to Asia. Even without a formal free trade agreement, China's entry into the World Trade Organization (WTO) in 2001, and the consequent lowering of tariffs on China's products, had a massive effect on domestic industries around the world. Textile and other clothing industries were particularly devastated, including in America, along with machinery production. One study by a left-leaning economics think tank concluded that in the decade between

2001, when China joined the WTO, and 2011, 2.7 million U.S. jobs were "lost or displaced," with the computer, electronics, and parts industries particularly hard hit.[40] Another study, conducted by the Yale School of Management, concluded that the United States lost 3.5 million manufacturing jobs, almost exclusively to China, between 2000 and 2007.[41]

The benefits of free trade and comparative advantage are as strong as ever, but what has happened in the past several decades is unique. China's rise and the development of its export markets have been so fast and so massive that the natural equilibrium whereby less efficient producers are forced to close down while the macroeconomy finds new production sectors has simply been overwhelmed. Economic shifts that normally take decades were compressed into years.[42] Added to this was the decades-long restructuring of the U.S. economy and its loss of manufacturing share to earlier modernizers like Japan and Korea. The collapses of the American steel and consumer electronics industries a generation ago were a precursor to the even more abrupt changes driven by China's emergence. The Bureau of Labor Statistics determined that from 1979 to 2007, U.S. manufacturing employment fell from 19.6 million to 13.7 million, a loss of nearly six million manufacturing jobs.[43] There has been no time for displaced workers to retrain or for new manufacturing sectors to be found. All this seems to mitigate against even closer trade relations. The reality, however, is more complex.

Taking Advantage of Asia

If there are so many ambiguities in trade, why should America help reshape Asia's economic risk map? Wouldn't it be better to let Asia continue to slow down, and then step into the gap? In a globalized world, such economic isolationism simply doesn't work, and following such a path makes everyone poorer over the long run. Instead, there are two compelling (and interlinked) reasons for reducing Asia's economic risk: the benefits of growth and the benefits of political stability.

It is perhaps easiest to appreciate the bottom line: the profit motive that drives all trade. "Look, I'll take China growing at 5 percent or less a year, because that's better than anywhere else," I'm told by an expat veteran doing private equity for twenty-five years in Shanghai. Until recently, the numbers supported his stance. A study by the HSBC banking and financial services organization projects 8 percent growth in U.S. exports to Asia (excluding Japan) during the 2020s, and an increase of 11 percent a year in exports to India.[44] Talk to American investors in Shanghai or exporters in Vietnam, and they will rave about long-term growth potential.

Now, however, business cannot be so complacent. They are beginning to grasp the economic challenges ahead, and they have a vested interest in pushing national governments farther down the road of trade liberalization, reform, and economic development. Given the needs of modernizing countries like Indonesia or India, these businessmen can't help but see a role for advanced Western technology, products, marketing, and knowledge transfer. An observer may be more skeptical, however, of their belief that the internal structure of Asia's economies is resilient enough to avoid stagnation, let alone a prolonged slump. The question now is where to find the most likely available opportunities, while pushing for continued liberalization.

One major driver of Asia's projected growth is urbanization, which will eventually begin slowing because of population decline but which still offers the prospect of years, maybe decades, of growth. Just as Japan in the twentieth century saw its population change from overwhelmingly rural to largely urban, China today is witnessing a massive internal migration, as are, on a smaller scale, Indonesia and India. Yet urbanization is a double-edged sword for Asian governments: though it may spur economic development, city populations make insistent political demands that can add to domestic instability. It will also remain highly sensitive to macroeconomic conditions, such as a prolonged slump.

Yet for domestic and foreign businesses alike, urbanization is for now an economic force, especially in China. With some three hundred million Chinese having moved to cities in the past two decades and another one hundred million expected to do so by 2025, the consumption needs of China's new urban class are enormous.[45] It is, a private equity type repeats, a "huge new market" that has just begun to be tapped. These new city dwellers need everything from machinery to medical instruments, electronics to cars. Add in India, Indonesia, Vietnam, and Malaysia, and the potential for growth remains strong for decades.

The opportunities for American investors as well are potentially huge. Thousands of Chinese companies need capital to function, and more will start up as cities in the interior expand, the more so if economic slowdown makes moving to the coasts less attractive. American manufacturers may have a harder time cracking the market, but even they will be needed, especially for higher-end products. It will be a continuing struggle, requiring constant U.S. government pressure, to ensure fair market access for American companies throughout the Indo-Pacific. A firm and consistent policy on this issue will in turn promote economic liberalization more broadly throughout developing countries.

Another opportunity is provided by online retailing, which is increasingly serving the needs of millions of middle-class, urban Asian consumers. In 2014, according to Goldman Sachs, Japan's e-commerce sector racked up nearly $49 billion, while in China it reached $143 billion.[46] That Chinese number currently is predicted to nearly double, to $265 billion by 2017. McKinsey and Company expects online sales to reach $350 billion by the mid-2010s, while Japan's Nippon Telephone and Telegraph (NTT) estimates Asia's e-commerce market is already $525 billion, making it the world's largest.[47] Giant Internet commerce companies like Japan's Rakuten or China's Alibaba provide an online sales portal for hundreds of thousands of small businesses. Even if this market slows down, U.S. firms will benefit by being aggressive players, in part to drive the competition that will benefit Asian consumers. U.S. financial firms, as well, will have a role to play, especially if domestic credit gets tight in China or remains underdeveloped in other countries. Economic restructuring, including e-commerce that moves consumption away from brick-and-mortar stores, will be an investment opportunity as Asia's economies mature.

Opportunity is a plus only if one is able to take advantage of it. The danger for U.S. companies is that they are being left behind. That means both playing more effectively and reducing barriers to trade. American businesses are competing with Asian companies that also see their home region as their largest growth market. American e-commerce firms, for example, still struggle to gain market share in China, where Amazon is only the fifth-biggest player. Intra-Asian trade makes up by far the largest share of exchange for all Asian countries; close to 40 percent of ASEAN's trade is with China, while trade with American firms had dropped to just 10 percent of ASEAN's total by 2011.[48]

This pattern is repeated throughout the region. After years of growth, American firms are seeing sales drop in the Indo-Pacific. Only 64 percent of U.S. companies in China made a profit in 2015, according to the American Chamber of Commerce, the lowest number since 2010.[49] Even well-established companies are facing economic headwinds. IBM's revenue in Asia dropped 11.8 percent from 2013 to 2014, and Coca-Cola took a 3.4 percent hit in sales over the same period.[50]

U.S. firms in particular face high-value competition from Japan and Korea, and make an increasing percentage of their profits from lower-value goods, such as cheaper cars in China. Asians continue to see Asia as their key market. Of the Japanese exporters receiving loans from the Japan Bank for International Cooperation, almost 50 percent were focused on Asian markets, while China, India, Indonesia, Thailand, and Vietnam held the top five spots of countries the bank considered "promising" for Japanese exports. The same Japanese manufacturers chose India, China, and Indonesia as the most promising countries over the next ten years.[51] In an economic environment that is both tightening and becoming more crowded, U.S. businesses will have to compete better, but the opportunities are there to cater to Asia's middle class, work with its leading corporations, and drive innovation.

How to increase the pie, then, for all players in the Indo-Pacific economic ecosystem? If trade is a net good, the primary risk in Asia is that its expectations of future growth will be unrealized. As we saw in chapter 2, productivity remains held back by malinvestment, protectionism, corruption, and inefficient regulations and tax laws, among other problems. From mature economies like Japan to developing ones like Indonesia, a host of market reforms are needed to push domestic restructuring and foreign exposure—in other words, to make reality meet the economists' projections.

No outsider can clean up domestic risk factors like corruption or force foreign leaders to change regulations. But foreign trade partners can work to create a vibrant, open, rules-based global trade architecture and expand economic ties. This, in turn, can make the logic of reform part of the broader economic environment. One of the key tools for achieving this is political agreements for free trade. It is here that America, along with other states, should take a leading role.

Trans-Pacific Partnership Member States. Artwork by Claude Aubert.

Despite the debate in America, the proposition that more trade is better for a country is still generally accepted. While carve-outs to shelter particular sectors and protectionist impulses remain in every negotiation, the ideals of a more open global trading system animate much of the thinking about economics today. But the politics of free trade lags behind. Groundbreaking agreements to follow the 1970s General Agreement on Tariffs and Trade (GATT) or the 1990s North American Free Trade Agreement (NAFTA) have stalled, and the latest round of global trade talks, the WTO-sponsored Doha Round, ended in deadlock in 2011.[52]

In the Asia-Pacific area, however, the world's only large, regional free trade negotiation is nearing reality. Begun with a 2006 agreement by New Zealand, Singapore, Brunei, and Chile, the Trans-Pacific Partnership (TPP) started with modest goals. When the United States expressed interest in joining the group in early 2008, it suddenly became a potentially major trade deal. Australia, Canada, Mexico, Peru, Malaysia, and Vietnam also joined the negotiations, and Japan finally agreed to enter in early 2013.[53] In October 2015, the twelve nations completed a high-standard pact protecting intellectual property rights, opening agricultural markets, liberalizing telecommunications, improving consumer safety, and reducing the role of state-owned enterprises. With Japan in the pact, the TPP comprises 38 percent of global GDP, and it could add some $14 billion to the American economy and as much as $33 billion to Japan's GDP by 2025.[54]

Yet the TPP is not a done deal. Even though some of its provisions will not come into force for decades, it faces significant challenges in being ratified in the United States, thanks to anti-free trade feelings. An American failure to approve the pact could doom it. Moreover, even if it is ratified, signatories will have to ensure that it is fully implemented once the world's attention turns elsewhere. Full implementation means changing the economic culture of countries like Japan, which retains highly protected agricultural markets. Vietnam, which is eager to be in the TPP as a way both to expand its global markets and to gain access to technology and best practices, also faces significant questions how much it will reduce its state-owned enterprises and its regulatory barriers.[55]

Linking advanced and developing economies in the world's most vibrant trade sector has enormous long-term benefits. These go beyond the simple numbers that would be added to the participants' national incomes. In setting high standards for intellectual property, clarifying regulatory regimes, and establishing coherent "rules of origin" for regional suppliers so as to strengthen supply chains, the TPP has the potential to set a much broader framework for liberal economic ties. Developing countries such as Malaysia and Vietnam will serve as models for other Southeast Asian nations that are considering the costs and benefits of liberalizing their markets. Moreover, the size of the TPP market will attract other major economies, such as South Korea. It can also serve as a political mechanism to encourage states just beginning to open their economies, like Burma, to continue liberalization.

The TPP may also serve as a basis for even larger agreements. For example, South Korea should be encouraged to join, and be accepted if it makes the first move. Similarly, the Philippines and Mongolia should be seen as potential partners, thus bringing together more of the region's democracies. Ultimately, the TPP could be a gateway to a truly pan-Asian trade pact, though years of negotiations will be required to get China and India to the level of openness required. Thus, it is particularly important to get the current TPP fully ratified and in force, so that it can serve as the "starter yeast" of a larger agreement.

Similar ideas are already afoot. Planners in Tokyo see the TPP as a gateway to a comprehensive Free Trade Area of the Asia-Pacific (FTAAP), a pan-Asian, regional liberal trade bloc. The Chinese are pushing another ASEAN concept, a "Regional Comprehensive Economic Partnership" that would link the ten ASEAN states and their FTA partners (Australia, China, India, Japan, Korea and New Zealand).[56] Ultimately, Washington and its partners will have to ensure that liberal norms and high standards undergird any larger trade agreements. That can happen only if a strong framework is already working for many of the leading economies of the area. Transparency, high standards, and reliable arbitration mechanisms will be crucial to the success of the TPP, and to the hope of building an FTAAP that includes China.

In areas like free trade, the United States does not have to go it alone as the only non-Asian participant. Europe also has a role in Asia's economic future. Collectively, the European Union is one of Asia's largest external trade partners, with over $1 trillion in trade. Nearly 30 percent of the European Union's imports come from Asia, while just over 20 percent of its exports head to the Indo-Pacific.[57] China is the European Union's second-largest individual trading partner after the United States, totaling over $550 billion in 2015, while the Europeans traded over $130 billion with Japan.[58] India was the European Union's ninth-largest trading partner, with nearly $100 billion in 2015, and the two are currently negotiating a free trade agreement patterned on the EU–South Korea FTA, which increased trade to $100 billion in 2015.[59]

Yet Europe could do more to promote trade and economic liberalization in the region. While the European Union is ASEAN's third-largest trading partner, with over $220 billion in goods and services exchanged in 2015, FTA negotiations between the two organizations have stalled out.[60] Bilateral negotiations with Malaysia and Singapore are under way, but both parties should revive the goal of a full EU-ASEAN free trade agreement. Such an agreement would complement American efforts and even expand them, promoting economic liberalization throughout the region.

Whether in concert with European nations or not, the United States can play other roles in economic relations that help reduce economic risk.

For example, foreign direct investment should be promoted on both sides of the Pacific. Despite Japan's impressive totals, Asian investment in U.S. companies still lags that of other regions. China overtook the United States as the top destination for foreign direct investment in 2014, pulling in $128 billion to America's $86 billion, while Hong Kong attracted $111 billion.[61] According to U.S. government figures, South Korea invested only $6.6 billion in the United States in 2013, while China added a comparatively minuscule $2.4 billion, a 31 percent decrease from the previous year.[62] Yet because foreign companies and governments hold billions of dollars, Asian companies have a great capacity to invest in America, if the U.S. tax and regulatory environment becomes more welcoming.

Investment barriers continue to exist on the other side of the Pacific. Japan still lags woefully in attracting foreign investors. Only $2.3 billion was spent by foreign firms on Japanese companies in 2013, and the total foreign direct investment (FDI) in Japan represents only 5 percent of GDP.[63] This is one reason Japanese corporations have been so resistant to innovation and change. India does even worse, with just over $2 billion in FDI inflows in 2014, thanks in part to the continuing drag of the license raj regime described in chapter 2.[64] The United States should make it a primary mission to push for more openness in Asia's investment climate, whether as part of broader free trade agreements or individually. A good step in that direction would be a carefully crafted bilateral investment treaty (BIT), such as the one being negotiated currently between the United States and China. A Sino-U.S. BIT would help protect the rights of U.S. companies in China and open China's economy up further to Western participation. That could lead to greater free trade negotiations between the world's two largest economies.

Promoting the exchange of skilled labor should be another priority. Since 1990, the U.S. Congress has capped new H-1B visas for skilled workers to eighty-five thousand per fiscal year. Given that the entire telecommunications and personal computer revolution has taken place in that quarter-century, the fact that the number of skilled immigrant visas has not changed does not reflect economic reality. Moreover, after the terrorist attacks of 9/11, skilled labor visa approvals (new visas plus renewals) dropped from 331,200 to 197,500. Over a decade later, the number still had not returned to 2001 levels, resting at 262,500 in 2012.[65] Washington should encourage the movement of skilled labor across borders and welcome Asians with advanced degrees to the United States. These workers not only add to U.S. innovation and competitiveness, they often maintain ties with research institutes and businesses in their home countries. All of this creates more possibilities for trade and collaboration.

Labor movement is a two-way street, just as needed in some Asian countries as in America. For a country like Japan, allowing skilled labor into the country offers the same opportunity as FDI and free trade. Access to some of the world's best minds and most experienced business leaders has multiplier effects throughout society. Prime Minister Shinzo Abe has made increasing the number of foreign skilled workers in Japan a serious policy for perhaps the first time since the Meiji Restoration, when hundreds of foreign experts were hired to help modernize the country.[66] Something similar is needed in Japan today, and it is encouraging that Tokyo is waking up to the problem.[67]

For all Asian nations, competing to attract the best talent, regardless of origin, will become the more important as economic pressures mount. More liberal foreign labor policies across the region may help in managing economic risk. More, however, needs to be done to free up the flow of skilled labor in Asia, and both U.S. businesses and Washington need to push their foreign partners to reduce restrictions on labor.

These are but some suggestions meant to spark a larger debate over what kind of economic growth strategy Asian nations can adopt along with their main trading partners, especially the United States. The more committed that countries in the Indo-Pacific become to opening up and modernizing their economies, the more likely it is that Asia's fantastic growth over the past decades continues. Yet securing the fruits of that growth requires more than just economic policy. It needs a political environment favorable to cooperation and development. Realizing such an environment would reshape many of Asia's risk regions over the long term.

The End of Risk?

The deeper we navigate into Asia's risk regions, the longer our timeframe becomes. If the dangers of military conflict are greatest in the near term and that of economic stagnation over the midterm, the threat of domestic political disorder is more of a long-term concern, though it also could be the "black swan" that upends all other calculations. Even if political upheaval seems far off, it may be the most serious risk region of all, since it can bring radical disruption both inside a country and outside.

Here is where our risk regions truly intersect. History is littered with examples of economic disruption and military conflict pushing societies into revolution and political collapse. The 1917 Bolshevik Revolution, the 1933 Nazi rise to power, and the 1949 Chinese Communist Revolution are just three of the most infamous examples. The reverse is also true. Political revolution in a major country can result in regional or global war. The French Revolution unleashed the forces that brought about the rise of Napoleon, and Hitler's dreams of world domination brought about World War II. In the case of Nazi Germany, the cycle turned completely, as the tides of destruction flowed from World War I first to Weimar economic depression, and thence to Hitler's coup and the catastrophe of an even more destructive world war.

In mentioning such examples, I am in no way predicting a similar upheaval in Asia. Yet these episodes give us a deeper appreciation of the risks posed by Asia's unfinished political revolutions. The Indo-Pacific has enjoyed general political stability for four decades, yet the challenges that vex both democratic and authoritarian governments should not be dismissed. Nor, if we want to avoid yet more strategic surprise, should we shrug our shoulders and say that such dangers are so far in the future that there's no sense worrying about them now. It is a cliché, but no less true, that an ounce of prevention is worth a pound of cure.

Betting on Democracy

How then, should we seek to redraw the map of political risk in Asia?

In asking this question, we have arrived at the end of our journey through the entirety of Asia's risk map. The best way to reduce risk across the board—be it economic, demographic, security, or other—is to pursue the most idealistic goal: to encourage wider liberalization throughout the region. That, as it turns out, is also the most difficult end to achieve.

A more democratic Indo-Pacific will be a more prosperous and stable one. No one pretends that democracy is perfect, but it offers the best opportunities for long-term social and economic growth. Even Japan has maintained its standards of living and kept social stability during its long period of stagnation, due in no small part to its liberal society. The more democracies a region has, the better the chance of peacefully resolving disputes and creating robust mechanisms of cooperation as well. The next generation therefore should be dedicated to nurturing a more democratic Asia, with untiring support from the region's current democracies, the United States, and Europe. This may be the most idealistic suggestion of how to reduce risk, but it must be undertaken in realistic ways.

Such a goal is made more important by the growing cooperation among authoritarian and illiberal powers. From China's longtime support for North Korea, to Russia's invasion of Ukraine and intervention in the Syrian civil war, to an informal Iran–North Korea axis, challengers to the post-World War II liberal international order are increasingly providing each other moral support, and are cooperating to undermine international institutions and norms.[68] While authoritarian nations do not have a good track record of maintaining extended alliances, they can nonetheless be very successful at undermining regional and global stability. This process can be short circuited only by increasing the number and strength of liberal states supporting regional and global order.

Nurturing democracy inside a country is intimately related to forging a community of liberal nations. It is rare for democracy to flower in a sterile garden. Long-term domestic stability and prosperity can be encouraged by the regional spread of democratic norms, including civil rights, rule of law, gender equality, and a free press. Just as our strategy for reducing security risk was to develop a nascent regional security community, a vibrant regional political environment will both encourage and be grown by stronger and more confident democracies. Again, Europe is a model for how a stable regional environment helps ensure democracy's long-term viability.

Many things can be done to nurture democracy in Asia. First, the region's leading liberal states, Japan, India, and South Korea, along with Taiwan, should take the lead in self-consciously promoting liberal ideas. As discussed earlier in this chapter, these "outer triangle" countries should form an alliance of democracies and hold annual summits on civil society and democratic governance. These should be smaller than pan-Asia gatherings and specifically concerned with promoting democratic growth.

Asia's leading liberal states, especially Japan and Australia, can promote grassroots gatherings and fund legislative, legal, media, and student exchanges to build the infrastructure of democracy.

The United States can play a major role in such an endeavor. The U.S. State Department should partner with the National Endowment for Democracy and its affiliate organizations to institute democracy summits in Asia in concert with those organized by Asia's liberal leaders. European states can do the same, and the United States and European democracies can lend their expertise to an Asian agenda that includes everything from best electoral practices to writing liberal legal codes. Younger European democracies, such as Poland and the Czech Republic, which have far less exposure to Asian nations, should be given formal opportunities to share with Asia's liberalizing states their experiences of adopting democracy. Asia's own newer democracies, such as South Korea and Taiwan, can and should do the same.

At the bilateral level, Washington should encourage liberalization by developing special aid and trade packages for governments that are willing to contribute to Asian democracy and security by hosting regional democracy meetings, participating in joint security exercises, or developing their own exchange programs.

Another area where both the U.S. government and business can cooperate is in promoting the exchange of young people. In 2010–11, just over thirty-eight thousand American students studied in China, Australia, India, Japan, New Zealand, and South Korea. This accounted for only 14 percent of the 274,000 American overseas students.[69] Yet given that Asia accounts for close to 30 percent of America's total trade, it would seem a good idea to get more young Americans to study in the region, learn the languages, and intern or work in American and Asian companies there.

On top of this, the U.S. government should increase funding for its cultural exchange programs, which have been repeatedly cut since the Clinton administration. Today there are just seven full-fledged American Centers in the entire Indo-Pacific, just over a fifth of the thirty-three centers worldwide. These centers offer talks, movies, social gatherings, and other programs, and are an important means of exposing Asians to American values. Expanding many of the tiny "American Corners," which are often just a bookshelf of pamphlets, in places like Dhaka, Bangladesh; Jakarta, Indonesia; rural China; and even Tokyo, Japan, will help publicize liberal values of tolerance, pluralism, gender equality, and the like. Cultural quasi-governmental actors such as the National Endowment for Democracy should be brought in as partners.

Such outreach is a particularly important way to influence the younger generation of Asians, who are generally better traveled and educated than their elders. Expanding the Fulbright Program's Asian scholarships from its current level of 1,100 Asian and American recipients is one path, as are other exchanges run by the U.S. State Department's Bureau of Educational and Cultural Affairs.[70] Educational exchange can be particularly useful, as these prestigious programs and fellowships target future political, business, and social elites, producing a multiplier effect in later years.

Not everything can or should be done at the official level. Because the long-term goal of this policy is to nurture liberal societies, focusing directly on unofficial and voluntary associations is as important as working with governments. American think tanks and advocacy groups can sponsor grassroots gatherings and aid civil society activists from liberalizing nations in the hope of encouraging liberal growth. European states can take the same approach, and private think tanks and public interest groups from Europe should promote liberalizing programs and exchanges with Asian states.

The importance of "people power" to the health of a liberal Asia cannot be overestimated. Special emphasis should be given to creating a network of nongovernmental organizations (NGOs) in Asia's emerging democracies. As an example of civil society, professional NGOs can start the long-term process of carving out a separate sphere that can both work with and, if necessary, oppose their governments. This is a growing need given recent crackdowns on NGOs by both democratic and authoritarian Asian governments.[71] Washington, along with countries like the United Kingdom, which have well-developed civil society organizations, can help make connections between their countries' NGOs and partners in the Indo-Pacific. American foundations like the Ford Foundation, the Bill and Melinda Gates Foundation, and others should increase their support for Asian NGOs that promote democracy and civil society, along with education and health issues. Developing deep-rooted NGOs that can tap the talents of citizens who have traveled abroad or received higher education in America or Europe is key to the liberalization of Asian nations.

At the government-to-government level, the United States and other Western nations should encourage Asian governments to liberalize rules regarding the establishment and running of NGOs, including ensuring their tax-exempt status. This is a problem even in countries as developed as Japan, where NGOs have yet to play as large a role as they do in America.[72] At the same time, leaders like Australia and Japan should host pan-Asian NGO conferences, provide funding, and establish a regional network that can trade expertise, provide assistance, and ensure constant communication among liberalizers.

Can China Join the Party?

Critics of the approach proposed above may call it provocative and claim that it will inflame political tensions in Asia by attempting to encircle China with a ring of liberal democracies. The ideas offered in this chapter are in no way incompatible with greater American engagement with China and its citizens. In fact it complements what should be an increased public and private commitment to reaching out to ordinary Chinese. This is all the more needed as public views of the other worsen in both America and China. In a 2012 Pew survey, for example, just 30 percent of respondents felt that China was trustworthy, highlighting the deep suspicion with which most Americans view that nation.[73] Yet if China changed, would those numbers change?

"We're dropping the ball," says the longtime China expert at the private dinner where he predicted the fall of the Communist Party. "When was the last time you heard Washington criticize Beijing's human rights record or labor practices?" We need to get more involved in contacting nongovernment Chinese, he passionately asserts.

Almost all of America's senior China watchers, from both sides of the political spectrum, argue that the United States can and should do more to engage with ordinary Chinese. The same approach toward promoting democratic liberalization in the Indo-Pacific region can also be taken with mainland China. Private NGOs from the Indo-Pacific and the West should enhance their contact, and the trend in student exchanges should be continued, along with media exchanges, business links, and even local legislator programs. In each case, the liberal side must demand full and free conversation and resist any type of official or self-censorship. The goal is to share or make available liberal ideas and viewpoints that ordinary Chinese normally do not experience. No one expects miracles from such an approach, but that does not make it any less important. As the hoary Chinese proverb puts it, a journey of a thousand miles starts with a single step.

Beijing will work hard to frustrate such attempts. Under President Xi Jinping, the government has already tightened control of foreign NGOs and cracked down on the country's few indigenous NGOs.[74] It will intimidate or forcibly prevent its citizens from having free contact with Americans and other liberals, but that is all the more reason to make it a priority. The goal is not to change the Chinese government, which wants only to keep its iron grip on power. Rather, the goal is to provide an insight into democratic thinking, to encourage those voices in China struggling for civil society, and to let them know they are not alone. These labors may not bear fruit for years, but it is the wisest policy, at once the most idealistic and the most realistic.

The prescriptions in this chapter will not automatically reduce Sino-U.S. tensions, just as they will not solve all of Asia's economic problems or suddenly bring a new era of harmony and cooperation among Asian nations themselves. But Asia and the rest of the world must begin the difficult task of navigating risk, seeking to mitigate it where possible, and preparing to manage it if the worst happens.

The long game in Asia is to promote and nurture liberalization and democracy. True and enduring stability can come about only when a community of democratic nations is preponderant in the Indo-Pacific. No country can be forced to accept democracy, but the liberal states of Asia, in conjunction with America, should do all they can to encourage and assist democratization. Eventually, that will lead to ties of interest, bonds of trust, and possibly even the preservation of the Asian Century.

When I began researching this book, I expected to write a triumphalist account of America's role in the new Asian Century. I was one of those who largely dismissed the idea that the Indo-Pacific might face significant dangers. My research and travel convinced me otherwise. Today the zeitgeist has changed dramatically, and everyone from military planners to business leaders now accepts that the risks to Asia's future are real.[75] If anything, our new sensitivity to Asia's challenges means that we will over-react to its problems, panicking that a golden era is slipping away or that war is imminent. Perhaps this represents the real end of the Asian Century, as the sudden and radical shift in our collective mindset about Asia's future leads us to lose hope and begin expecting the worst.

Whatever our opinions, the challenges are real. Mapping risk in Asia reveals a complex terrain of overlapping regions, immediate obstacles and long-term challenges. The point is not to predict what will happen, but to understand the most important underlying trends and prepare ourselves for any number of possibilities. For almost a half-century, the world has been used to seeing Asia as a success story, and indeed its achievements rank among the most impressive in modern times. Yet we no longer can ignore the cracks and fissures in Asia's dynamic surface, now that they have the potential of opening up massive sinkholes.

Navigating these risks is above all the job of Asians themselves, and many of the suggestions in this chapter are meant for political, business, and military leaders from Tokyo and Jakarta to Beijing to New Delhi. Yet Americans, along with other Westerners, have a great stake in the future of the Indo-Pacific. Their economic, political, and security ties mean they also must be aware of the pitfalls ahead. The United States in particular, thanks to its long history, enduring links, and public and private commit-ments to the region, has a unique role to play. Some will call that typical American hubris or simpleminded idealism.

But there can be no positive future for the Indo-Pacific without a path that combines both idealism and realism. Hard-hearted policies to main-tain stability are needed to instill confidence in the region that no one country will dominate the seas and skies of the Indo-Pacific or change its borders by force. Pushing for greater economic liberalization will lock in the gains of the hundreds of millions who have entered the middle class and extend wealth to tens of millions more, improving their health and living standards, and allowing them to live fuller lives. A constant drum-beat of encouraging political liberalization will help strengthen democ-racy in those nations that have chosen that path, while offering hope to the hundreds of millions who yearn for freedom. Aiming at the reduction of tensions, the deepening of wealth, and the spread of liberal democracy is a goal worthy of the aspirations of Asia's four billion people, and of the world's liberal nations that already enjoy such gifts.

Our suggestions have ranged from the realistic to the self-interested to the idealistic. Yet they are all interdependent, creating a holistic approach that recognizes the risks we face and acts in response. Should these attempts, or others like them, be successful, the twenty-first century will indeed be an Asian Century, and will change the course of world history for the benefit of all nations.

NOTES

Preface

1. Martin Jacques, *When China Rules the World: The End of the Western World and the Birth of a New Global Order* (New York: Penguin Books, upd. exp. ed. 2012).

2. See her article of the same title in *Foreign Policy*, October 11, 2011, http:// foreignpolicy.com/2011/10/11/americas-pacific-century/.

3. Julian Ryall, "US-China War 'Inevitable' unless Washington Drops Demands over South China Sea," *The Telegraph*, May 26, 2015, http://www.telegraph.co.uk /news/worldnews/asia/china/11630185/US-China-war-inevitable-unless -Washington-drops-demands-over-South-China-Sea.html.

4. "Population Dynamics," United Nations Economic and Social Commission for Asia and the Pacific, http://www.unescap.org/our-work/social-development/pop-ulation-dynamics, accessed July 1, 2015.

5. "Regional Economic Outlook: Asia and Pacific," International Monetary Fund, April 2015, http://www.imf.org/external/pubs/ft/reo/2015/apd/eng/ pdf/area0415c1.pdf, 1.

6. See Nassim Nicholas Taleb, *The Black Swan: The Impact of the Highly Improbable*, 2nd ed. (New York: Random House, 2010). Another discussion of this idea is in Paul Bracken, Ian Bremmer, and David Gordon, "Conclusion: Managing Strategic Surprise," in *Managing Strategic Surprise: Lessons from Risk Management and Risk Assessment*, ed. Paul Bracken, Ian Bremmer, and David Gordon (Cambridge: Cambridge University Press, 2008), ch. 10, 302–11.

1. Mapping Risk in Asia

1. Early examples of this include Herman Kahn, *The Emerging Japanese Superstate: Challenge and Response* (New York: Prentice Hall, 1970) and Ezra Vogel, *Japan as Number One: Lessons for America* (New York: Harper, 1979). Summers describes this phenomenon in Lant Pritchett and Lawrence H. Summers, "Asiaphoria Meet

Regression to the Mean," *Proceedings of the Federal Reserve Bank of San Francisco* (November 2013), 1–35.

2. See, for example, Kishore Mahbubani, *The New Asian Hemisphere: The Irresistible Shift of Global Power to the East* (New York: Public Affairs, 2009); Martin Jacques, *When China Rules the World: The End of the Western World and the Birth of a New Global Order*, 2nd ed. (New York: Penguin, 2012).

3. World Trade Organization, International Trade Statistics 2014, https://www.wto .org/english/res_e/statis_e/its2014_e/its14_highlights2_e.pdf, accessed April 26, 2016.

4. A general argument about the importance of regions in post–Cold War politics is Peter J. Katzenstein, *A World of Regions: Asia and Europe in the American Imperium* (Ithaca, NY: Cornell University Press, 2005).

2. The Asian Miracle at Risk

1. Sophia Yan, "China's Stock Market Is Now Worth $10 Trillion," CNN, June 15, 2015, http://money.cnn.com/2015/06/15/investing/china-stocks-10-trillion/.

2. The literature is large and heavily dependent on a liberal perspective, but see, for example, Jurgen Osterhammel and Niels P. Peterson, *Globalization: A Short History* (Princeton, NJ: Princeton University Press, 2009); Manfred Steger, *Globalization: A Very Short Introduction* (Oxford: Oxford University Press, 2013); Samuel S. Kim, ed., *East Asia and Globalization*, 2nd ed. (Lanham, MD: Rowman and Littlefield, 2000); Anthony Elson, *Globalization and Development: Why East Asia Surged Ahead and Latin America Fell Behind* (New York: Palgrave MacMillan, 2013), esp. chs. 1, 2, and 4; Anjum Siddiqui, ed., *India and South Asia: Economic Developments in the Age of Globalization* (New York: Routledge, 2015), esp. chs. 3 and 14; and Mark Berger, *The Battle for Asia: From Decolonization to Globalization* (New York: Routledge, 2003).

3. See, for example, William H. McNeill, *The Pursuit of Power: Technology, Armed Force, and Society since A.D. 1000* (Chicago: University of Chicago Press, 1984).

4. It is true that this growth began in Japan during the Korean War when the U.S. military placed orders for light vehicles and other goods that jump-started Japan's economy.

5. Dexter Roberts, "Where Made-in-China Textiles Are Emigrating," *Bloomberg Business*, January 12, 2012, http://www.bloomberg.com/bw/magazine/where -madeinchina-textiles-are-emigrating-01122012.html; Edward S. Steinfeld, *Playing Our Game: Why China's Economic Rise Doesn't Threaten the West* (New York: Oxford University Press, 2010), 86. See also "Textile Manufacturing Services by Country," *UNdata*, last updated April 24, 2015, http://data.un.org/Data.aspx?d=ICS&f =cmID%3a88121-0.

6. "Top 50 World Container Ports," World Shipping Council, http://www .worldshipping.org/about-the-industry/global-trade/top-50-world-container -ports, accessed January 15, 2016.

7. Kyoungwha Kim, "China's Stocks Decline in Biggest Three-Week Plunge since 1992," *Bloomberg Business*, July 2, 2015, http://www.bloomberg.com/news/articles

/2015-07-03/china-s-stocks plunge-to-three-month-lows-as-bear-market-deepens -ibmyolol.

8. "Capital Flows to Emerging Markets," Institute of International Finance, January 19, 2016, https://images.magnetmail.net/images/clients/IIF_2/attach /CF_0116_Press(3).pdf.

9. "If China Catches a Cold," *The Economist*, last modified August 24, 2012, http://www.economist.com/blogs/graphicdetail/2012/08/daily-chart-9.

10. Ranjit Teja, "2012 Spillover Report," International Monetary Fund, July 9, 2012, https://www.imf.org/external/np/pp/eng/2012/070912.pdf.

11. Michael J. De La Merced, "Alibaba Raised $21.8 Billion in Initial Public Offering," *New York Times*, September 18, 2014, http://dealbook.nytimes.com/2014 /09/18/alibaba-raises-21-8-billion-in-initial-public-offering/?_r=0.

12. See, for example, Martin Jacques, *When China Rules the World* (New York: Penguin 2012) and Henry Kissinger, *On China* (New York: Penguin 2012).

13. "China Lowers Growth Target to 'around 7 Percent,'" *Financial Times*, March 5, 2015, http://www.ft.com/intl/cms/s/0/1bc73e72-c2d7-11e4-ad89 -00144feab7de.html#axzz3v9sUysPt.

14. See Derek Scissors, "China's Stall: Testimony before the House Committee on Foreign Affairs," June 17, 2015, http://www.aei.org/publication/chinas -stall/.

15. Among the books on the end of the USSR, see Serhii Plokhy, *The Last Empire: The Final Days of the Soviet Union* (New York: Basic Books, 2015).

16. For a study of Deng's policies, see Ezra Vogel, *Deng Xiaoping and the Transformation of China* (Cambridge, MA: Belknap Press, 2013). On Tiananmen, see Philip J. Cunningham, *Tiananmen Moon: Inside the Chinese Student Uprising of 1989* (Lanham, MD: Rowman and Littlefield, 2010).

17. "GDP Per Capita (Current US$)," World Bank, http://data.worldbank.org /indicator/NY.GDP.PCAP.CD, accessed December 10, 2015. Ami Sedghi, "China GDP: How It Has Changed since 1980," *The Guardian*, March 23, 2012, http:// www.theguardian.com/news/datablog/2012/mar/23/china-gdp-since-1980.

18. Patrick Chovanec, "The Nine Nations of China," *The Atlantic*, November 2009, http://www.theatlantic.com/magazine/archive/2009/11/the-nine-nations-of -china/307769/.

19. For one account, see Kevin Kelly, "The Post-Productive Economy," The Technium, http://kk.org/thetechnium/the-post-produc/, accessed August 2, 2015.

20. World Bank and the Development Research Center of the State Council, P. R. China, *China 2030: Building a Modern, Harmonious, and Creative Society* (Washington, DC: World Bank, 2013), http://www.worldbank.org/content/dam/World bank/document/China-2030-complete.pdf. For a classic economic discussion, see W. W. Rostow, *The Stages of Economic Growth: A Non-Communist Manifesto*, 3rd ed. (Cambridge: Cambridge University Press, 1991).

21. "China's Next Revolution," *The Economist*, March 8, 2007, http://www .economist.com/node/8815075.

22. "China Pledges Further Reforms for State-Dominated Sectors," *Xinhua*, October 24, 2012, http://news.xinhuanet.com/english/indepth/2012-10/24/c_131928023.htm.

23. "Fixing China Inc," *The Economist*, August 30, 2014, http://www.economist.com/news/china/21614240-reform-state-companies-back-agenda-fixing-china-inc.

24. "China's Global 500 Companies Are Bigger than Ever—and Mostly State-Owned," *Fortune*, July 22, 2015, http://fortune.com/2015/07/22/china-global-500-government-owned/.

25. See Derek Scissors, "Chinese State Owned Enterprises and the US Policy on China," *Testimony for the U.S.-China Economic and Security Review Commission*, February 15, 2013, available via the Heritage Foundation, http://www.heritage.org/research/testimony/2012/03/chinese-state-owned-enterprises-and-the-us-policy-on-china.

26. This point is debated, but many experts on the Chinese economy have pointed to the many measures by which state influence is growing in the economy. See "Section 2: Chinese State-Owned Enterprises and U.S.-China Bilateral Investment," *2011 Report to Congress*, U.S.-China Economic and Security Review Commission, (Washington, DC: U.S.-China Economic and Security Review Commission, November 2011), 40–50. For an argument that the role of SOEs is decreasing; see Junyeop Lee, "State Owned Enterprises in China: Review the Evidence," *OECD Working Group on Privatization and Corporate Governance of State Assets Occasional Paper* (Paris, France: January 26, 2009), http://www.oecd.org/corporate/ca/corporategovernanceofstate-ownedenterprises/42095493.pdf.

27. Lingling Wei and Brian Spegele, "China Considers Merger among Its Big State Oil Companies," *Wall Street Journal*, February 17, 2015, http://www.wsj.com/articles/china-considering-mergers-among-its-big-state-oil-companies-1424176242.

28. Peter S. Goodman, "Huawei Founder Ren Zhengfei Dismisses Chinese Military Connections," *International Business Times*, January 22, 2015, http://www.ibtimes.com/huawei-founder-ren-zhengfei-dismisses-chinese-military-connections-1791228; Charles Arthur, "China's Huawei and ZTE Pose National Security Threat, Says US Committee," *The Guardian*, October 8, 2012, http://www.theguardian.com/technology/2012/oct/08/china-huawei-zte-security-threat.

29. David Barboza, "China Unveils $586 Billion Stimulus Plan," *New York Times*, November 10, 2008, http://www.nytimes.com/2008/11/10/world/asia/10iht-10china.17673270.html; see also Ariana Eunjung Cha and Maureen Fan, "China Unveils $586 Billion Stimulus Plan," *Washington Post*, November 10, 2008, http://articles.washingtonpost.com/2008-11-10/world/36812387_1_zhou-xiaochuan-china-s-state-council-stimulus-plan.

30. Jack Perkowski, "China's Debt: How Serious Is It?" *Forbes*, January 21, 2014, http://www.forbes.com/sites/jackperkowski/2014/01/21/chinas-debt-how-serious-is-it/.

31. "How Strong Is China's Economy?" *The Economist*, May 26, 2012, http://www
.economist.com/node/21555915; "China to Cap Local Government Debt at $2.5
Trillion: Xinhua," *Reuters*, August 29, 2015, http://www.reuters.com/article/us
-china-economy-debt-idUSKCN0QY0BY20150829.

32. Kelvin Soh and Aileen Wang, "Special Report: China's Debt Pileup Raises Risk
of Hard Landing," *Reuters*, October 10, 2011, http://www.reuters.com/article/2011
/10/10/us-china-debt-idUSTRE79901L20111010.

33. "Hitting the Kerb," *The Economist*, November 9, 2011, http://www.economist
.com/node/21533412.

34. "People's Republic of China: 2011 Article IV Consultation," International
Monetary Fund, July 2011, http://www.imf.org/external/pubs/ft/scr/2011
/cr11192.pdf, 74.

35. Simon Rabinovitch, "Gap Widens in China's Property Market," *Financial
Times*, February 26, 2013, http://www.ft.com/intl/cms/s/0/e3459a76-7f26-11e2
-89ed-00144feabdc0.html#axzz2M6mS3ZX0. For China's over-investment broadly,
see Il Houng Lee, Murtaza Syed, and Liu Xueyan, "Is China Over-Investing and
Does It Matter?" *IMF Working Paper*, Working Paper 12/277, November 2012,
http://www.imf.org/external/pubs/ft/wp/2012/wp12277.pdf; also, "More than
1 in 5 Homes in Chinese Cities Are Empty, Survey Says," *Wall Street Journal*, June 11,
2014, http://www.wsj.com/articles/more-than-1-in-5-homes-in-chinese-cities-are
-empty-survey-says-1402484499.

36. See Wade Shepard, *Ghost Cities of China: The Story of Cities without People in
the World's Most Populated Country* (London: Zed Books, 2015).

37. Tom Hancock, "China's 'Dubai' Has Turned into a Deserted Island," *Business
Insider*, February 25, 2013, http://www.businessinsider.com/china-phoenix-island
-deserted-2013-2.

38. Patrick Chovanec, "BBC: China's 2011 GDP Numbers," *An American Perspective from China* (blog), January 17, 2012, http://chovanec.wordpress.com/2012/01
/17/bbc-chinas-2011-gdp-numbers/; Tom Orlik and Bob Davis, "China's Economic
Growth Slows amid Global Turmoil," *Wall Street Journal*, July 13, 2012, http://online
.wsj.com/article/SB10001424052702303740704577523202849328184.html.

39. "Gross Domestic Product (GDP) (First Quarter, 2013)," *National Bureau of
Statistics of China*, March 28, 2013, http://www.stats.gov.cn/english/statisticaldata
/Quarterlydata/201304/t20130428_56809.html.

40. Malhar Nabar and Olaf Unteroberdoerster, "A Change in Focus," *Finance &
Development*, September 2012, vol. 49, no. 3, http://www.imf.org/external/pubs/ft
/fandd/2012/09/nabar.htm.

41. "An Understated Recovery," *The Economist*, December 13, 2012, http://www
.economist.com/news/china/21568405-although-economy-mend-lingering
-worries-remain-understated-recovery.

42. "China—The World Factbook," Central Intelligence Agency, https://www.cia
.gov/library/publications/the-world-factbook/geos/ch.html, accessed October 3,
2015.

43. "European Union, Trade in Goods with China," European Commission, October 4, 2015, http://trade.ec.europa.eu/doclib/docs/2006/september/tradoc_113366.pdf.

44. See Paul Mozur, "Life inside Foxconn's Facility in Shenzhen," *Wall Street Journal*, December 19, 2012, http://blogs.wsj.com/chinarealtime/2012/12/19/life-inside-foxconns-facility-in-shenzhen/.

45. "Bangladesh Factory Collapse Toll Passes 1,000," *BBC*, May 10, 2013, http://www.bbc.com/news/world-asia-22476774.

46. United Nations Commission on Trade and Development (UNCTAD), *World Investment Report 2012*, United Nations (2012), 23. These are the latest data available from UNCTAD.

47. "The End of Cheap China," *The Economist*, March 10, 2012, http://www.economist.com/node/21549956.

48. Rahul Jacob, "China Factories Eye Cheaper Labour Overseas," *Financial Times*, November 8, 2011, http://www.ft.com/intl/cms/s/0/f3e4e612-061d-11e1-a079-00144feabdc0.html#axzz3ZZMr9UXO.

49. Chris Hogg, "Chinese Migrant Job Losses Mount," *BBC News*, February 2, 2009, http://news.bbc.co.uk/2/hi/asia-pacific/7864293.stm; see also Chris Buckley, "China Official Says 20 Million Migrants Lost Jobs," Reuters, February 2, 2009, http://www.reuters.com/article/2009/02/02/us-china-economy-migrants-sb-idUSTRE51117920090202, and Tomas Etzler and Jaime FlorCruz, "Road to Riches Ends for 20 Million Chinese Poor," CNN, February 20, 2009, http://www.cnn.com/2009/WORLD/asiapcf/02/20/china.economy.family/index.html.

50. Jeremy Page, "Wave of Unrest Rocks China," *Wall Street Journal*, June 14, 2011, http://online.wsj.com/article/SB10001424052702304665904576383142907232726.html?mod=ITP_pageone_0.

51. "More Arbitrators Needed as Labor Disputes Soar," *China Daily*, June 9, 2011, http://www.chinadaily.com.cn/china/2011-06/09/content_12662445.htm.

52. Bob Davis, "China Tries to Shut Rising Income Gap," *Wall Street Journal*, December 10, 2012, http://online.wsj.com/article/SB1000142412788732464010457816149385872288884.html.

53. For two examples, see "Analysing Chinese Grey Income," Credit Suisse, August 6, 2010, available at http://www.institutionalinvestorchina.com/arfy/uploads/soft/100925/1_1732139941.pdf; Xiaolu Wang and Wing Thye Woo, "The Size and Distribution of Hidden Household Income in China," Chinese Research Society for Economic System Reform, December 25, 2010, http://www.econ.ucdavis.edu/faculty/woo/9.Wang-Woo.Hidden%20Income%20in%20China.2010-12-25.pdf.

54. "Gini Index," World Bank Data, http://data.worldbank.org/indicator/SI.POV.GINI?page=2, accessed September 15, 2015; see also "China Survey Shows Wealth Gap Soaring as Xi Pledges Help," *Bloomberg News*, December 9, 2012, http://www.bloomberg.com/news/2012-12-09/china-s-wealth-gap-soars-as-xi-pledges-to-narrow-income-divide.html; "China Gini Coefficient Was 0.474 in 2012," *Xinhua*

News, January 18, 2013, http://www.chinadaily.com.cn/bizchina/2013-01/18 /content_16140018.htm.

55. "To Each, not According to His Needs," *The Economist*, December 15, 2012, http://www.economist.com/news/finance-and-economics/21568423-new-survey -illuminates-extent-chinese-income-inequality-each-not.

56. See Nargiza Salidjanova and Iacob Koch-Weser, "Third Plenum Economic Reform Proposals: A Scorecard," U.S.-China Economic and Security Review, November 19, 2013, http://origin.www.uscc.gov/sites/default/files/Research/Backgrounder _Third%20Plenum%20Economic%20Reform%20Proposals--A%20Scorecard%20 %282%29.pdf.

57. Xiaoyi Shao and Sui-Lee Wee, "China Says Faster Economic Reforms Needed," Reuters, May 18, 2014, http://www.reuters.com/article/2014/05/18/us-china -economy-reform-idUSBREA4H01820140518.

58. Commission on the Theft of Intellectual Property, "The IP Commission Report," National Bureau of Asian Research, 2013, 23–31, http://www.ipcommission .org/report/ip_commission_report_052213.pdf.

59. Discussion with Microsoft officials, Washington, DC, June 2011; Craig Tolliver, "Chinese IP Theft Hits Microsoft's Bottom Line," *MarketWatch*, May 27, 2011, http://blogs.marketwatch.com/thetell/2011/05/27/chinese-ip-theft-hits -microsofts-bottom-line/.

60. Alexander Hammer and Katherine Linton, *China: Effects of Intellectual Property Infringement and Indigenous Innovation Policies on the U.S. Economy*, U.S. International Trade Commission Report no. 332–519, May 2011, http://www.usitc.gov /publications/332/pub4226.pdf.

61. Ibid.

62. Doug Palmer, "Theft of Trade Secrets Worsening in China-U.S. Business," Reuters, October 3, 2012, http://www.reuters.com/article/2012/10/03/us-usa -china-tradesecrets-idUSBRE89211920121003.

63. "Intellectual Property Rights and the Prospects for U.S.-Japan Cooperation in Asia," Columbia Business School, February 15, 2002, http://www.google.com /url?sa=t&rct=j&q=&esrc=s&source=web&cd=2&ved=0CDgQFjAB&url =http%3A%2F%2Facademiccommons.columbia.edu%2Fdownload%2Ffedora_conte nt%2Fdownload%2Fac%3A113288%2FCONTENT%2F4121.pdf&ei =Tl5HUfrlDIji4APlluGYDA&usg=AFQjCNHOxVTIPlyV2lZeF6JeowABNFL9 Gg&bvm=bv.43828540,d.dmg.

64. "APT1: Exposing One of China's Cyber Espionage Units," Mandiant, February 2013, http://intelreport.mandiant.com/Mandiant_APT1_Report.pdf.

65. Ellen Nakashima, "Confidential Report Lists U.S. Weapons System Designs Compromised by Chinese Cyberspies," *Washington Post*, May 27, 2013, http://www .washingtonpost.com/world/national-security/confidential-report-lists-us-weapons -system-designs-compromised-by-chinese-cyberspies/2013/05/27/a42c3e1c-c2dd -11e2-8c3b-0b5e9247e8ca_story.html.

66. Interviews with corporate security experts, Shanghai, China, December 2012.

67. "The SEC Caves on China," *Wall Street Journal,* February 26, 2015, http:// www.wsj.com/articles/the-sec-caves-on-china-1424967173.

68. See U.S. International Trade Commission report, xxi–xxiii.

69. Ibid.

70. Paul Merrion, "U.S. Probes Itasca Firm's Chinese Trade Dispute," *Chicago Tribune,* January 23, 2013, http://www.chicagobusiness.com/article/20130123 /NEWS05/130129890/u-s-probes-itasca-firms-chinese-trade-dispute.

71. "Notice of Institution of Investigation," United States International Trade Commission, January 22, 2013, http://www.usitc.gov/secretary/fed_reg_notices /337/337_863_notice01222013sgl_0.pdf.

72. "China's Drive for 'Indigenous Innovation'—A Web of Industrial Policies," U.S. Chamber of Commerce, July 27, 2010, https://www.uschamber.com /report/china%E2%80%99s-drive-indigenous-innovation-web-industrial-policies.

73. For a general history, see Marius B. Jansen, *The Making of Modern Japan* (Cambridge, MA: Belknap Press, 2000).

74. See, for example, David Halberstam, *The Reckoning* (New York: William Morrow, 1986) and Chalmers C. Johnson, *MITI and the Japanese Miracle: The Growth of Industrial Policy, 1925–1975* (Stanford, CA: Stanford University Press, 1982).

75. For a prescient analysis of Japan's weaknesses, see Bill Emmott, *The Sun Also Sets: The Limits to Japan's Economic Power* (New York: Touchstone, 1991).

76. James Brooke, "Korean Shipbuilders See China's Shadow," *New York Times,* January 6, 2005, http://www.nytimes.com/2005/01/05/business/worldbusiness /05iht-ships.html?_r=0; "MHI Eyes Stake in India's L&T / Move Aims to Catch Up to Chinese, S. Korean shipbuilding rivals," *Yomiuri Shimbun,* October 4, 2012.

77. "From Summit to Plummet," *The Economist,* February 18, 2012, http://www .economist.com/node/21547815.

78. Seven Japanese chip-making firms remain in the world's top twenty manufacturers. "Top 25 Semiconductor Company Rankings Reveal Big Winners, Big Losers," *Solid State Technology,* April 5, 2012, http://www.electroiq.com/articles/sst /2012/04/2011-semiconductor-sales-rankings.html.

79. Giovanni Ganelli, "Sharpening Abenomics' Third Srrow: Labour-Market Reform in Japan," *VOX,* January 15, 2014, http://www.voxeu.org/article/fixing-japan -s-labour-market.

80. "A Game of Leapfrog," *The Economist,* April 26, 2012, http://www.economist .com/node/21553498.

81. Reiji Yoshida, "Spot Price Plunges as Demand from Utilities Wanes," *Nikkei Asian Review,* December 5, 2014, http://asia.nikkei.com/Japan-Update/Spot-price -plunges-as-demand-from-utilities-wanes.

82. Reiji Yoshida, "JA-Zenchu Accepts Drastic Farm Cooperative Reforms," *Japan Times,* February 9, 2015, http://www.japantimes.co.jp/news/2015/02/09 /business/ja-zenchu-may-support-most-proposed-farm-cooperative-reforms/.

83. "Employment Outlook 2008—How Does JAPAN Compare?" OECD, 2008, http://www.oecd.org/employment/emp/40904611.pdf.

84. Kathy Matsui, Hiromi Suzuki, Christopher Eoyang, Tsumugi Akiba, and Kazunori Tatebe, "Womenomics 3.0: The Time Is Now," Goldman Sachs, October 1, 2010, http://www.goldmansachs.com/our-thinking/focus-on/investing-in-women/bios-pdfs/womenomics3_the_time_is_now_pdf.pdf.

85. Kana Inagaki, "Takeda CEO Hits Back at Dissident Shareholders," *Wall Street Journal*, June 27, 2014, http://www.wsj.com/articles/takeda-ceo-hits-back-at-dissident-shareholders-1403866136.

86. Antoni Slodkowski, "Abe's 'Drill Bit' Hits Resistance on Japan Labor," *Reuters*, June 23, 2014, http://www.reuters.com/article/2014/06/23/us-japan-growth-labour-insight-idUSKBN0EY17Q20140623.

87. Toru Fujioka and Mio Coxon, "Japan, Inc. Holds Italy-Sized Cash Pile as Abe Urges Spending," *Bloomberg Business*, June 19, 2013, http://www.bloomberg.com/news/articles/2013-06-19/japan-inc-sits-on-italy-sized-cash-pile-as-abe-urges-investment.

88. An early study of South Korean economic modernization is Charles. R. Frank, Jr., et al., "Economic Growth in South Korea since World War II," in *Foreign Trade Regimes and Economic Development: South Korea*, ed. Charles R. Frank et al. (Cambridge, MA: National Bureau of Economic Research, 1975), 6–24.

89. See, for example, Namhee Lee, *The Making of Minjung: Democracy and the Politics of Representation in South Korea* (Ithaca, NY: Cornell University Press, 2009).

90. A collection of essays can be found in Stephan Haggard et al., *Economic Crisis and Corporate Restructuring in Korea: Reforming the Chaebol* (Cambridge: Cambridge University Press, 2010).

91. "Waiting in the Wings," *The Economist*, September 27, 2014, http://www.economist.com/news/business/21620195-succession-looms-korean-conglomerate-much-has-change-waiting-wings.

92. "Exports of Goods and Services (% of GDP)," World Bank, http://data.worldbank.org/indicator/NE.EXP.GNFS.ZS, accessed June 2, 2015.

93. Yang Sung-Jin, "Korea's Stock Market Volatility Outpaces Major Countries," *Korea Herald*, December 19, 2011, http://nwww.koreaherald.com/view.php?ud=20111219000892; Kwanwoo Jun, "South Korea's Carrot-and-Stick on Capital Flows," *Wall Street Journal*, December 6, 2012, http://blogs.wsj.com/korearealtime/2012/12/06/south-koreas-carrot-and-stick-on-capital-flows/.

94. "Vietnam–The World Factbook," Central Intelligence Agency, https://www.cia.gov/library/publications/the-world-factbook/geos/vm.html, accessed October 3, 2015.

95. "Doing Business in Vietnam," Embassy of the Socialist Republic of Vietnam, http://vietnamembassy-usa.org/business, accessed April 26, 2016.

96. Interview, Finance Ministry, Vietnam, April 5, 2014.

97. Interview, Vietnam Chamber of Commerce and Industry, April 6, 2014.

98. "Vietnam," Office of the United States Trade Representative, May 8, 2014, http://www.ustr.gov/countries-regions/southeast-asia-pacific/vietnam.

99. "Viet Nam," World Trade Organization, http://stat.wto.org/CountryProfile /WSDBCountryPFView.aspx?Language=E&Country=VN, accessed March 3, 2015.

100. "GDP per Capita (Current US$)," World Bank, http://data.worldbank.org /indicator/NY.GDP.PCAP.CD, accessed March 4, 2015.

101. Bruce Vaughn, "Indonesia: Domestic Politics, Strategic Dynamics, and American Interests," Congressional Research Service, June 17, 2009, 17–18, research.policyarchive.org/2068_Previous_Version_2009-06-17.pdf; "What's Cooking?" *The Economist*, September 17, 2011, http://www.economist.com/node/2152 9085.

102. An example is Iain Marlow, "The Next China? Indonesia Emerging as a New Asian Powerhouse," *The Globe and Mail*, January 16, 2015, http://www.theglobe andmail.com/report-on-business/international-business/asian-pacific-business/the -next-china-indonesia-emerging-as-a-new-asian-powerhouse/article22496882/.

103. "Indonesia–The World Factbook," Central Intelligence Agency, https://www .cia.gov/library/publications/the-world-factbook/geos/id.html, accessed October 3, 2015.

104. David Pilling, "Islands of Hope Amid the Indonesian Hype," *Financial Times*, January 26, 2011, http://www.ft.com/intl/cms/s/0/72e60d3a-2986-11e0-bb9b -00144feab49a.html#axzz3ZZMr9UXO.

105. A good overview is Gurcharan Das, *India Unbound: The Social and Economic Revolution from Independence to the Global Information Age* (New York: Anchor Books, 2002).

106. Akash Kapur, "The Economic Crisis India Needs," *Bloomberg Business*, August 22, 2013, http://www.bloomberg.com/bw/articles/2013-08-22/the-economic -crisis-india-needs.

107. See the essays in Ishur Judge Ahluwalia and I. M. D. Little, eds., *India's Economic Reforms and Development: Essays for Manmohan Singh*, 2nd ed. (Oxford: Oxford University Press, 2012).

108. "India's Special Economic Zones: Cash Cows," *The Economist*, October 12, 2006, http://www.economist.com/node/8031219.

109. "India Has Largest Debt-to-GDP Ratio among BRIC Nations: Report," *Economic Times*, June 29, 2012, http://articles.economictimes.indiatimes.com/2012 -06-29/news/32472423_1_gdp-ratio-bric-nations-debt-payments.

110. Guarav Datt, "Poverty in India and Indian States: An Update," *International Food Policy Research Institute*, 1998, http://www.ifpri.org/sites/default/files/pubs /divs/fcnd/dp/papers/dp47.pdf.

111. "Poverty and Equity: India Country Dashboard," World Bank, http:// povertydata.worldbank.org/poverty/country/IND, accessed April 26, 2016.

112. Reeba Zacharia, "Mukesh Ready to Move into Mansion in the Sky," *Times of India*, October 13, 2010, http://articles.timesofindia.indiatimes.com/2010-10-13 /mumbai/28268270_1_antilia-mukesh-ambani-ambani-scion.

113. "Adventures in Capitalism," *The Economist*, October 22, 2011, http://www.economist.com/node/21532448.

114. "The Masala Mittelstand," *The Economist*, August 11, 2012, http://www.economist.com/printedition/2012-08-11.

115. "Trade in Goods with India," U.S. Census Bureau, https://www.census.gov/foreign-trade/balance/c5330.html, accessed April 26, 2016.

116. "Chennai: The Next Global Auto Manufacturing Hub?" Moneycontrol.com, October 13, 2011, http://www.moneycontrol.com/news/special-videos/chennai-the-next-global-auto-manufacturing-hub_539405.html.

117. "Michelin Tamilnadu," *Michelin*, updated August 14, 2014, http://www.michelin.in/Home/About-Michelin/Michelin-Tamilnadu.

118. "Seminar to Focus on Chennai's Growth Potential," *The Hindu*, August 21, 2008, http://www.thehindubusinessline.com/todays-paper/tp-economy/article1634650.ece?ref=archive.

119. Dhiraj Nayyar, "Modi's Budget Gets the Big Stuff Right," *BloombergView*, March 1, 2015, http://www.bloombergview.com/articles/2015-03-01/modi-s-india-budget-improves-climate-for-investment.

120. Saritha Rai, "Modi's Economic Reforms Agenda in India Hits Biggest Roadblock–Land," *Forbes*, April 22, 2015, http://www.forbes.com/sites/saritharai/2015/04/22/modis-economic-reforms-agenda-in-india-hits-biggest-roadblock-land/.

121. "India–The World Factbook," Central Intelligence Agency, https://www.cia.gov/library/publications/the-world-factbook/geos/in.html, accessed December 22, 2015.

122. Alexandra Niez, "Comparative Study on Rural Electrification Policies in Emerging Economies: Keys to Successful Policies," International Energy Agency, March 2010, http://www.iea.org/publications/freepublications/publication/rural_elect.pdf.

123. Tripti Lahiri, "How Many People Actually Lost Power?" *Wall Street Journal*, August 1, 2012, http://blogs.wsj.com/indiarealtime/2012/08/01/how-many-people-actually-lost-power in-india/. See also "Power Grid Failure: NTPC Says Complete Restoration Possible by Midnight," *Economic Times*, July 31, 2012, http://articles.economictimes.indiatimes.com/2012-07-31/news/32961545_1_grid-failure-power-grid-corporation-northern-grid.

124. "India," U.S. Energy Information Administration, http://www.eia.gov/countries/cab.cfm?fips=IN, accessed July 9, 2015.

125. "The Future Is Black," *The Economist*, January 21, 2012, http://www.economist.com/printedition/2012-01-21.

126. Shilpa Phandnis, "India Suffered Rs 36,400 cr Loss Due to Corruption: Report," *Times of India*, July 22, 2013, http://timesofindia.indiatimes.com/business/india-business/India-suffered-Rs-36400-cr-loss-due-to-corruption-Report/articleshow/21252592.cms.

127. Santosh Tiwari, "Black Money Estimated at 30% of GDP," *Business Standard*, January 13, 2013, http://www.business-standard.com/article/economy-policy/black-money-estimated-at-30-of-gdp-113011300067_1.html.

128. "Foreign Direct Investment Hits Record in 2014," Korea Net, January 5, 2016, http://www.korea.net/NewsFocus/Policies/view?articleId=124506.

3. The Goldilocks Dilemma

1. Peter K. Austin, ed., *One Thousand Languages: Living, Endangered, Lost* (Berkeley: University of California Press, 2008).

2. Names have been changed.

3. Associated Press, "Japan: More and More, a Land of Centenarians," *The Daily Mail*, September 14, 2014, http://www.dailymail.co.uk/wires/ap/article-2755940 /Japan-More-land-centenarians.html.

4. Roger Goodman and Sarah Harper, eds., *Aging in Asia: Asia's Position in the New Global Demography* (New York: Routledge, 2008), 1.

5. Krishnadev Calamur, "Japan's Population Declined in 2014 as Births Fell to a New Low," NPR.org, January 1, 2015, http://www.npr.org/blogs/thetwo-way /2015/01/01/374382369/japans-population-declined-in-2014-as-births-fell-to-a -new-low.

6. Keizo Mori, "Japan Population to Show Record Decline," UPI.com, January 1, 2013, http://www.upi.com/Top_News/World-News/2013/01/01/Japan-population -to-show-record-decline/UPI-22581357016770/.

7. Government of Japan, *Statistical Handbook of Japan 2008*, (Tokyo: Statistics Bureau, 2008), ch. 2, www.stat.go.jp/english/data/handbook/c02cont.htm.

8. Personal correspondence with Nicholas Eberstadt, based on official Japanese government figures at: Government of Japan, *Statistical Handbook of Japan 2014* (Tokyo: Statistics Bureau, 2014), ch. 2, http://www.stat.go.jp/english/data/nenkan /pdf/yhyou02.pdf. I am grateful to him for bringing this to my attention and correcting other demographic calculations in this chapter.

9. "Increase in Unmarried Childbearing Also Seen in Other Countries," Centers for Disease Control and Prevention, National Center for Health Statistics, Office of Communication, May 13, 2009, http://www.cdc.gov/nchs/pressroom/09new sreleases/unmarriedbirths.htm.

10. "Handbook of Health and Welfare Statistics 2013," Japan Ministry of Health, http://www.mhlw.go.jp/english/database/db-hh/1-2.html, accessed January 20, 2016.

11. Abigail Haworth, "Why Have Young People in Japan Stopped Having Sex?" *The Guardian*, October 20, 2013, http://www.theguardian.com/world/2013/oct /20/young-people-japan-stopped-having-sex.

12. See Mark Buckton, "A Hard Day's Grind for Porn's Professionals," *Japan Times*, January 20, 2014, http://www.japantimes.co.jp/community/2014/01/13/issues/a -hard-days-grind-for-porns-professionals/#.VYbYkWTBzGf.

13. "Handbook of Health and Welfare Statistics 2013," Japan Ministry of Health, http://www.mhlw.go.jp/english/database/db-hh/1-2.html, accessed January 20, 2016.

14. Ibid.

15. For more information on "parasite singles," see J. Sean Curtin, "Youth Trends in Japan: Part One—'Parasite Singles' in the International Context," *Global Communications Platform*, May 26, 2003, www.glocom.org/special_topics/social_trends /20030526_trends_s38/.

16. "Glitter Starts Wearing Off for Aging 'Parasite Singles,'" *Japan Today*, February 20, 2014, http://www.japantoday.com/category/kuchikomi/view/glitter-starts -wearing-off-for-aging-parasite-singles.

17. Government of Japan, *Statistical Handbook of Japan 2008*, (Tokyo: Statistics Bureau, 2008), ch. 2, www.stat.go.jp/english/data/handbook/c02cont.htm.

18. "Japan–The World Factbook," Central Intelligence Agency, https://www.cia .gov/library/publications/the-world-factbook/geos/ja.html, accessed November 2, 2015.

19. "Life Expectancy Data by Country," World Health Organization, http://apps .who.int/gho/data/view.main.680?lang=en, accessed December 8, 2015.

20. "TPP or No, Aging Farm Sector Needs True Reform," *Japan Times*, March 26, 2013, http://www.japantimes.co.jp/news/2013/03/26/business/economy-business /tpp-or-no-aging-farm-sector-needs-true-reform/#.Vq_akDYrJE5.

21. Richard Solomon, "Shinzo Abe's Olympic Challenge," *Beacon Reports*, September 30, 2014, http://beaconreports.net/shinzo-abes-olympic-challenge-road -map-fiscal-sustainability-2020-2/.

22. OECD, *Pensions at a Glance 2013: OECD and G20 Indicators*, http://www .oecd.org/pensions/public-pensions/OECDPensionsAtAGlance2013.pdf, accessed October 3, 2015.

23. Maggie Jones, "For Some in Japan, a Room Is Their World," *New York Times*, January 13, 2006, http://www.nytimes.com/2006/01/13/world/asia/13iht-shutins .html?pagewanted=all&_r=0.

24. For more information on NEETs, see Kosugi Reiko, "Youth Employment in Japan's Economic Recovery: 'Freeters' and 'NEETs,'" *Japan Focus*, May 11, 2006, www.japanfocus.org/products/details/2022.

25. Government of Japan, Ministry of Health, Labor and Welfare, "White Paper on Labor and the Economy 2005," ch. 2, www.mhlw.go.jp/english/wp/l-economy /2005/dl/02-02-01.pdf, accessed March 10, 2009.

26. "Japanese Restaurants Hungry for Part-Time Workers," *Nikkei Asian Review*, June 11, 2014, http://asia.nikkei.com/Business/Trends/Japanese-restaurants-hungry -for-parttime-workers.

27. Blaine Harden, "Once Drawn to U.S. Universities, More Japanese Students Staying Home," *Washington Post*, April 11, 2010, http://www.washingtonpost.com /wp-dyn/content/article/2010/04/10/AR2010041002835.html.

28. "International Students in the United States," Institute for International Education, http://www.iie.org/Services/Project-Atlas/United-States/International -Students-In-US, accessed January 5, 2016.

29. Among the best current demographers is Nicholas Eberstadt. See, for example, his "The Demographic Future: What Population Growth—and Decline—Means

for the Global Economy," *Foreign Affairs* (November–December 2010), https://www.foreignaffairs.com/articles/2010-11-01/demographic-future.

30. See Norimitsu Onishi, "A Leftover City of Day Laborers in Japan Faces a Grim Future, *New York Times*, October 12, 2008, http://www.nytimes.com/2008/10/12/world/asia/12iht-japan.1.16873838.html?pagewanted=all&_r=0; Hideo Aoki, *Japan's Underclass: Day Laborers and the Homeless*, trans. Teresa Castelvetere (Melbourne: Trans Pacific Press, 2006).

31. "Japan Stands by Immigration Controls Despite Shrinking Population," *Financial Times*, June 2, 2014, http://www.ft.com/intl/cms/s/0/32788ff0-ea00-11e3-99ed-00144feabdc0.html#axzz3diEbV0ET.

32. "Honda Unveils Self-Driving Car in Detroit," *Euronews*, September 16, 2014, http://www.euronews.com/2014/09/16/honda-unveils-self-driving-car-in-detroit/.

33. "Japan Plans Robot Revolution," *The Nation*, September 11, 2014, http://www.nationmultimedia.com/breakingnews/Japan-plans-robot-revolution-30243042.html.

34. Tanya Lewis, "World's First Robot-Staffed Hotel to Open in Japan," *Yahoo! TECH,* February 12, 2015, https://www.yahoo.com/tech/s/worlds-first-robot-staffed-hotel-open-japan-141900165.html.

35. Julian Ryall, "South Koreans 'Will be Extinct by 2750,'" *The Telegraph,* August 25, 2014, http://www.telegraph.co.uk/news/worldnews/asia/southkorea/11054817/South-Koreans-will-be-extinct-by-2750.html.

36. Kim So-youn, "Amid Budget Shortfall, South Korea's Social Welfare Spending at OECD Bottom," *The Hankyoreh*, November 8, 2014, http://www.hani.co.kr/arti/english_edition/e_national/663565.html.

37. Basil Hall Chamberlain, *Things Japanese: Being Notes on Various Subjects Connected with Japan* (Cambridge: Cambridge University Press, 2014), 1, orig. pub. 1890.

38. Ma Jiantang, Commissioner, "Press Release on Major Figures of the 2010 National Population Census," *National Bureau of Statistics of China*, April 28, 2011, http://www.stats.gov.cn/english/NewsEvents/201104/t20110428_26448.html; Infographic: China's Census Data, *US-China Today*, University of Southern California, http://www.uschina.usc.edu/article@usct?infographic_chinas_census_data_18065.aspx.

39. Thomas Lam, "Measuring the Rise of China's Cities," *Business Now,* American Chamber of Commerce China, April 9, 2013, http://www.amchamchina.org/article/11135. For a complete list of China's most populous cities, see "China 2010 Census Data Release," China Data Center, University of Michigan, September 29, 2011, http://chinadatacenter.org/Announcement/AnnouncementContent.aspx?id=470.

40. "Population of Provinces, Municipalities, and Autonomous Region, 2010 Census of China, and Change in the Percent Distribution by Area, 2000–2010," *Population Reference Bureau*, 2011, http://www.prb.org/pdf11/china-2010-census-results-table.pdf. The figure for Chongqing includes the city itself and surrounding districts and suburbs.

41. Xinhua, "Car Ownership Tops 154 Million in China in 2014," *China Daily,* January 28, 2015, http://www.chinadaily.com.cn/business/motoring/2015-01/28 /content_19424673.htm.

42. Karl Gerth, *As China Goes, So Goes the World: How Chinese Consumers Are Transforming Everything* (New York: Hill and Wang, 2011), 38.

43. "China–The World Factbook," Central Intelligence Agency, https://www.cia .gov/library/publications/the-world-factbook/geos/ch.html, accessed September 20, 2015; "Top 20 Countries with the Highest Number of Internet Users," *Internet Word Stats–Usage and Population Statistics,* http://www.internetworldstats.com/top20 .htm; Kenneth Rapoza, "China's Weibos vs US's Twitter: And the Winner IS?" *Forbes,* May 17, 2011, http://www.forbes.com/sites/kenrapoza/2011/05/17/chinas-weibos -vs-uss-twitter-and-the-winner-is/. See also "Sina Reports First Quarter 2011 Finan- cial Results," Sina Corporation, May 11, 2011, http://phx.corporate-ir.net/phoenix .zhtml?c=121288&p=irol-newsArticle&ID=1562873&highlight.

44. Daniel A. Bell, "The Spirit of Chinese Cities," AmCham China, April 18, 2012, http://www.amchamchina.org/article/9511; Richard Dobbs, Sven Smit, Jaana Remes, James Manyika, Charles Roxburgh and Alejandra Restrepo, "Urban World: Mapping the Economic Power of Cities," *McKinsey Global Institute,* March 2011, http://www.mckinsey.com/insights/urbanization/urban_world.

45. Joseph Kahn and Jim Yardley, "As China Roars, Pollution Reaches Deadly Ex- tremes," *New York Times,* August 26, 2007, http://www.nytimes.com/2007/08 /26/world/asia/26china.html?pagewanted=print&_r=0.

46. Henry Sanderson, "Beijing Air Tops Hazardous Levels Days before Congress," *Bloomberg,* February 28, 2013, http://www.bloomberg.com/news/2013-02-28 /beijing-air-pollution-tops-hazardous-levels-days-before-congress.html.

47. Peter Walker, "Beijing Olympics: 1.15m Cars Banned from Roads in Last-Ditch Smog Effort," *The Guardian,* July 21, 2008, http://www.guardian.co.uk/world /2008/jul/21/china.olympicgames2008.

48. Adam Rose, "China Smog Emergency Shuts City of 11 Million People," *Yahoo News,* October 21, 2013, http://ca.news.yahoo.com/latest-china-smog-emergency -shuts-city-11-million-055104682.html.

49. Gonghuan Yang, Yu Wang, et al., "Rapid Health Transition in China, 1990– 2010: Findings from the Global Burden of Disease Study 2010," *The Lancet,* June 8, 2013, DOI: http://dx.doi.org/10.1016/S0140-6736(13)61097 1.

50. World Bank and the State Environmental Protection Administration (China), *Costs of Pollution in China: Economic Estimates of Physical Damage,* 2007; "Cost of Pollution in China, Economic Estimates of Physical Damages," World Bank, Febru- ary 2007, http://www-wds.worldbank.org/external/default/WDSContentServer /WDSP/IB/2007/03/30/000090341_20070330141612/Rendered/PDF/3923 60CHA0Cost1of1Pollution01PUBLIC1.pdf. Apparently, China forced the World Bank to remove from the report data regarding the number of premature deaths, citing concerns about potential political instability; Peony Lui, "Pollution Is One

Reason Guangzhou People's Lungs Are Turning Black, Warns Expert," *South China Morning Post,* March 12, 2013, http://www.scmp.com/news/china/article /1185398/pollution-one-reason-guangzhou-peoples-lungs-are-turning-black-warns; Kahn and Yardley, "As China Roars"; Richard McGregor, "750,000 a Year Killed by Chinese Pollution," *Financial Times,* July 2, 2007, http://www.ft.com/intl/cms /s/0/8f40e248-28c7-11dc-af78-000b5df10621.html#axzz2SFIPBfS2.

51. Edward Wong, "Air Pollution Linked to 1.2 Million Premature Deaths in China," *New York Times,* April 2, 2013, http://www.nytimes.com/2013/04/02 /world/asia/air-pollution-linked-to-1-2-million-deaths-in-china.html?_r=0.

52. Edward Wong, "Pollution Leads to Drop in Life Span in Northern China, Research Finds," *New York Times,* July 8, 2013, http://www.nytimes.com/2013/07/09 /world/asia/pollution-leads-to-drop-in-life-span-in-northern-china-study-finds.html.

53. Edward Wong, "Thousands of Dead Pigs Found in River Flowing into Shanghai," *New York Times,* March 11, 2013, http://www.nytimes.com/2013/03/12 /world/asia/thousands-of-dead-pigs-found-in-chinese-river.html?_r=0.

54. Kahn and Yardley, "As China Roars."

55. "Pollution Status: Rivers, Groundwater and Lakes," China Water Risk, 2013, http://chinawaterrisk.org/big-picture/pollution-status/.

56. Ibid.

57. World Bank, "Cost of Pollution in China."

58. Andrew Jacobs, "In China, Pollution Worsens Despite New Efforts," *New York Times,* July, 28, 2010, http://www.nytimes.com/2010/07/29/world/asia/29china .html. In general, see Elizabeth Economy, *The River Runs Black: The Environmental Challenge to China's Future* (Ithaca, NY: Cornell University Press, 2004).

59. Meena Thiruvengadam, "Pollution Is Costing China's Economy More than $100 Billion a Year," *Business Insider,* March 4, 2013, http://www.businessinsider .com/cost-of-china-smog-2013-3.

60. Alexa Olessen, "Experts Challenge China's 1-Child Population Claim," *Associated Press,* October 27, 2011, http://www.boston.com/news/world/asia/articles /2011/10/27/chinas_touting_of_1_child_rules_draws_challenges/.

61. "Demography: China's Achilles Heel," *The Economist,* April 21, 2012, http:// www.economist.com/node/21553056.

62. Data taken from the U.S. Census Bureau, with author's calculations. China recorded 16,301,000 births in 2000. That number increases through 2015, and then drops precipitously to 11,655,000 by 2050. Data are available at "Demographic Overview—Custom Region—China," U.S. Census Bureau, http://www.census.gov /population/international/data/idb/region.php?N=%20Results%20&T=13&A =separate&RT=0&Y=2000,2010,2012,2025,2050&R=-1&C=CH, accessed April 26, 2016.

63. "China's Achilles Heel"; Adele Hayutin, "China Demographic Shifts: The Shape of Things to Come," *Stanford Center for Longevity,* October 24, 2008, http:// longevity3.stanford.edu/wp-content/uploads/2012/10/Chinas-Demographic -Shifts_Hayutin-r-10-2008.pdf.

64. Based on data on midyear population estimate from the U.S. Census Bureau, http://www.census.gov/population/international/data/idb/region.php?N=%20 Results%20&T=13&A=separate&RT=0&Y=2010,2020,2025,2030,2040,2050&R =-1&C=CH, accessed April 26, 2016; Andrea den Boer and Valerie M. Hudson, "The Security Risks of China's Abnormal Demographics," April 30, 2014, http://www .washingtonpost.com/blogs/monkey-cage/wp/2014/04/30/the-security-risks-of -chinas-abnormal-demographics/.

65. Chris Buckley, "China Ends One-Child Policy, Allowing Families Two Children," *New York Times*, October 29, 2015, http://www.nytimes.com/2015/10 /30/world/asia/china-end-one-child-policy.html?_r=0.

66. "China's Population: Peak Toil," *The Economist*, January 26, 2013, http://www .economist.com/news/china/21570750-first-two-articles-about-impact-chinas-one -child-policy-we-look-shrinking.

67. "China to Employ Another 20,000 N. Korean Workers," *The Chosunilbo*, June 22, 2012, http://english.chosun.com/site/data/html_dir/2012/06/22 /2012062201146.html.

68. "China's Achilles Heel."

69. Andrew den Boer and Valerie M. Hudson, "The Security Risks of China's Abnormal Demographics."

70. Rob Brooks, "China's Biggest Problem? Too Many Men," CNN, March 4, 2013, http://www.cnn.com/2012/11/14/opinion/china-challenges-one-child-brooks.

71. "Communique of the National Bureau of Statistics of People's Republic of China on Major Figures of the 2010 Population Census (No. 1)," National Bureau of Statistics, April 28, 2011, http://www.stats.gov.cn/english/newsandcomingevents /t20110428_402722244.htm. See also Laurie Burkitt and Josh Chin, "China's Race with the Gender Gap," *Wall Street Journal*, April 29, 2011, http://blogs.wsj.com /chinarealtime/2011/04/29/china%E2%80%99s-race-with-the-gender-gap/.

72. "GDP Per Capita (Current US$)," World Bank, http://data.worldbank.org /indicator/NY.GDP.PCAP.CD, accessed April 26, 2016.

73. "Adult Literacy Rate, Population 15+ Years, Both Sexes (%)," World Bank, http://data.worldbank.org/indicator/SE.ADT.LITR.ZS, accessed April 26, 2016.

74. "Rethinking the Welfare State: Asia's Next Revolution," *The Economist*, September 8, 2012, http://www.economist.com/node/21562195.

75. "India 'To Overtake China's Population by 2022'–UN," *BBC*, July 30, 2015, http://www.bbc.com/news/world-asia-33720723.

76. Much of this section is taken from Michael Auslin, "Passing through India," *National Review Online*, July 1, 2011, http://m.nationalreview.com/corner/270963 /passing-through-india-michael-auslin.

77. Diana Farrell and Eric Beinhocker, "Next Big Spenders: India's Middle Class," McKinsey Global Institute, May 19, 2007, http://www.mckinsey.com/Insights /MGI/In_the_news/Next_big_spenders_Indian_middle_class.

78. Ankita Rao, "Welcome to Modicare," *Foreign Policy*, March 4, 2015, http:// foreignpolicy.com/2015/03/04/india-healthcare-modi-chhattisgarh/.

79. Aditya Kalra, "Insight–Deserted New Delhi Hospitals Sour India's Healthcare Dream," Reuters, February 12, 2015, http://in.reuters.com/article/2015/02/11/india-healthcare-hospitals-idINKBN0LF2G220150211.

80. Much of this section is drawn from Michael Auslin, "India's Missing Women," *The American*, January 10, 2013 http://www.american.com/archive/2013/january/indias-missing-women.

81. Sonali Das, Sonali Jain-Chandra, Kalpana Kochhar, and Naresh Kumar, "Women Workers in India: Why So Few among So Many?" IMF Working Paper, March 2015, https://www.imf.org/external/pubs/ft/wp/2015/wp1555.pdf.

82. "India's Man Problem," *New York Times*, January 16, 2013, http://india.blogs.nytimes.com/2013/01/16/indias-man-problem/.

4. Asia's Mesdames Defarges

1. General treatments can be found in John King Fairbank, *China: A New History* (Cambridge, MA: Belknap Press, 1992), esp. ch. 12 for the Qing collapse; and Jonathan D. Spence, *The Search for Modern China*, 2nd ed. (New York: W. W. Norton, 1999), esp. ch. 11. For a study of China's global history, see Joanna Waley-Cohen, *The Sextants of Beijing: Global Currents in Chinese History* (New York: W. W. Norton, 1999). For the Qing's regional dominance, see Warren I. Cohen, *East Asia at the Center: Four Thousand Years of Engagement with the World* (New York: Columbia University Press, 2000), ch. 7.

2. See Lucien Bianco, *Origins of the Chinese Revolution, 1915–1949*, trans. Muriel Bell (Stanford, CA: Stanford University Press, 1971); William G. Beasley, *The Meiji Restoration* (Stanford, CA: Stanford University Press, 1972); Michael R. Auslin, *Negotiating with Imperialism: The Unequal Treaties and the Culture of Japanese Diplomacy* (Cambridge, MA: Harvard University Press, 2004).

3. For a discussion, see Robert Kagan, *Dangerous Nation: America's Foreign Policy from Its Earliest Days to the Dawn of the Twentieth Century* (New York: Vintage, 2007). For the religious elements in America's worldview, see Andrew Preston, *Sword of the Spirit, Shield of Faith: Religion in American War and Diplomacy* (New York: Anchor Books, 2012).

4. The triumphalist view was summed up by Francis Fukuyama in *The End of History and the Last Man*, reissue ed. (New York: Free Press, 2006). The contrasting position was set out by Samuel P. Huntington, *The Clash of Civilizations and the Remaking of World Order* (New York: Simon and Schuster, 1996).

5. See, for example, Thomas L. Friedman and Michael Mandelbaum, *That Used to Be Us: How America Fell Behind in the World It Invented and How We Can Come Back* (New York: Picador, 2012).

6. Susan Shirk, *China: Fragile Superpower* (Oxford: Oxford University Press, 2008). See also Evan Osnos, *Age of Ambition: Chasing Fortune, Truth and Faith in the New China* (New York: Farrar, Straus and Giroux, 2015).

7. See William A. Joseph, *Politics in China: An Introduction*, 2nd ed. (Oxford: Oxford University Press, 2012). For a study of China's top officials, see David M.

Lampton, *Following the Leader: Ruling China, from Deng Xiaoping to Xi Jinping* (Berkeley: University of California Press, 2014).

8. The best book on the CCP is by Richard McGregor, *The Party: The Secret World of China's Communist Rulers* (New York: HarperCollins, 2010).

9. For an in-depth look at Xi's life and first years in power, see Evan Osnos, "Born Red," *The New Yorker*, April 6, 2015, http://www.newyorker.com/magazine /2015/04/06/born-red.

10. Chris Buckley, "Xi Jinping Assuming New Status as China's 'Core Leader,'" *New York Times*, February 4, 2016, http://mobile.nytimes.com/2016/02/05/world /asia/china-president-xi-jinping-core.html?_r=1&referer=.

11. "China's Billionaires Double in Number," *The Telegraph*, September 7, 2011, http://www.telegraph.co.uk/news/worldnews/asia/china/8746445/Chinas -billionaires-double-in-number.html. By a different calculation, known as Purchasing Power Parity (PPP), a country is ranked on the comparative cost of an average "basket of goods." On this measure, China ranks higher, around $13,200 according to the World Bank; see "GDP Per Capita (Current US$)," World Bank, http://data.worldbank .org/indicator/NY.GDP.PCAP.CD, accessed September 10, 2015; and "GDP Per Capita, PPP (Current International $)," World Bank, http://data.worldbank.org /indicator/NY.GDP.PCAP.PP.CD, accessed September 10, 2015.

12. See Spence, *Search for Modern China*, ch. 26, for an overview.

13. See McGregor, *Party*, ch. 2. For a firsthand account, see James R. Lilley and Jeffrey Lilley, *China Hands: Nine Decades of Adventure, Espionage, and Diplomacy in Asia* (New York: Public Affairs, 2005), ch. 19.

14. Max Fisher, "How China Stays Stable despite 500 Protests Every Day," *The Atlantic*, January 5, 2012, http://www.theatlantic.com/international/archive/2012 /01/how-china-stays-stable-despite-500-protests-every-day/250940/.

15. See Yuri Pines, *The Everlasting Empire: The Political Culture of Ancient China and Its Imperial Legacy* (Princeton, NJ: Princeton University Press, 2012), esp. ch. 1.

16. For a recent history of Xinjiang, see James A. Millward, *Eurasian Crossroads: A History of Xinjiang* (London: C. Hurst, 2007), ch. 7.

17. Michael Forsythe, "Deadly Clash between Police and Ethnic Uighurs Reported in Xinjiang Region of China," *New York Times*, June 25, 2015, http://www.nytimes .com/2015/06/25/world/asia/deadly-clash-between-police-and-ethnic-uighurs -reported-in-xinjiang-region-of-china.html?_r=0.

18. Carrie Gracie, "Xinjiang: Has China's Crackdown on 'Terrorism' Worked?" *BBC News*, January 2, 2015, http://www.bbc.com/news/world-asia-30373877. See also Ian Johnson, "China: What the Uighurs See," *New York Review of Books*, April 13, 2015, http://www.nybooks.com/blogs/nyrblog/2015/apr/13/wild -pigeon-what-uighurs-see/.

19. See, for example, Phelim Kine, "Beijing's Broken Promises on Human Rights," *Wall Street Journal*, January 10, 2011, http://www.hrw.org/en/news/2011/01/10 /beijings-broken-promises-human-rights-0; also "China: Alarming New Surveillance,

Security in Tibet," Human Rights Watch, March 20, 2013, http://www.hrw.org /news/2013/03/20/china-alarming-new-surveillance-security-tibet.

20. *New York Times* Editorial Board, "Blacklisting Scholars," *New York Times*, July 17, 2014, http://www.nytimes.com/2014/07/18/opinion/blacklisting-scholars .html.

21. Carrie Gracie, "China Jails Prominent Uighur Academic Ilham Tohti for Life," *BBC News*, September 23, 2014, http://www.bbc.com/news/world-asia-29321701.

22. Jonathan Kaiman, "Hong Kong's Umbrella Revolution–the *Guardian* Briefing," *The Guardian*, September 30, 2014, http://www.theguardian.com/world /2014/sep/30/-sp-hong-kong-umbrella-revolution-pro-democracy-protests.

23. "Sichuan Earthquake," *New York Times*, updated May 6, 2009, http://topics .nytimes.com/top/news/science/topics/earthquakes/sichuan_province_china /index.html.

24. Edward Wong, "Chinese Stifle Grieving Parent's Protest of Shoddy School Construction," *New York Times*, June 4, 2008, http://www.nytimes.com/2008/06 /04/world/asia/04china.html?_r=1&.

25. Tania Branigan, "Chinese Anger over Alleged Cover-Up of High-Speed Rail Crash," *The Guardian*, July 25, 2011, http://www.theguardian.com/world/2011 /jul/25/chinese-rail-crash-cover-up-claims.

26. Jeremy Page and Brian Spegele, "Land Dispute in China Town Sparks Revolt," *Wall Street Journal*, December 15, 2011, http://www.wsj.com/articles/SB1000142 4052970203518404577097532246936046.

27. Jamil Anderlini, "Chinese National People's Congress Has 83 Billionaires, Report Says," *Washington Post*, March 7, 2013, http://www.washingtonpost.com /world/asia_pacific/chinese-national-peoples-congress-has-83-billionaires-report -says/2013/03/07/d8ff4a4e-8746-11e2-98a3-b3db6b9ac586_story.html.

28. Andrew Flowers, "Why the Chinese Are Snapping Up Real Estate in the U.S.," *FiveThirtyEight*, July 11, 2014, http://fivethirtyeight.com/datalab/why-the-chinese -are-snapping-up-real-estate-in-the-u-s/.

29. James Griffiths, "Half of China's Millionaires 'Plan to Leave Country within Five Years,'" *South China Morning Post*, September 16, 2014, http://www.scmp.com /news/china/article/1592975/47-cent-chinese-super-rich-want-leave-country -barclays-survey?page=all. See also Rachel Wang, "Why China's Rich Want to Leave," *The Atlantic*, April 11, 2013, http://www.theatlantic.com/china/archive/2013/04 /why-chinas-rich-want-to-leave/274920/.

30. See McGregor, *Party*, 94–100; Bao Tong, "How Deng Xiaoping Helped Create a Corrupt China," *New York Times*, June 3, 2015, http://www.nytimes.com /2015/06/04/opinion/bao-tong-how-deng-xiaoping-helped-create-a-corrupt -china.html.

31. David Barboza, "Billions in Hidden Riches for Family of Chinese Leader," *New York Times*, October 25, 2012, http://www.nytimes.com/2012/10/26 /business/global/family-of-wen-jiabao-holds-a-hidden-fortune-in-china.html ?pagewanted=all.

32. Jeremy Page, "Bo Xilai Found Guilty, Sentenced to Life in Prison," *Wall Street Journal*, September 22, 2013, http://www.wsj.com/articles/SB100014240527023 03730704579090080547591654.

33. Minxin Pei, "Crony Communism in China," *New York Times*, October 17, 2014, http://www.nytimes.com/2014/10/18/opinion/crony-communism-in-china.html.

34. Jaime A. FlorCruz, "Corruption as China's Top Priority," CNN, January 6, 2013, http://www.cnn.com/2013/01/06/world/asia/florcruz-china-corruption; see also Osnos, "Born Red."

35. Matt Schiavera, "Why Xi Jinping's 'Anti-Corruption Campaign' Is Hollow, Unserious, and Ultimately Doomed," *The Atlantic*, July 18, 2013, http://www .theatlantic.com/china/archive/2013/07/why-xi-jinpings-anti-corruption -campaign-is-hollow-unserious-and-ultimately-doomed/277908/; see also James Leung, "Xi's Corruption Crackdown," *Foreign Affairs*, April 20, 2015, https://www .foreignaffairs.com/articles/china/2015-04-20/xis-corruption-crackdown.

36. Andrea Peterson, "China Has Almost Twice as Many Internet Users as the U.S. Has People," *Washington Post*, January 31, 2014, http://www.washingtonpost.com /blogs/the-switch/wp/2014/01/31/china-has-almost-twice-as-many-internet -users-as-the-u-s-has-people/; Charles Custer, "The Demise of Sina Weibo: Censorship or Evolution?" *Forbes*, February 4, 2014, http://www.forbes.com/sites/ccuster/2014 /02/04/the-demise-of-sina-weibo-censorship-or-evolution/. For an earlier look at Sina Weibo's social role, see Rachel Dewoskin, "East Meets Tweet," *Vanity Fair*, February 17, 2012, http://www.vanityfair.com/news/tech/2012/02/weibo-china -twitter-chinese-microblogging-tom-cruise-201202.

37. Andrew Jacobs, "China Further Tightens Grip on the Internet," *New York Times*, January 29, 2015, http://www.nytimes.com/2015/01/30/world/asia/china -clamps-down-still-harder-on-internet-access.html?_r=0.

38. Francis Fukuyama, *Trust: The Social Virtues and the Creation of Prosperity* (New York: Free Press, 1996).

39. A fascinating study of how this worked in prior decades is by Anne-Marie Brady, *Making the Foreign Serve China: Managing Foreigners in the People's Republic* (Lanham, MD: Rowman and Littlefield, 2003).

40. See, for example, Xiao Shu, "China's Veil of Civil Rights Oppression," *New York Times*, November 26, 2013, http://www.nytimes.com/2013/11/27/opinion /chinas-veil-of-civil-rights-oppression.html.

41. See Tom Friedman, "Our One-Party Democracy," *New York Times*, September 8, 2009, http://www.nytimes.com/2009/09/09/opinion/09friedman.html?_r=0.

42. An interesting argument is in Sungmoon Kim, *Confucian Democracy in East Asia: Theory and Practice* (Cambridge: Cambridge University Press, 2014); also Mark R. Thompson, "Modernization Theory's Last Redoubt: Democratization in East and Southeast Asia," in Yin-wah Chu and Siu-lun Wong, *East Asia's New Democracies: Deepening, Reversal, Non-liberal Alternatives* (New York: Routledge, 2010), 85–101. A more detailed discussion of elections and parties is in Jungug Choi, *Votes, Party Systems and Democracy in Asia* (New York: Routledge, 2012), esp. ch. 1.

43. Jean-Pierre Lehmann, "Asia's Democratic Dramas," *Japan Times*, February 14, 2014, http://www.japantimes.co.jp/opinion/2014/02/14/commentary/world-commentary/asias-democratic-dramas/#.VZ115kYYEsI.

44. Pronounced "AH-bay."

45. Reiji Yoshida, "Low Voter Turnout Mars Abe's Claim of Election Triumph," *Japan Times*, December 17, 2014, http://www.japantimes.co.jp/news/2014/12/17/national/politics-diplomacy/low-voter-turnout-mars-abes-claim-election-triumph/#.VYq-g2TBzGd.

46. See, for example, Ezra Vogel, *Japan as Number One: Lessons for America* (Cambridge, MA: Harvard University Press, 1979).

47. This claim has been central to the debate over "modernization theory" during the Cold War and after. For a detailed discussion, see Mark T. Berger, *The Battle for Asia: From Decolonization to Globalization* (London: RoutledgeCurzon, 2004), 93–94, 107–8; see also Laura E. Hein, "Free Floating Anxieties on the Pacific: Japan and the West Revisited," *Diplomatic History* 20, no. 3 (Summer 1996): esp. 415–19.

48. "The Man Who Remade Japan," *The Economist*, September 14, 2006, http://www.economist.com/node/7916942.

49. See its 2009 election manifesto: Yukio Hatoyama, "Make Politics Work for People's Lives," Democratic Party of Japan, August 18, 2009, http://www.dpj.or.jp/english/manifesto/manifesto2009.html.

50. "DPJ's Weak, Confusing Platform, *Japan Times*, November 30, 2012, http://www.japantimes.co.jp/opinion/2012/11/30/editorials/dpjs-weak-confusing-platform/#.VYrJd2TBzGd.

51. Patrick Koellner, "The Triumph and Fall of the Democratic Party of Japan," in *Party Politics in Japan: Political Chaos and Stalemate in the Twenty-First Century*, ed. Ronald J. Hrebenar and Akira Nakamura (New York: Routledge, 2015), ch. 4, 80–117.

52. Roland Kelts, "The Identity Crisis That Lurks behind Japan's Right-Wing Rhetoric," *Time*, May 31, 2013, http://world.time.com/2013/05/31/the-identity-crisis-that-lurks-behind-japans-right-wing-rhetoric/.

53. Michael Auslin, "Shinzo Won't Go," *Foreign Policy*, April 23, 2014, http://foreignpolicy.com/2014/04/23/shinzo-wont-go/.

54. See, for example, contrasting articles such as Jeff Kingston, "Right-Wing Witch Hunt Signals Dark Days in Japan," *Japan Times*, November 8, 2014, http://www.japantimes.co.jp/opinion/2014/11/08/commentary/japan-commentary/right-wing-witch-hunt-signals-dark-days-japan/#.VYrLUGTBzGd; and Yoshihisa Komori, "Japan not Becoming Right-Wing, Returning from the Left," *JBPress*, February 11, 2013, http://jbpress.ismedia.jp/articles/-/37121.

55. Akira Nakamura and Ronald J. Hrebenar, "The Liberal Democratic Party: The Persistent Ruling Party of Japan," in Hrebenar and Nakamura, *Party Politics in Japan*, ch. 5, 118–47.

56. See Gregg A. Brazinsky, *Nation Building in South Korea: Koreans, Americans, and the Making of a Democracy* (Durham: University of North Carolina Press, 2009);

Carl Saxer, *From Transition to Power Alternation: Democracy in South Korea, 1987–1997* (New York: Routledge, 2013); and Sunhyuk Kim, "State and Civil Society in South Korea's Democratic Consolidation: Is the Battle Really Over?" *Asian Survey* 37, no. 12 (December 1997): 1135–44.

57. Jae H. Ku, "The Decline of Political Participation in Korea between 2000 and 2011," in *Incomplete Democracies in the Asia-Pacific: Evidence from Indonesia, Korea, The Philippines and Thailand*, ed. Giovanna Maria Dora Dore, Jae H. Ku, and Karl D. Jackson (New York: Palgrave MacMillan, 2014), ch. 4; Chong-Min Park, "South Korea's Disaffected Democracy," in *Democracy in Eastern Asia: Issues, Problems and Challenges in a Region of Diversity*, ed. Edmund S. K. Fung and Steven Drakeley (New York: Routledge, 2014), 38–59.

58. Jaeyeon Woo, "South Korea President Apologizes for Scandals," *Wall Street Journal*, July 24, 2012, http://www.wsj.com/articles/SB10000872396390443570 904577546422236761092.

59. Ian Allen, "South Korean Court Convicts Ex-Spy Director of Interfering in Elections," *Intel News*, September 12, 2014, http://intelnews.org/2014/09/12/11321/.

60. Se-Woong Koo, "South Korea's Invasion of Privacy," *New York Times*, April 2, 2015, http://www.nytimes.com/2015/04/03/opinion/south-koreas-invasion-of -privacy.html?_r=0.

61. "South Korea Protests: Seoul Rally against Park Geun-hye," BBC.com, December 5, 2015, http://www.bbc.com/news/world-asia-35014582.

62. "Disputing Korean Narrative on 'Comfort Women,' a Professor Draws Fierce Backlash," *New York Times*, December 18, 2015, http://www.nytimes.com/2015/12 /19/world/asia/south-korea-comfort-women-park-yu-ha.html.

63. Kim Hyo-jin, "Park's Approval Rating Shows Signs of Rebounding," *Korea Times*, June 22, 2015, http://www.koreatimes.co.kr/www/news/nation/2015/06 /116_181356.html.

64. Joshua Hall, "How Unhappy Are South Koreans?" *Wall Street Journal*, September 26, 2014, http://blogs.wsj.com/korearealtime/2014/09/26/how-unhappy -are-south-koreans/.

65. Anna Fifield, "Young South Koreans Call Their Country "Hell" and Look for Ways Out," *Washington Post*, January 31, 2016, https://www.washingtonpost.com /world/asia_pacific/young-south-koreans-call-their-country-hell-and-look-for -ways-out/2016/01/30/34737c06 b967-11e5-85cd-5ad59bc19432_story.html ?utm_content=bufferc181a&utm_medium=social&utm_source=twitter.com&utm _campaign=buffer.

66. Michael Auslin, "The Return of North Korea," *Commentary Magazine*, February 2015, https://www.commentarymagazine.com/article/the-return-of-north -korea/.

67. "Don't Scare North Korea Off a Pyongyang Spring," *The Independent*, January 2, 2013, http://www.independent.co.uk/voices/editorials/editorial-dont-scare -north-korea-off-a-pyongyang-spring-8435923.html.

68. Chico Harlan, "South Korean Youth Grow Wary of Unification," *Washington Post*, October 17, 2011, http://www.washingtonpost.com/world/south-korean -youth-grow-wary-of-unification/2011/10/14/gIQA3ujmqL_story.html.

69. Simon Mundy, "S Korea Lawyers Seek 20-Year Jail Term for Treason Case Politician," *Financial Times*, February 3, 2014, http://www.ft.com/intl/cms/s/0 /c4b021ea-8ccb-11e3-ad57-00144feab7de.html#axzz3Dydmt7a1.

70. "Association of Southeast Asian Nations (ASEAN)," USTR Fact Sheet, http:// www.ustr.gov/countries-regions/southeast-asia-pacific/association-southeast-asian -nations-asean.

71. A good introduction to the region is Milton Osborne, *Southeast Asia: An Introductory History* (London: Allen and Unwin, 2013); see also Robert D. Kaplan, *Asia's Cauldron: The South China Sea and the End of a Stable Pacific* (New York: Random House, 2014).

72. "Asia's Aging Population," East-West Center, http://www.eastwestcenter.org /fileadmin/stored/misc/FuturePop08Aging.pdf. That number is expected to quadruple by 2050, however.

73. "Suharto": Indonesians traditionally went by just one name, though that is now changing. A recent general survey is Adrian Vickers, *A History of Modern Indonesia*, 2nd ed. (Cambridge: Cambridge University Press, 2014).

74. Karl D. Jackson, "Democratization and the Indonesia Middle Class: Waiting for Godot?" in Dore et al., *Incomplete Democracies in the Asia-Pacific*, ch. 3, 63–118.

75. "Amnesty: Indonesia 'Failing to Uphold' Aceh Peace Terms," BBC, April 18, 2013, http://www.bbc.co.uk/news/world-asia-22198860.

76. Tito Summa Siahaan, "Minister Admits Indonesia to Fall Short on Infrastructure Goals," *Jakarta Globe*, July 24, 2013, http://www.thejakartaglobe.com/business /minister-admits-indonesia-to-fall-short-on-infrastructure-goals/.

77. Tom Pepinski, "The Key to Understanding Indonesia's Upcoming Elections? The Jokowi Effect," *Washington Post*, March 17, 2014, http://www.washingtonpost .com/blogs/monkey-cage/wp/2014/03/17/the-key-to-understanding-indonesias -upcoming-elections-the-jokowi-effect/.

78. "Indonesian Parliament Scraps Direct Elections, Undermining Joko Widodo," *The Guardian*, September 25, 2014, http://www.theguardian.com/world/2014 /sep/26/indonesian-parliament-scraps-direct-elections-undermining-joko -widodo.

79. Elizabeth Pisani, "Widodo's Desperate Executions," *The New Yorker*, May 1, 2015, http://www.newyorker.com/news/news-desk/widodos-desperate-executions.

80. "Approval Ratings Boost Marks Indonesia's Widodo's First Year in Office," *Reuters*, October 20, 2015, http://www.reuters.com/article/us-indonesia-president -idUSKCN0SE12H20151020.

81. A general history is C. M. Turnbull, *A Modern History of Singapore: 1895–2005*, rev. ed. (Singapore: NUS Press, 2010); see also Jim Baker, *Crossroads: A Popular History of Malaysia and Singapore*, 2nd ed. (Singapore: Marshall Cavendish International, 2008).

82. The prime minister currently receives an annual salary of $1.7 million, which has been cut from $2.8 million because of public anger over income disparity. Jerin Mathew, "Singapore PM Lee Hsien Loong Remains Highest Paid Country Leader with $1.7m Annual Salary," *International Business Times*, March 28, 2015, http:// www.ibtimes.co.uk/singapore-pm-lee-hsien-loong-remains-highest-paid-country -leader-1-7m-annual-salary-1493952.

83. Derived from interviews with Singaporean government officials and business leaders and foreign business leaders. See also Prashanth Parameswaran, "Singapore Faces Challenges both Near and Far in Post-Lee Kuan Yew Era," *World Politics Review*, April 1, 2015, http://www.worldpoliticsreview.com/articles/15429/singapore -faces-challenges-near-and-far-in-post-lee-kuan-yew-era.

84. See Diane K. Mauzy and R. S. Milne, *Malaysian Politics under Mahathir* (New York: Routledge, 1999). 2014 per capita income figures at: "GDP Per Capita, PPP (Current International $)," World Bank, http://data.worldbank.org/indicator/NY .GDP.PCAP.PP.CD, accessed April 26, 2016.

85. A brief review of his case is at "Profile: Anwar Ibrahim," *BBC*, February 10, 2015, http://www.bbc.com/news/world-asia-16440290.

86. Thomas Fuller and Louise Story, "Power Struggle in Malaysia Pits Former Premier against a Protégé," *New York Times*, June 17, 2015, http://www.nytimes.com /2015/06/18/world/asia/malaysia-prime-minister-najib-razak-mahathir -mohamad.html.

87. Joe Cochrane, "In a Nation of Muslims, Political Islam Is Struggling to Win Votes," *New York Times*, April 17, 2014, http://www.nytimes.com/2014/04/08 /world/asia/political-islam-indonesia.html?_r=0.

88. Al-Zaquan Amer Hamzah and Trinna Leong, "Malaysian Move toward Harsher Islamic Law Divides Opposition," *Reuters*, March 18, 2015, http://www.reuters.com /article/2015/03/18/us-malaysia-islam-law-idUSKBN0ME0JJ20150318.

89. Thomas Fuller, "Malaysian Premier Says Sedition Act Will Stand," *New York Times*, November 28, 2014, http://www.nytimes.com/2014/11/28/world/asia /malaysian-premier-says-sedition-act-will-stand.html.

90. A basic history is Chris Baker and Pasuk Phongpaichit, *A History of Thailand*, 3rd ed. (Cambridge: Cambridge University Press, 2014).

91. For a detailed account, see Andrew MacGregor Marshall, *A Kingdom in Crisis: Thailand's Struggle for Democracy in the Twenty-First Century* (London: Zed Books, 2014).

92. Prinat Apirat, "From Subject to Citizens: Democratic Consolidation in Thailand between 2000 and 2011," in Dore et al., *Incomplete Democracies in the Asia-Pacific*, ch. 5, 143–85.

93. Christian Caryl, "Can Thailand Move beyond the Coup?" *Foreign Policy*, November 22, 2014, http://foreignpolicy.com/2014/11/22/can-thailand-move-beyond -the-coup/.

94. See Rena Pederson, *The Burma Spring: Aung San Suu Kyi and the New Struggle for the Soul of a Nation* (New York: Pegasus, 2015); a general history is Michael W.

Charney, *A History of Modern Burma* (Cambridge: Cambridge University Press, 2009).

95. *New York Times* Editorial Board, "Backsliding on Reform in Myanmar," *New York Times*, March 21, 2015, http://www.nytimes.com/2015/03/21/opinion/backsliding-on-reform-in-myanmar.html?gwh=C5F3E84CAA485327C93850F5B0DEC858&gwt=pay&assetType=opinion.

96. Among numerous works, see John Keay, *India: A History*, rev. ed. (New York: Grove, 2011).

97. See Nisid Hajari, *Midnight's Furies: The Deadly Legacy of India's Partition* (New York: Houghton Mifflin Harcourt, 2015).

98. Ramachandra Guha, *India after Gandhi: The History of the World's Largest Democracy* (New York: Harper, 2008).

99. Ibid., ch. 24.

100. A brief study is Nirupam Bajpai, "Economic Crisis, Structural Reforms, and the Prospects of Growth in India," Harvard Institute for International Development, 1996, http://www.cid.harvard.edu/hiid/530.pdf; see also Charan Wadhva, "India Trying to Liberalize: Economic Reforms since 1991," in *The Asia-Pacific: A Region in Transition*, ed. Jim Rolfe (Honolulu: Asia-Pacific Center for Security Studies, 2004), 259–84.

101. For background, see Barney Henderson, "Mumbai Terror Attacks: The Making of a Monster," *The Telegraph*, April 12, 2013, http://www.telegraph.co.uk/news/worldnews/asia/india/9985109/Mumbai-terror-attacks-the-making-of-a-monster.html.

102. For the optimistic view, see A. Gary Schilling, "Why India Will Displace China as Global Growth Engine," *Bloomberg View*, December 16, 2012, http://www.bloombergview.com/articles/2012-12-16/why-india-will-displace-china-as-global-growth-engine.

103. See, for example, Jason Burke, "India's Congress Party Suffers Local Election 'Meltdown,'" *The Guardian*, December 8, 2013, http://www.theguardian.com/world/2013/dec/08/india-congress-party-local-election-defeat.

104. See results of April 2014 Gallup poll at: Andrew Dugan, "Corruption Concerns All Generations of Indian Voters," Gallup, April 14, 2014, http://www.gallup.com/poll/168488/corruption-concerns-generations-indian-voters.aspx.

105. Vikas Bajaj, "Indian Court Cancels Contentious Wireless Licenses," *New York Times*, February 2, 2012, http://www.nytimes.com/2012/02/03/business/global/india-supreme-court-cancels-2g-licenses.html?_r=1&.

106. "Delhi Commonwealth Games Organiser Arrested in Corruption Investigation," *The Guardian* through the *Associated Press*, April 25, 2011, http://www.theguardian.com/world/2011/apr/25/delhi-commonwealth-games-organiser-arrested.

107. "A Bad Boom," *The Economist*, March 15, 2014, http://www.economist.com/news/briefing/21598967-graft-india-damaging-economy-country-needs-get-serious-about-dealing-it.

108. Corruption Perceptions Index 2012, Transparency International, http://www
.transparency.org/cpi2012/results, accessed June 2, 2015.

109. Shilpa Phadnis, "India Suffered Rs 36,400 cr Loss Due to Corruption: Report," *Times of India*, July 22, 2013, http://timesofindia.indiatimes.com/business
/india-business/India-suffered-Rs-36400-cr-loss-due-to-corruption-Report
/articleshow/21252592.cms.

110. See Jennifer Bussell, *Corruption and Reform in India: Public Services in the
Digital Age* (Cambridge: Cambridge University Press, 2013), chs. 4–5.

111. See Sadanand Dhume, "Out with a Whisper," *Foreign Policy*, January 13,
2014, http://foreignpolicy.com/2014/01/13/out-with-a-whimper-2/.

112. Derek Scissors, "Modinomics at One," *Foreign Affairs*, May 24, 2015, https://
www.foreignaffairs.com/articles/india/2015-05-24/modinomics-one;   see   also
Dhiraj Nayyar, "Modi's Window for Reform Is Closing," *Bloomberg View*, June 21,
2015, http://www.bloombergview.com/articles/2015-06-21/modi-s-window-for
-reform-is-closing.

5. Why Can't We All Just Get Along?

1. Some studies exploring this question include Ellen Frost, *Asia's New Regionalism* (Boulder, CO: Lynne Rienner, 2008); Robyn Lim, *The Geopolitics of East
Asia: The Search for Equilibrium*, new ed. (New York: Routledge, 2005), esp. ch. 6;
Gilbert Rozman, *Northeast Asia's Stunted Regionalism: Bilateral Distrust in the
Shadow of Globalization* (Cambridge: Cambridge University Press, 2004); and essays in David Shambaugh and Michael Yahuda, eds., *International Relations of Asia*,
2nd ed. (New York: Rowman and Littlefield, 2014).

2. Among others, see Ronald Spector, *In the Ruins of Empire: The Japanese Surrender and the Battle for Postwar Asia* (New York: Random House, 2008); and
Mark T. Berger, *The Battle for Asia: From Decolonization to Globalization* (New York:
Routledge, 2003).

3. Bruce Russett, *Grasping the Democratic Peace: Principles for a Post–Cold War
World* (Princeton, NJ: Princeton University Press, 1993).

4. Thorough studies are Warren I. Cohen, *East Asia at the Center: Four Thousand
Years of Engagement with the World* (New York: Columbia University Press, 2000);
and Odd Arne Westad, *Restless Empire: China and the World since 1750* (New York:
Basic Books, 2012), esp. chs. 1–2. See also Morris Rossabi, *China among Equals: The
Middle Kingdom and Its Neighbors, 10th–14th Centuries* (Berkeley: University of California Press, 1983).

5. A general survey is Gary D. Allinson, *Japan's Postwar History*, 2nd ed. (Ithaca,
NY: Cornell University Press, 2004). See also Karl van Wolferen, *The Enigma of
Japanese Power: People and Politics in a Stateless Nation* (New York: Vintage, 1989),
esp. chs. 15–16.

6. Kevin Cooney, *Japan's Foreign Policy since 1945* (Armonk, NY: M. E. Sharpe,
2007), esp. ch. 3.

7. Tomohito Shinoda, *Koizumi Diplomacy: Japan's Kantei Approach to Foreign and Defense Affairs* (Seattle: University of Washington Press, 2007).

8. Pre-9/11 expressions of hope for a new alliance can be found in Richard L. Armitage and Joseph S. Nye, "The U.S.-Japan Alliance: Getting Asia Right through 2020," Center for Strategic and International Studies, 2000.

9. See, for example, Balbina Y. Hwang, "Japan's Troop Dispatch to Iraq: The End of Checkbook Diplomacy," The Heritage Foundation, February 9, 2004, http:// www.heritage.org/research/reports/2004/02/japans-troop-dispatch-to-iraq-the -end-of-checkbook-diplomacy.

10. See, for example, his keynote address at the 2014 Shangri-La Dialogue, https:// www.iiss.org/en/events/shangri%20la%20dialogue/archive/2014-c20c/opening -remarks-and-keynote-address-b0b2/keynote-address-shinzo-abe-a787.

11. Sueo Sudo, *The International Relations of Japan and South East Asia: Forging a New Regionalism* (New York: Routledge, 2001).

12. Kirk Spitzer, "War's Legacy Plagues Japan and Its Neighbors," *Time*, August 16, 2012, http://nation.time.com/2012/08/16/wars-legacy-plagues-japan -and-its-neighbors/.

13. Jean Yoon and Tony Munroe, "South Korea's Park Says Door Open for Talks with North," *Reuters*, September 16, 2014, http://www.reuters.com/article/2014 /09/16/us-southkorea-president-interview-idUSKBN0HB2P420140916.

14. A general overview is Don Oberdorfer and Robert Karlin, *The Two Koreas: A Contemporary History*, rev. ed. (New York: Basic Books, 2013). See also Mark Tudor, *Korea: The Impossible Country* (North Clarendon, VT: Tuttle Books, 2013), esp. chs. 5–6, 13–15.

15. Scott A. Snyder, *Global Korea: South Korea's Contributions to International Security* (New York: Council on Foreign Relations Press, 2012).

16. See Michael R. Auslin, "Japan and South Korea: The New East Asian Core," *Orbis* 49, no. 3 (Summer 2005): 459–73.

17. This is an old question. See, for example, Usha Mahajani, "Is Australia a Part of Asia?" *Australian Quarterly* 36, no. 2 (June 1964): 25–34.

18. This is discussed in the Australian government's 2012 White Paper, "Australia in the Asian Century" (Canberra, October 2012), document hosted by Murdoch University, http://www.murdoch.edu.au/ALTC-Fellowship/_document/Resources /australia-in-the-asian-century-white-paper.pdf.

19. On the FTA, see "Outcomes at a Glance," Department of Foreign Affairs and Trade, http://dfat.gov.au/trade/agreements/chafta/fact-sheets/Pages/key-outcomes .aspx.

20. Hugh White, *The China Choice: Why America Should Share Power* (Melbourne: Black, 2012).

21. Private conversation with senior Australian defense official, Washington, DC, September 2012; see also Greg Sheridan, "US President Barack Obama's Pivotal Absence in Asia," *The Australian*, May 23, 2015, http://www.theaustralian.com.au

/opinion/columnists/us-president-barack-obamas-pivotal-absence-in-asia/story
-e6frg76f-1227365819331.

22. Frank Frost, "Australia's Proposal for an 'Asia Pacific Community': Issues and Prospects," Parliament of Australia, Department of Parliamentary Services, December 1, 2009, https://www.aph.gov.au/binaries/library/pubs/rp/2009-10/10rp13.pdf.

23. See Avinash Kumar, "Lessons of Experience in International Democracy Promotion: The Case of Australia in Post-Coup Fiji," *Journal of Pacific Studies* 33, no. 1 (2013): 62–77. On East Timor, see "Australia—Timor-Leste Country Strategy 2009 to 2014," Department of Foreign Affairs and Trade, http://dfat.gov.au/about-us /publications/Pages/australia-timor-leste-country-strategy-2009-to-2014.aspx.

24. On refugees, see "Australia Asylum: Why Is It Controversial?" *BBC News*, December 5, 2014, http://www.bbc.com/news/world-asia-28189608.

25. A general history is Burjor Avari, *India: The Ancient Past: A History of the Indian-Subcontinent from 7000 BC to AD 1200* (New York: Routledge, 2007), esp. chs. 8–9.

26. See, for example, Stephen Sherlock, "Asia's Next Emerging Giant?: Political Change and Economic Reform in India," Research Paper 5, Parliament of Australia, 1995–96, http://www.aph.gov.au/About_Parliament/Parliamentary_Departments /Parliamentary_Library/pubs/rp/RP9697/97rp5; Amitav Acharya, "China, India, Japan—Who Will Speak for Asia?" Asia Pacific Foundation of Canada, November 30, 2009, http://www.asiapacific.ca/op-eds/china-india-japan-who-will-speak-asia.

27. Jayshree Sengupta, "India, Bangladesh and Nepal: Learning Lessons, Facing Challenges," *ORF Issue Brief* 64, November 2013, http://orfonline.org/cms/export /orfonline/modules/issuebrief/attachments/Issuebrief64_1385545948867.pdf; "Almost All Quiet on the Eastern Front," *The Economist*, April 18, 2011, http:// www.economist.com/blogs/banyan/2011/04/indias_border_bangladesh.

28. See C. Raja Mohan, *Crossing the Rubicon: The Shaping of India's New Foreign Policy* (New York: Palgrave Macmillan, 2004).

29. Thongkholal Haokip, *India's Look East Policy and the Northeast* (New York: Sage, 2015); and David Brewster, *India's Ocean: The Story of India's Bid for Regional Leadership* (New York: Routledge, 2014).

30. A dated but interesting study is P. F. Power, *India's Nonalignment Policy: Strengths and Weaknesses* (Lexington, MA: D. C. Heath, 1968).

31. For a recent study, see Andrew Small, *The China-Pakistan Axis: Asia's New Geopolitics* (Oxford: Oxford University Press, 2015).

32. Titli Basu, "India-Japan Relations: New Times, Renewed Expectations," Institute for Defence Studies and Analyses, September 4, 2014, http://www.idsa.in /idsacomments/IndiaJapanRelations_tbasu_040914.html.

33. Shinzo Abe and Manmohan Singh, "Joint Statement: Towards Japan-India Strategic and Global Partnership," December 15, 2006, http://japan.kantei.go.jp /abespeech/2006/12/15joint.pdf; see also Shihoko Goto, ed., *The Rebalance within Asia: The Evolution of Japan-India Relations*, Wilson Center, 2014, http://www

.wilsoncenter.org/sites/default/files/ASIA_140905_Rebalance%20Within%20 Asia%20rpt.pdf.

34. "PM: India Not Part of 'Contain China' Effort," *The Hindu*, January 11, 2008, http://www.thehindu.com/todays-paper/tp-national/article1177057.ece; see also Brahma Chellaney, "The U.S.-India-Japan-Australia Quadrilateral Initiative: A New Great Game," *Asian Age*, June 2, 2007, http://chellaney.net/2007/06/01/the-u-s -india-japan-australia-quadrilateral-initiative/.

35. Ministry of Foreign Affairs of Japan, "General Information on East Asia Summit (EAS)," December 2005, http://www.mofa.go.jp/region/asia-paci/eas/outline .html.

36. "Making Things Normal," *The Economist*, June 8, 2015, http://www.econo mist.com/news/asia/21653790-tidying-up-their-border-should-be-only-first-order -business-making-things-normal.

37. Anil Sasi, " 'Look East' Has Become 'Act East' Policy, Says PM Modi at ASEAN Summit," http://indianexpress.com/article/india/india-others/look-east-has-become -act-east-policy-pm-modi-at-asean/.

38. See Joshua Kurlantzick, "ASEAN's Future and Asian Integration," Working Paper, Council on Foreign Relations, November 2012, http://www.cfr.org/content /publications/attachments/IIGG_WorkingPaper10_Kurlantzick.pdf.

39. Christopher Banks, *ASEAN Regionalism: Cooperation, Values and Institutionalization* (New York: Routledge, 2012).

40. "Belgrade Declaration of Non-Aligned Countries, 1961," Belgrade, September 6, 1061, http://namiran.org/wp-content/uploads/2013/04/Declarations-of-All -Previous-NAM-Summits.pdf.

41. See Christopher B. Roberts, *ASEAN Regionalism: Cooperation, Values, and Institutionalization* (New York: Routledge, 2013), ch. 2.

42. For a study of the limitations of nonintervention, see Lee Jones, *ASEAN, Sovereignty, and Intervention in Southeast Asia* (New York: Palgrave Macmillan, 2012).

43. See David Rosenberg, "The Maritime Borderlands: Terrorism, Piracy, Pollution, and Poaching in the South China Sea," in *The Borderlands of Southeast Asia: Geopolitics, Terrorism, and Globalization*, ed. James Clad, Sean M. McDonald, and Bruce Vaughn (Washington, DC: National Defense University Press, 2013), 107–26.

44. "Why Are So Many Rohingyan Migrants Stranded at Sea?" *BBC News*, May 18, 2015, http://www.bbc.com/news/world-asia-32740637; Jane Perlez, "Myanmar's Policy Message to Muslims: Get Out," *New York Times*, November 6, 2014, http:// www.nytimes.com/2014/11/07/world/asia/rohingya-myanmar-rakhine-state -thailand-malaysia.html.

45. Rhoda Margesson, "Indian Ocean Earthquake and Tsunami: Humanitarian Assistance and Relief Operations," Congressional Research Service, February 10, 2005, https://www.fas.org/sgp/crs/row/RL32715.pdf.

46. See Amitav Acharya, *Constructing a Security Community in Southeast Asia: ASEAN and the Problem of Regional Order*, 3rd ed. (New York: Routledge, 2014), esp. ch. 7.

47. Seth Mydans, "Thailand and Cambodia Clash Again in Border Dispute," *New York Times*, April 24, 2011, http://www.nytimes.com/2011/04/25/world/asia /25temples.html.

48. ASEAN Regional Forum, "About the ASEAN Regional Forum," http:// aseanregionalforum.asean.org/about.html.

49. Hillary Rodham Clinton, "Remarks at Press Availability," 2014 ASEAN Regional Forum, July 23, 2010, http://www.state.gov/secretary/20092013clinton/rm /2010/07/145095.htm.

50. ASEAN, "Overview: ASEAN plus Three Cooperation," January 22, 2014, http://www.asean.org/asean/external-relations/asean-3/item/asean-plus-three -cooperation.

51. Alan Burns, "U.S. Joins East Asia Summit: Implications for Regional Cooperation," National Bureau of Asian Research, November 17, 2011, http://www.nbr .org/research/activity.aspx?id=183.

52. Carol J. Williams, "Obama's Absence at Asia-Pacific Summits Lets China Dominate," *Los Angeles Times*, October 10, 2013, http://articles.latimes.com/2013/oct /10/world/la-fg-wn-asia-pacific-obama-china-20131010.

53. See Nick Bisley and Malcolm Cook, "How the East Asia Summit Can Achieve Its Potential," Institute of Southeast Asian Studies, October 2014, http://www.iseas .edu.sg/documents/publication/ISEAS_perspective_2014_56.pdf.

54. John Pomfret, "U.S. Takes a Tougher Tone with China," *Washington Post*, July 30, 2010, http://www.washingtonpost.com/wp-dyn/content/article/2010/07 /29/AR2010072906416.html.

55. Joanna-Waley Cohen, *The Sextants of Beijing: Global Currents in Chinese History* (New York: W. W. Norton, 1999).

56. A thorough study is Lorenz M. Luthi, *The Sino-Soviet Split: Cold War in the Communist World* (Princeton, NJ: Princeton University Press, 2008).

57. See Steven J. Hood, *Dragons Entangled: Indochina and the China-Vietnam War* (New York: Routledge, 1992).

58. See, for example, Akira Iriye, "Chinese-Japanese Relations, 1945–1990," in *China and Japan: History, Trends, and Prospects*, ed. Christopher Howe (New York: Oxford University Press, 1996), 46–59; Caroline Rose, *Interpreting History in Sino-Japanese Relations: A Case-Study in Political Decision Making* (New York: Routledge, 2005), ch. 3; Jae Ho Chung, *Between Ally and Partner: Korea-China Relations and the United States* (New York: Columbia University Press, 2006), ch. 4.

59. Zheng Bijian is one of the most prominent voices in the peaceful rise debate. See his "China's 'Peaceful Rise' to Great-Power Status," *Foreign Affairs*, September–October 2005, https://www.foreignaffairs.com/articles/asia/2005-09-01/chinas -peaceful-rise-great-power-status. A collection of his writings and speeches is Zheng Bijian, *China's Road to Peaceful Rise: Observations on Its Cause, Basis, Connotation and Prospect* (New York: Routledge, 2011).

60. See, for example, Joshua Kurlantzick, *Charm Offensive: How China's Soft Power Is Transforming the World* (New Haven, CT: Yale University Press, 2007).

61. ASEAN, "ASEAN–China Free Trade Area," http://www.asean.org/communities/asean-economic-community/item/asean-china-free-trade-area-2.

62. See Shanthi Kalathil, "Influence for Sale? China's Trade, Investment and Assistance Policies in Southeast Asia," *East and South China Seas Bulletin 4*, Center for a New American Security, September 2012, http://www.cnas.org/files/documents/publications/CNAS_ESCA_bulletin4.pdf; Prak Chan Sul, "China Pledges $548 Million in Aid to Ally Cambodia," *Reuters*, April 10, 2013, http://www.reuters.com/article/2013/04/10/us-cambodia-china-idUSBRE93909D20130410.

63. A representative take on China's influence over North Korea is by Christopher R. Hill, "Strategic Clarity on North Korea," Project Syndicate, December 30, 2014, http://www.project-syndicate.org/commentary/north-korea-us-strategy-by-christopher-r-hill-2014-12.

64. See, for example, John Lee, "The End of Smile Diplomacy?" *National Interest*, September 23, 2010, http://nationalinterest.org/commentary/the-end-smile-diplomacy-4122.

65. Two recent examples of changes of heart are by Michael Pillsbury, *The Hundred-Year Marathon: China's Secret Strategy to Replace America as the Global Superpower* (New York: Henry Holt, 2015); and Robert D. Blackwill and Ashley J. Tellis, "Revising U.S. Grand Strategy toward China," Council on Foreign Relations, 2015, http://carnegieendowment.org/files/Tellis_Blackwill.pdf.

66. See, for example, "China's New Development Bank: How Obama Blew It in the Pacific (Again)," *Fiscal Times*, March 23, 2015, http://www.thefiscaltimes.com/Columns/2015/03/23/China-s-New-Development-Bank-How-Obama-Blew-It-Pacific-Again.

67. Geoff Dyer and George Parker, "US Attacks UK's 'Constant Accommodation' with China," *Financial Times*, March 12, 2015, http://www.ft.com/intl/cms/s/0/31c4880a-c8d2-11e4-bc64-00144feab7de.html#axzz3dzjy30gp.

68. On Africa, see Yun Sun, "Africa in China's Foreign Policy," Brookings Institution, 2014, http://www.brookings.edu/~/media/research/files/papers/2014/04/africa-china-policy-sun/africa-in-china-web_cmg7.pdf; Howard W. French, "The Next Empire," *The Atlantic* (May 2010), http://www.theatlantic.com/magazine/archive/2010/05/the-next-empire/308018/; "China Is Besting the U.S. in Africa," *U.S. News and World Report*, March 24, 2015, http://www.usnews.com/opinion/economic-intelligence/2015/03/24/china-beating-us-in-race-to-invest-in-africa. On Latin America, see Rebecca Ray et al., "China in Latin America: Lessons for South-South Cooperation and Sustainable Development," Global Economic Governance Initiative, Boston University, 2015, http://www.bu.edu/pardeeschool/files/2014/12/Working-Group-Final-Report.pdf; Adrian Hearn et al., *China Engages Latin America: Tracing the Trajectory* (Boulder, CO: Lynne Rienner, 2011); Gonzalo Sebastian Paz, "China, the United States, and Hegemonic Challenge in Latin America," in *From the Great Wall to the New World: China and Latin America in the 21st Century*, ed. Julia C. Strauss and Ariel C. Armony, *China Quarterly* Special Issues, no. 11 (Cambridge: Cambridge University Press, 2012), 18–34.

69. For some examples, see news reports at Lizzie Dearden, "Chinese and Japanese Ambassadors Trade Voldemort Insults in Row over Shrine Visit," *The Independent*, January 6, 2014, http://www.independent.co.uk/news/world/asia/chinese -and-japanese-ambassadors-trade-voldemort-insults-in-row-over-shrine-visit -9040996.html; Julian Ryall, "US-China War 'Inevitable' Unless Washington Drops Demands over South China Sea," *The Telegraph*, May 26, 2015, http://www.telegraph .co.uk/news/worldnews/asia/china/11630185/US-China-war-inevitable-unless -Washington-drops-demands-over-South-China-Sea.html.

6. *Hic Sunt Dracones*

1. Anthony Capaccio and Angela Greiling Keane, "Chinese Jet Barrel-Rolls over U.S. Plane Bringing Protest," *Bloomberg*, August 22, 2014, http://www.bloomberg .com/news/2014-08-22/chinese-jet-barrel-rolls-over-u-s-plane-bringing-protest.html.

2. Shirley A. Kan, Richard Best, Christopher Bolkcom, Robert Chapman, Richard Cronin, Kerry Dumbaugh, Stuart Goldman, Mark Manyin, Wayne Morrison, and Ronald O'Rourke, "China-U.S. Aircraft Collision Incident of April 2001: Assessments and Policy Implications," Congressional Research Service, October 10, 2001, https://www.fas.org/sgp/crs/row/RL30946.pdf.

3. P. W. Singer and August Cole, *Ghost Fleet: A Novel of the Next World War* (New York: Houghton Mifflin Harcourt, 2015).

4. See Kishore Mahbubani, "East Asia Will Avoid War in 2015: Here's Why," *Financial Times*, December 30, 2014, http://blogs.ft.com/the-exchange/2014/12 /30/east-asia-will-avoid-war-in-2015-heres-why/.

5. See, for example, Kishore Mahbubani, *The New Asian Hemisphere: The Irresistible Shift of Global Power to the East* (New York: Public Affairs, 2009). For the history of pre–World War I Europe, see Barbara W. Tuchman, *The Proud Tower: A Portrait of the World before the War, 1890–1914* (New York: Random House, 1996); Christopher Clark, *The Sleepwalkers: How Europe Went to War in 1914* (New York: HarperPerennial, 2014).

6. This is more properly understood as "structural realism" or "neorealism"; see Kenneth Waltz, *Theory of International Politics* (New York: McGraw-Hill, 1979). For a classic exposition of realism, see Hans Morgenthau, *Politics among Nations*, 6th ed. (New York: McGraw-Hill, 1985).

7. Tai Yong Tan and Gyanesh Kudasiya, *The Aftermath of Partition in South Asia* (New York: Routledge, 2004); see also John Keay, *Midnight's Descendants: A History of South Asia since Partition* (New York: Basic Books, 2014).

8. On Cambodia, see Elizabeth Becker, *When the War Was Over: Cambodia and the Khmer Rouge Revolution*, rev. ed. (New York: Public Affairs, 1998). For the Korean War, see Max Hastings, *The Korean War* (New York: Simon and Schuster, 1988).

9. Robert Kaplan, *Asia's Cauldron: The South China Sea and the End of a Stable Pacific* (New York: Random House, 2014), ch. 6, for a discussion of the Philippines.

10. The immediate postwar history is recounted in Ronald Spector, *In the Ruins of Empire: The Japanese Surrender and the Battle for Postwar Asia* (New York: Random House, 2008).

11. Ippei Yamazawa, *Economic Integration in the Asia Pacific Region* (New York: Routledge, 2000); Ki-Wai Li, *Capitalist Development and Economism in East Asia: The Rise of Hong Kong, Singapore, Taiwan and South Korea* (New York: Routledge, 2002).

12. An older but still useful edited volume is Eun Mee Kim, ed., *The Four Asian Tigers: Economic Development and the Global Political Economy* (Bingley, UK: Emerald Group Publishing Limited, 1999).

13. I am influenced by the idea of the "security dilemma," first proposed in John H. Herz, *Political Realism and Political Idealism* (Chicago: University of Chicago Press, 1951).

14. The classic study is Barbara Tuchman, *The Guns of August* (New York: Macmillan, 1962); see also Paul W. Schroeder, "World War I as Galloping Gertie: A Reply to Joachim Remak," *Journal of Modern History* 44, no. 3 (September 1972): 319–45.

15. Shreeya Sinha and Susan Beachy, "Timeline on North Korea's Nuclear Program," *New York Times*, November 20, 2014, http://www.nytimes.com/interactive/2014/11/20/world/asia/northkorea-timeline.html?_r=0#/#time238_10529.

16. Julian Ryall, "Japan Agrees to Buy Disputed Senkaku Islands," *The Telegraph*, September 5, 2012, http://www.telegraph.co.uk/news/worldnews/asia/japan/9521793/Japan-agrees-to-buy-disputed-Senkaku-islands.html.

17. Wendell Minnick, "Is China Laying Down Stakes at Disputed Scarborough Shoal?" *DefenseNews*, September 6, 2013, http://archive.defensenews.com/article/20130906/DEFREG03/309060013/Is-China-Laying-Down-Stakes-Disputed-Scarborough-Shoal-.

18. Michael D. Mosettig, "Asia Now Spends More for Defense than Europe," *The European Institute*, April 15, 2014, http://www.europeaninstitute.org/index.php/component/content/article?id=1713:asia-now-spends-more-for-defense-than-europe-415.

19. Instead, experts contend that the Democratic People's Republic of Korea's January 2016 nuclear test was a fission weapon.

20. Among others, see Melanie Kirkpatrick, *Escape from North Korea: The Untold Story of Asia's Underground Railroad* (New York: Encounter Books, 2012).

21. Bruce Bechtol, *The Last Days of Kim Jong-Il* (Lincoln, NE: Potomac Books, 2013).

22. See, for example, "Don't Scare North Korea off a Pyongyang Spring," *The Independent*, January 2, 2013, http://www.independent.co.uk/voices/editorials/editorial-dont-scare-north-korea-off-a-pyongyang-spring-8435923.html.

23. Chico Harlan, "North Korea Announces Execution of Kim Jong Un's Uncle," *Washington Post*, December 12, 2013, http://www.washingtonpost.com/world/asia_pacific/north-korea-announces-execution-of-kim-jong-uns-uncle-jang-song-thaek/2013/12/12/060b18ac-637d-11e3-91b3-f2bb96304e34_story.html.

24. International Institute for Strategic Studies, *The Military Balance: 2015* (London: Routledge, 2015), 261; Blaine Harden, "North Korea Massively Increases Its Special Forces," *Washington Post*, October 9, 2009, http://www.washingtonpost.com/wp-dyn/content/article/2009/10/08/AR2009100804018.html.

25. Office of the Secretary of Defense, "*Military and Security Developments Involving the Democratic People's Republic of Korea*," U.S. Department of Defense, February 2013, http://www.defense.gov/Portals/1/Documents/pubs/North_Korea _Military_Power_Report_2013-2014.pdf.

26. John S. Park, "The Leap in North Korea's Ballistic Missile Program," *NBR Analysis Brief*, December 19, 2012, http://www.nbr.org/publications/analysis/pdf /Brief/121812_Park_NKoreaMissile.pdf.

27. Anthony Capaccio, "North Korea Can Miniaturize a Nuclear Weapon, U.S. Says," *Bloomberg*, April 7, 2015, http://www.bloomberg.com/news/articles/2015 -04-07/n-korea-can-mount-miniature-nuclear-weapon-u-s-admiral-says.

28. A profile of North Korea's weapons proliferation by the Arms Control Association can be found at: "Arms Control and Proliferation Profile: North Korea," Arms Control Association, https://www.armscontrol.org/factsheets/northkoreaprofile, accessed October 5, 2015. See also Paul K. Kerr, Steven A. Hildreth and Mary Beth D. Nikitin, "Iran-North Korea-Syria Ballistic Missile and Nuclear Cooperation," Congressional Research Service, May 11, 2015, http://www.fas.org/sgp /crs/nuke/R43480.pdf.

29. Michael Auslin, "The Return of North Korea," *Commentary Magazine*, February 2015, https://www.commentarymagazine.com/article/the-return-of-north-korea/.

30. Andrew Scobell and Mark Cozad, "China's North Korea Policy: Rethink or Recharge?" in *Parameters* (Spring 2014), http://www.strategicstudiesinstitute.army .mil/pubs/Parameters/issues/Spring_2014/5_ScobellCozad.pdf.

31. Michael Rubin, *Dancing with the Devil: The Perils of Engaging Rogue Regimes* (New York: Encounter Books, 2014), 126.

32. Denny Roy, *Taiwan: A Political History* (Ithaca, NY: Cornell University Press, 2002). For a political history of the island's first decades, see Jay Taylor, *The Generalissimo: Chiang Kai-shek and the Struggle for Modern China* (Cambridge, MA: Harvard University Press, 2011).

33. For one recounting, see Gordon H. Chang, "To the Nuclear Brink: Eisenhower, Dulles, and the Quemoy-Matsu Crisis," *International Security* 12, no. 4 (Spring 1988), 96–123.

34. James Mann, *About Face: A History of America's Curious Relationship with China, from Nixon to Clinton* (New York: Vintage Books, 1998), chs. 1–4.

35. *Report to Congress of the U.S.-China Economic and Security Review Commission* (Washington, DC: Government Printing Office, 2010), 149.

36. Jim Mann, "U.S. Carrier Group Sails near China as Tensions over Taiwan Mount," *Los Angeles Times*, January 27, 1996, http://articles.latimes.com/1996-01 -27/news/mn-29246_1_taiwan-strait.

37. "China Sends Warning to Taiwan with Anti-Secession Law," *Washington Post*, March 8, 2005, http://www.washingtonpost.com/wp-dyn/articles/A15294-2005 Mar7.html.

38. See, for example, Brett V. Benson and Emerson M. S. Niou, "Comprehending Strategic Ambiguity: US Security Commitment to Taiwan," unpublished paper, Duke

University, November 2001, http://people.duke.edu/~niou/teaching/strategic%20 ambiguity.pdf.

39. Charles Hutzler and Jake Maxwell Watts, "China's Xi Jinping and Taiwan's Ma Ying-jeou Meet in Singapore," *Wall Street Journal*, November 8, 2015, http:// www.wsj.com/articles/china-s-xi-jinping-and-taiwan-s-ma-ying-jeou-meet-in -singapore-1446880724.

40. Abraham M. Denmark and Richard Fontaine, "Taiwan's Gamble: The Cross-Strait Rapprochement and Its Implications for U.S. Policy," Center for a New American Security, December 2009, http://www.cnas.org/files/documents/publications /Taiwan_Denmark_Dec2009_code502_policybrief_1.pdf.

41. Ninety-Sixth United States Congress, "Taiwan Relations Act, Public Law 96–8," U.S. Government Publishing Office, April 10, 1979, http://www.gpo.gov/fdsys /pkg/STATUTE-93/pdf/STATUTE-93-Pg14.pdf.

42. Mann, *About Face*, chs. 6–7.

43. Saurabh Shukla, "Beijing Games," *India Today*, June 13, 2008, http://indiatoday .intoday.in/story/Beijing%20games/0/9754.html.

44. Tom Mitchell and James Crabtree, "China Criticizes Narendra Modi Visit to Disputed Arunachal Pradesh," *Financial Times*, February 22, 2015, http://www.ft .com/intl/cms/s/0/cf82ad8e-ba5d-11e4-945d-00144feab7de.html#axzz3ee U6uDtJ.

45. "Unsettled for a Long Time Yet," *The Economist*, October 20, 2012, http:// www.economist.com/news/asia/21564861-fifty-years-after-nasty-high-altitude -war-border-dispute-remains-unresolved.

46. Mohan Malik, *China and India: Great Power Rivals* (Boulder, CO: Lynne Rienner, 2011).

47. Andrew Small, *The China-Pakistan Axis: Asia's New Geopolitics* (Oxford: Oxford University Press, 2015).

48. "Cambodia PM Calls Border Clashes with Thailand 'Real War,'" *Xinhuanet*, February 9, 2011, http://news.xinhuanet.com/english2010/world/2011-02/09/c _13724507.htm.

49. "UN Court Rules for Cambodia in Preah Vihear Temple Dispute with Thailand," *UN News Centre*, November 11, 2013, http://www.un.org/apps/news/story .asp?NewsID=46461#.VZQKnmTBzGc. See also Greg Raymond, "Thai-Cambodia Relations One Year after the ICJ Judgment," *East Asia Forum*, November 11, 2014, http://www.eastasiaforum.org/2014/11/11/thai-cambodia-relations-one-year -after-the-icj-judgement/.

50. Anggatira Golmer, "Indonesia's Role in the Thai-Cambodia Border Dispute Still Unclear," *DW*, March 25, 2011, http://www.dw.com/en/indonesias-role-in-the -thai-cambodia-border-dispute-still-unclear/a-6483440.

51. Michael Auslin, "Russia Fears China, Not Japan," *Wall Street Journal*, March 4, 2011, http://www.wsj.com/articles/SB100014240527487035596045761756609 16870214.

52. Kareem Fahim, "On City's Plastic Bags, an Old and Distant Dispute," *New York Times*, March 20, 2009, http://www.nytimes.com/2009/03/21/nyregion/21islands.html?_r=0.

53. Barbara Demick, "A Cluster of Rocks Erupts into a Mountain of Emotion in S. Korea," *Los Angeles Times*, March 17, 2005, http://articles.latimes.com/2005/mar/17/world/fg-islets17.

54. See Caitlin Campbell, "China's 'Core Interests' and the East China Sea," U.S.-China Economic and Security Review Commission Staff Research Backgrounder, May 10, 2013, http://www.uscc.gov/sites/default/files/Research/China's%20Core%20Interests%20and%20the%20East%20China%20Sea.pdf.

55. Martin Fackler and Ian Johnson, "Arrest in Disputed Seas Riles China and Japan," *New York Times*, September 19, 2010, http://www.nytimes.com/2010/09/20/world/asia/20chinajapan.html?_r=0.

56. Jane Perlez, "China Accuses Japan of Stealing after Purchase of Group of Disputed Islands," *New York Times*, September 11, 2012, http://www.nytimes.com/2012/09/12/world/asia/china-accuses-japan-of-stealing-disputed-islands.html.

57. See Obama-Abe press conference transcript, https://www.whitehouse.gov/the-press-office/2014/04/24/joint-press-conference-president-obama-and-prime-minister-abe-japan.

58. Simon Denyer, "China Withdraws Oil Rig from Waters Disputed with Vietnam, but Warns It Could Return," *Washington Post*, July 16, 2014, http://www.washingtonpost.com/world/china-withdraws-oil-rig-from-waters-disputed-with-vietnam-but-warns-it-could-return/2014/07/16/51f584a0-6128-4cd4-bad0-cb547907be30_story.html.

59. Mohan Malik, "Historical Fiction: China's South China Sea Claims," *World Affairs Journal* (May–June 2013), http://www.worldaffairsjournal.org/article/historical-fiction-china%E2%80%99s-south-china-sea-claims.

60. David Alexander, "China Land Reclamation in South China Sea Creates 'New Facts': US," *Reuters*, May 29, 2015, http://www.reuters.com/article/2015/05/29/us-asia-usa-carter-idUSKBN0OD1FF20150529.

61. Julian Ryall, "US-China War 'Inevitable' Unless Washington Drops Demands over South China Sea," *The Telegraph*, May 26, 2015, http://www.telegraph.co.uk/news/worldnews/asia/china/11630185/US-China-war-inevitable-unless-Washington-drops-demands-over-South-China-Sea.html.

62. Marcus Hand, "Malacca Straits Transits Hit All Time High in 2013, Pass 2008 Peak," Seatrade Maritime News, February 10, 2014, http://www.seatrade-maritime.com/news/asia/malacca-straits-transits-hit-all-time-high-in-2013-pass-2008-peak.html.

63. Donald B. Freeman, *The Straits of Malacca: Gateway or Gauntlet?* (Montreal: McGill Queens University Press, 2003).

64. Johnny Langenheim, "Preventing Ecocide in South China Sea," *The Guardian*, July 15, 2015, http://www.theguardian.com/environment/the-coral-triangle/2015/jul/15/preventing-ecocide-in-south-china-sea.

65. Sui Lee Wee, "China Defends Vessels' Actions against Philippines in South China Sea," *Reuters*, April 22, 2015, http://www.reuters.com/article/2015/04/22/us-southchinasea-china-philippines-idUSKBN0ND0XA20150422.

66. Tama Salim, "RI Flexes Muscle, Sinks Chinese Boat, a Big One," *Jakarta Post*, May 20, 2015, http://www.thejakartapost.com/news/2015/05/20/ri-flexes-muscle-sinks-chinese-boat-a-big-one.html.

67. James Kraska, *Maritime Power and the Law of the Sea: Expeditionary Operations in World Politics* (Oxford: Oxford University Press, 2011).

68. An accessible account is in Louise Levathes, *When China Ruled the Seas: The Treasure Fleet of the Dragon Throne, 1405–1433* (New York and Oxford: Oxford University Press, 1994).

69. Min Gyo Koo, *Island Disputes and Maritime Regime Building in East Asia* (New York: Springer, 2009), 153.

70. See Daniel J. Dzurek, "China Occupies Mischief Reef in Latest Spratly Gambit," *IBRU Boundary and Security Bulletin* (April 1995), 65–71.

71. A copy of the U.S. House of Representatives' Cox Report on China's theft of missile and nuclear technology is at http://www.house.gov/coxreport/cont/gncont.html; for a critique of the Cox Report, see M. M. May, ed., "The Cox Report: An Assessment," http://fsi.stanford.edu/sites/default/files/cox.pdf.

72. For a recent view on China's long-term strategy, see Michael Pillsbury, *The Hundred-Year Marathon: China's Secret Strategy to Replace America as the Global Superpower* (New York: Henry Holt, 2015). An older treatment is Alastair Iain Johnston, *Culture Realism: Strategic Culture and Grand Strategy in Chinese History* (Princeton, NJ: Princeton University Press, 1998).

73. Edward Wong and Chris Buckley, "China's Military Budget Increases 10% for 2015, Official Says," *New York Times*, March 4, 2015, http://www.nytimes.com/2015/03/05/world/asia/chinas-military-budget-increasing-10-for-2015-official-says.html.

74. See, for example, Liu Mingfu, *The China Dream: Great Power Thinking and Strategic Posture in the Post-American Era* (New York: CN Times Books, 2015).

75. There is not yet a comprehensive recounting of China's post-1992 challenges to regional order, but see Pillsbury, *Hundred-Year Marathon* or Geoff Dyer, *The Contest of the Century: The New Era of Competition with China—How America Can Win* (New York: Knopf, 2014).

76. "China Sub Stalked U.S. Fleet," *Washington Times*, November 13, 2006, http://www.washingtontimes.com/news/2006/nov/13/20061113-121539-3317r/?page=all.

77. Marc Kaufman and Dafna Linzer, "China Criticized for Anti-Satellite Missile Test," *Washington Post*, January 19, 2007, http://www.washingtonpost.com/wp-dyn/content/article/2007/01/18/AR2007011801029.html.

78. Nick Macfie, "Japan Jets Scramble at Cold War Levels as Chinese and Russian Incursions Increase," *Reuters*, April 15, 2015, http://www.reuters.com/article/2015/04/15/japan-airforce-scramble-idUSL4N0XC2ZC20150415.

79. "China's Defense Budget," *Global Security*, March 2015, http://www.globalsecurity.org/military/world/china/budget.htm.

80. Richard D. Fisher, *China's Military Modernization: Building for Regional and Global Reach* (Westport, CT: Greenwood, 2008), 16.

81. Bernard D. Cole, *The Great Wall at Sea: China's Navy Enters the 21st Century* (Annapolis, MD: Naval Institute Press, 2001).

82. Ronald O'Rourke, "China Naval Modernization: Implications for U.S. Navy Capabilities—Background and Issues for Congress," *Congressional Research Service*, December 23, 2014, http://www.fas.org/sgp/crs/row/RL33153.pdf, 49.

83. Robert Haddick, "China's Most Dangerous Missile (So Far)," *War on the Rocks*, July 2, 2014, http://warontherocks.com/2014/07/chinas-most-dangerous-missile-so-far/.

84. For a general discussion, see Toshi Yoshihara and James R. Holmes, *Red Star over the Pacific: China's Rise and the Challenge to U.S. Maritime Strategy* (Annapolis, MD: Naval Institute Press, 2013). See also Robert Haddick, *Fire on the Water: China, America, and the Future of the Pacific* (Annapolis, MD: Naval Institute Press, 2014).

85. Peter A. Dutton and Ryan D Martinson, eds., *Beyond the Wall: Chinese Far Seas Operations*, China Maritime Studies 13 (Newport, RI: U.S. Naval War College, 2015).

86. See "China's Military Strategy," May 2015, http://eng.mod.gov.cn/Database/WhitePapers/.

87. International Institute for Strategic Studies, *The Military Balance: 2010* (London: Routledge, 2010) 403–4. See also Phillip C. Saunders and Joshua K. Wiseman, "Buy, Build, Steal: China's Quest for Advanced Military Aviation Technologies," Institute for National Strategic Studies, December 2011, http://ndupress.ndu.edu/Media/News/NewsArticleView/tabid/7849/Article/717785/buy-build-or-steal-chinas-quest-for-advanced-military-aviation-technologies.aspx.

88. Kenneth Allen, "The Ten Pillars of the People's Liberation Army Air Force: An Assessment," Jamestown Foundation, April 2011, http://www.jamestown.org/programs/recentreports/single/?tx_ttnews%5Btt_news%5D=37846&tx_ttnews%5BbackPid%5D=7&cHash=94d0d69fec9f98fd6449c7a5b6acd19a#.Vx-_IXErJpg.

89. A full discussion of the drone revolution is in Peter W. Singer, *Wired for War: The Robotics Revolution and Conflict in the 21st Century* (New York: Penguin Books, 2009); Peter Singer, "Inside China's Secret Arsenal," *Popular Science*, December 20, 2012, http://www.popsci.com/technology/article/2012-12/inside-chinas-secret-arsenal.

90. See, for example, US-Taiwan Business Council, "The Balance of Air Power in the Taiwan Strait," ed. Lotta Danielsson-Murphy, May 2010, http://www.us-taiwan.org/reports/2010_may11_balance_of_air_power_taiwan_strait.pdf; and David A. Shlapak, "Questions of Balance: The Shifting Cross-Strait Balance and Implications for the U.S.," *RAND Corporation*, March 2010, http://www.rand.org/content/dam/rand/pubs/testimonies/2010/RAND_CT343.pdf.

91. Anthony Capaccio, "China Has World's Most Active Missile Programs, U.S. Says," *Bloomberg*, July 11, 2013, http://www.bloomberg.com/news/2013-07-10 /china-has-world-s-most-active-missile-programs-u-s-says.html. See also Andrew S. Erickson, "Showtime: China Reveals Two 'Carrier-Killer' Missiles," *The National Interest*, September 3, 2015, http://nationalinterest.org/feature/showtime-china -reveals-two-carrier-killer-missiles-13769.

92. Joseph Kahn, "Chinese General Threatens Use of A-Bombs If U.S. Intrudes," *New York Times*, July 15, 2005, http://www.nytimes.com/2005/07/15/international /asia/15china.html?_r=0.

93. James M. Acton, "Is China Changing Its Position on Nuclear Weapons?" *New York Times*, April 18, 2013, http://www.nytimes.com/2013/04/19/opinion /is-china-changing-its-position-on-nuclear-weapons.html?_r=0.

94. AFP, "U.S. Admiral Calls for Hotline with China to Prevent Conflict in Disputed Waters," *ABC News* (Australia), January 23, 2014, http://www.abc.net .au/news/2014-01-24/an-us-admiral-calls-for-china-hotline/5216712.

95. David Finkelstein, "China's National Military Strategy: An Overview of the 'Military Strategic Guidelines,'" in *Right-Sizing the People's Liberation Army: Exploring the Contours of China's Military,* ed. Roy Kamphausen and Andrew Scobell (Carlisle, PA: Strategic Studies Institute, 2006), 69–140, http://www.strategicstudie sinstitute.army.mil/pdffiles/PUB784.pdf.

96. Bryan Krekel, "Capability of the People's Republic of China to Conduct Cyber Warfare and Computer Network Exploitation," US-China Economic and Security Review Commission, October 9, 2009, http://www2.gwu.edu/~nsarchiv /NSAEBB/NSAEBB424/docs/Cyber-030.pdf.

97. A fictional treatment of a U.S.-China cyber clash can be found in Singer and Cole, *Ghost Fleet.*

98. On Georgia, see David Hollis, "Cyberwar Case Study: Georgia 2008," *Small Wars Journal*, January 6, 2011, http://smallwarsjournal.com/blog/journal/docs -temp/639-hollis.pdf.

99. Mandiant, "APT1: Exposing One of China's Cyber Espionage Units," January 2013, http://intelreport.mandiant.com/.

100. David Perera, "Jason Chaffetz: OPM Data Breaches May Affect 32 Million," *Politico*, June 24, 2015, http://www.politico.com/story/2015/06/opm-data-breach -jason-chaffetz-119374.html.

101. Jonah Goldberg, "Why Are We Ignoring a Cyber Pearl Harbor?" *Los Angeles Times*, June 16, 2015, http://www.latimes.com/opinion/op-ed/la-oe-0616-goldberg -china-cyber-hack-20150616-column.html.

102. David Alexander, "Theft of F-35 Design Data Is Helping U.S. Adversaries–Pentagon," *Reuters*, June 19, 2013, http://www.reuters.com/article/2013/06/19 /usa-fighter-hacking-idUSL2N0EV0T320130619.

103. Ellen Nakashima, "Confidential Report Lists U.S. Weapons System Designs Compromised by Chinese Cyberspies," *Washington Post*, May 27, 2013, https://www .washingtonpost.com/world/national-security/confidential-report-lists-us-weapons

-system-designs compromised-by-chinese-cyberspies/2013/05/27/a42c3e1c-c2dd-11e2-8c3b-0b5e9247e8ca_story.html.

104. See Haddick, *Fire on the Water* for a discussion.

105. Wendell Minnick, "Asia's Naval Procurement Sees Major Growth," *Defense News*, May 19, 2013, http://www.defensenews.com/article/20130519/DEFREG03/305190004/Asia-s-Naval-Procurement-Sees-Major-Growth.

106. "Abe Seeking Record Y4.98 Trillion in Defense Spending to Counter China," *Japan Times*, January 14, 2015, http://www.japantimes.co.jp/news/2015/01/14/national/japan-passes-record-defense-budget-in-bid-to-defend-senkakus-counter-china/#.VZVTPmTBzGd.

107. A comprehensive look at Japan's military capabilities is in its White Paper, "Defense of Japan 2014," Ministry of Defense of Japan, http://www.mod.go.jp/e/publ/w_paper/2014.html.

108. "Japan Scrambles Warplanes at Cold War Levels," *Sky News*, April 15, 2015, http://news.sky.com/story/1465557/japan-scrambles-warplanes-at-cold-war-levels.

109. See Abhijit Singh, "China: Getting Ready to Dominate the Indian Ocean?" *The National Interest*, January 27, 2015, http://nationalinterest.org/blog/the-buzz/china-getting-ready-dominate-the-indian-ocean-12130; and Go Yamada, "As China Rises, India Asserts Itself," *Nikkei Asian Review*, April 2, 2015, http://asia.nikkei.com/Politics-Economy/International-Relations/As-China-rises-India-asserts-itself.

110. Rajat Pandit, "India to Slowly but Steadily Boost Military Presence in Andaman and Nicobar Islands," *Times of India*, May 7, 2015, http://timesofindia.indiatimes.com/india/India-to-slowly-but-steadily-boost-military-presence-in-Andaman-and-Nicobar-Islands/articleshow/47182151.cms.

111. Sureesh Mehta, "Indian Navy to Grow to 160-Plus by 2022," *ThaIndian News*, http://www.thaindian.com/newsportal/business/indian-navy-fleet-to-grow-to-160-plus-by-2022_10081924.html.

112. "India to Invest USD 46.96 Billion on 101 Naval Ships," *India Post*, May 16, 2011, http://www.indiapost.com/india-to-invest-usd-46-96-billion-on-101-naval-ships/.

113. Jeremy Bender, "India Is Co-Developing a Fifth-Generation Fighter Plane alongside Russia," *Business Insider*, June 24, 2014, http://www.businessinsider.com/india-is-bankrolling-russias-t-50-2014-6.

114. The term is most often applied to Taiwan. See William S. Murray, "Revisiting Taiwan's Defense Strategy," *Naval War College Review* 61, no. 3 (Summer 2008): 13–38.

115. Andrew Jacobs, "China, Updating Military Strategy, Puts Focus on Projecting Naval Power," *New York Times*, May 26, 2015, http://www.nytimes.com/2015/05/27/world/asia/china-updating-military-strategy-puts-focus-on-projecting-naval-power.html.

7. Managing Risk in Asia

1. See, for example, William H. Overholt, *Asia, America, and the Transformation of Geopolitics* (Cambridge: Cambridge University Press, 2008), ch. 9.

2. "Public's Policy Priorities Reflect Changing Conditions at Home and Abroad," Pew Research Center, January 15, 2015, http://www.people-press.org/2015/01/15/publics-policy-priorities-reflect-changing-conditions-at-home-and-abroad/.

3. Eleven countries were polled, but I have not included Pakistan here because I do not consider it part of the Indo-Pacific. The report can be found at "Global Opposition to U.S. Surveillance and Drones, but Limited Harm to America's Image," Pew Research Center, July 14, 2014, http://www.pewglobal.org/2014/07/14/global-opposition-to-u-s-surveillance-and-drones-but-limited-harm-to-americas-image/.

4. Julian Ryall, "U.S.-China War 'Inevitable' Unless Washington Drops Demands over South China Sea," *The Telegraph*, May 26, 2015, http://www.telegraph.co.uk/news/worldnews/asia/china/11630185/US-China-war-inevitable-unless-Washington-drops-demands-over-South-China-Sea.html.

5. Aaron Mehta, "U.S.: N. Korean Nuclear ICBM Achievable," *Defense News*, April 8, 2015, http://www.defensenews.com/story/defense/policy-budget/budget/2015/04/08/north-korea-icbm-nuclear-weapon/25422795/.

6. Victor D. Cha, "Powerplay: Origins of the U.S. Alliance System in Asia," *International Security*, vol. 34, no. 3 (Winter 2009–2010), 161.

7. "Area of Responsibility," USPACOM, http://www.pacom.mil/AboutUSPACOM/USPACOMAreaofResponsibility.aspx, accessed November 12, 2015.

8. "About USPACOM," USPACOM, http://www.pacom.mil/AboutUSPACOM.aspx, accessed November 12, 2015.

9. "PACAF Factsheets," USPACOM, http://www.pacaf.af.mil/Info/FactSheets.aspx, accessed November 12, 2015.

10. David Berteau and Michael Green, "U.S. Force Posture Strategy in the Asia Pacific Region: An Independent Assessment," Center for Strategic and International Studies, August 2012, http://csis.org/files/publication/120814_FINAL_PACOM_optimized.pdf.

11. Barack Obama, "Remarks By President Obama to the Australian Parliament," White House, November 17, 2011, https://www.whitehouse.gov/the-press-office/2011/11/17/remarks-president-obama-australian-parliament.

12. Mark E. Manyin, "Pivot to the Pacific? The Obama Administration's 'Rebalancing' toward Asia," Congressional Research Service, March 28, 2012, archived at https://www.fas.org/sgp/crs/natsec/R42448.pdf.

13. A variety of news stories on U.S. budget restrictions and their impact on defense can be found here: "Sequestration," U.S. Department of Defense, http://www.defense.gov/home/features/2013/0213_sequestration/, accessed April 26, 2016.

14. A fuller discussion is in Michael Auslin, *Security in the Indo-Pacific Commons: Toward a Regional Strategy*, AEI, 2010, http://www.aei.org/publication/security-in-the-indo-pacific-commons/. For a discussion of the next-generation bomber, see

Jeremiah Gertler, "U.S. Air Force Bomber Sustainment and Modernization: Background and Issues for Congress," Congressional Research Service, June 4, 2014, archived at http://www.fas.org/sgp/crs/weapons/R43049.pdf.

15. For cyber, see Martin C. Libicki, *Brandishing Cyberattack Capabilities*, RAND, 2013, http://www.rand.org/pubs/research_reports/RR175.html.

16. Jessica Mendoza, "Cyclone Pam: Why Japan Is a Leader in Disaster Relief," *Christian Science Monitor*, March 14, 2015, http://www.csmonitor.com/World/Global-News/2015/0314/Cyclone-Pam-Why-Japan-is-a-leader-in-disaster-relief-video.

17. Akhilesh Pillalamarri, "India, Japan, and the US Hold Joint Naval Exercises," *The Diplomat*, July 25, 2014, http://thediplomat.com/2014/07/india-japan-and-the-us-hold-joint-naval-exercises/.

18. Prashanth Parameswaran, "US Launches New Maritime Security Initiative at Shangri-La Dialogue 2015," *The Diplomat*, June 2, 2015, http://thediplomat.com/2015/06/us-launches-new-maritime-security-initiative-at-shangri-la-dialogue-2015/.

19. Yuka Hayashi and Chieko Tsuneoka, "Japan Open to Joining U.S. in South China Sea Patrols," *Wall Street Journal*, June 25, 2015, http://www.wsj.com/articles/japan-may-join-u-s-in-south-china-sea-patrols-1435149493. See also "U.S. Says Open to Patrols with Philippines in Waters Disputed with China," *Reuters*, February 3, 2016, http://www.reuters.com/article/us-southchinasea-philippines-usa-idUSKCN0VC0MU.

20. See an analysis of recent trends in "Annual Report to Congress: Military and Security Developments Involving the People's Republic of China 2015," Department of Defense, April 7, 2015, http://www.defense.gov/pubs/2015_China_Military_Power_Report.pdf.

21. "Ten Years On: How Asia Shrugged Off Its Economic Crisis," *The Economist*, July 4, 2007, http://www.economist.com/node/9432495.

22. Derek Scissors, "China's Real GDP Is Slower than Official Figures Show," *Financial Times*, January 20, 2015, http://blogs.ft.com/beyond-brics/2015/01/20/guest-post-chinas-real-gdp-is-slower-than-official-figures-show/.

23. Extrapolating from the following report: Laura M. Baughman and Joseph F. Francois, "Trade and American Jobs: The Impact of Trade on U.S. and State Level Employment: An Update," Trade Partnership Worldwide, July 2010, http://www.tradepartnership.com/pdf_files/Trade_and_American_Jobs7.2010.pdf.

24. "U.S. Census Bureau News," U.S. Department of Commerce, May 6, 2014, https://www.census.gov/foreign-trade/Press-Release/2013pr/aip/related_party/rp13.pdf.

25. "Outlook for U.S. Agricultural Trade," U.S. Department of Agriculture, http://usda.mannlib.cornell.edu/usda/ers/AES/2010s/2011/AES-05-26-2011.pdf.

26. "US-Asia Imports and Exports," Asia Matters for America, http://www.asiamattersforamerica.org/asia/data/trade/importexport, accessed November 1, 2015.

27. Not surprisingly, the number of positive responses drops the lower the income level polled. Those making $30,000 or less supported free trade by only 38 percent. The poll can be found at "Free Trade Agreements Seen as Good for U.S., but Concerns Persist," Pew Research Center, May 27, 2015, http://www.people-press.org /2015/05/27/free-trade-agreements-seen-as-good-for-u-s-but-concerns-persist/.

28. "JAMA in America: More American than Ever," Japan Automobile Manufacturers Association (JAMA), January 6, 2015, http://www.jama.org/publications /2014-jama-contributions-report/.

29. "Foreign Direct Investment in the United States, 2014 Report," Organization for Foreign Direct Investment, http://www.ofii.org/sites/default/files/FDIUS2014 .pdf, p. 4.

30. David Faber, "Game-Changer in US Wireless: Softbank Buys 70% of Sprint," *Business Insider*, October 14, 2012, http://www.businessinsider.com/softbank-buys -sprint-2012-10-b.

31. "China Overtakes US for Foreign Direct Investment," *BBC News*, January 30, 2015, http://www.bbc.com/news/business-31052566.

32. Steven Weisman, "Sale of 3Com to Huawei Is Derailed by U.S. Security Concerns," *New York Times*, February 21, 2008, http://www.nytimes.com/2008/02/21 /business/worldbusiness/21iht-3com.1.10258216.html?pagewanted=all&_r=0.

33. Howard Schneider and Brady Dennis, "Smithfield Foods to Be Bought by Chinese Firm Shuanghui International," *Washington Post*, May 29, 2013, http://www .washingtonpost.com/business/economy/smithfield-foods-to-be-taken-over-by -chinese-firm/2013/05/29/a520434a-c873-11e2-9245-773c0123c027_story .html.

34. "Trade Goods with Asia," U.S. Census Bureau, http://www.census.gov /foreign-trade/balance/c0016.html, accessed November 2, 2015.

35. Ian Talley, "Did Japan Really Overtake China as the Biggest Foreign Holder of U.S. Treasury Debt? A Deeper Look at the Math," *Wall Street Journal*, April 15, 2015, http://blogs.wsj.com/economics/2015/04/15/did-japan-really-overtake -china-as-the-biggest-foreign-holder-of-u-s-treasury-debt-a-deeper-look-at-the -math/.

36. "Many iPhone 5 Components Change, but Most Suppliers Remain the Same, Teardown Reveals," *IHS Technology*, September 25, 2012, http://www.isuppli.com /Teardowns/News/pages/Many-iPhone-5-Components-Change-But-Most -Suppliers-Remain-the-Same-Teardown-Reveals.aspx.

37. Yuqing Xing and Neal Detert, "How iPhone Widens the US Trade Deficits with PRC," *GRIPS Discussion Paper, National Graduate Institute for Policy Studies* (2010), http://www3.grips.ac.jp/%7Epinc/data/10-21.pdf; totals of component parts and sales/profit have changed since 2010, but not dramatically.

38. Mark J. Perry, "Using Value-Added Trade Estimates, We Have a +$32.25B Trade SURPLUS with China for 2011," *CARPE DIEM Blog*, August 12, 2011, http://mjperry.blogspot.com/2011/08/using-value-added-estimates-we-have .html.

39. "iPadded," *The Economist*, January 21, 2012, http://www.economist.com/node/21543174.

40. Robert E. Scott, "The China Toll," *Economic Policy Institute*, August 23, 2012, http://www.epi.org/publication/bp345-china-growing-trade-deficit-cost/.

41. Justin R. Pierce and Peter K. Schott, "The Surprisingly Swift Decline of U.S. Manufacturing Employment," *Research Paper* (2012 Draft), http://faculty.som.yale.edu/peterschott/files/research/papers/manuf_229.pdf.

42. See David H. Autor et al., "The China Shock: Learning from Labor Market Adjustment to Large Changes in Trade," National Bureau of Economic Research, *NBER Working Paper* No. 21906 (January 2016), http://www.nber.org/papers/w21906.

43. Ibid.

44. Steve Minter, "U.S. Trade Opportunities Ramp Up in India, Asia," *Industry-Week*, November 12, 2012, http://www.industryweek.com/trade/us-trade-opportunities-ramp-india-asia?page=1.

45. Shannon Tiezzi, "Urbanization with Chinese Characteristics," *The Diplomat*, February 12, 2015, http://thediplomat.com/2015/02/urbanization-with-chinese-characteristics/.

46. Heath Terry et al., "eCommerce Expected to Accelerate Globally in 2014," Goldman Sachs Equity Research Report, March 5, 2014, http://boletines.prisadigital.com/Global_ecommerce.pdf.

47. Yougang Chen, Daniel Hui, and Jeongmin Seong, "Click by Click: How Consumers Are Changing China's e-Commerce Landscape," *McKinsey & Company*, July 2012, http://csi.mckinsey.com/Home/Knowledge_by_topic/Digital_consumer/How_consumers_are_changing_Chinas_ecommerce_landscape.aspx; "Whitepaper–Breaking into the e-Commerce Market in Asia: Opportunities and Challenges," NTT Communications, June 13, 2014, http://www.hk.ntt.com/en/resources/white-papers/slideshow-breaking-into-the-e-commerce-market-in-asia.html.

48. Véronique Salze-Lozac'h, Nina Merchant-Vega, Katherine Loh, and Sarah Alexander, "The Key to Asia's Future," *The Diplomat*, January 18, 2013, http://thediplomat.com/2013/01/integration-is-key-to-asias-future/.

49. *2016 Business Climate Survey*, American Chamber of Commerce in China, http://www.amchamchina.org/policy-advocacy/business-climate-survey/.

50. Jeffrey Rothfeder, "The Great Unraveling of Globalization," *Washington Post*, April 26, 2015, http://www.washingtonpost.com/business/reconsidering-the-value-of-globalization/2015/04/24/7b5425c2-e82e-11e4-aae1-d642717d8afa_story.html.

51. "Survey Report on Overseas Business Operations by Japanese Manufacturing Companies," JBIC, 2013, https://www.jbic.go.jp/wp-content/uploads/press_en/2013/11/15929/FY2013_Survey2.pdf, pp. 22, 25.

52. "WTO Talks End with Doha Round Still Deadlocked," *ABC News*, December 17, 2011, http://www.abc.net.au/news/2011-12-18/wto-talks-end-with-doha-round-still-deadlocked/3736840.

53. Reiji Yoshida, "Abe Declares Japan Will Join TPP Free-Trade Process," *Japan Times*, March 16, 2013, http://www.japantimes.co.jp/news/2013/03/16/business/abe-declares-japan-will-join-tpp-free-trade-process/#.VZL6EflVikp.

54. Joshua Meltzer, "The Significance of the Trans-Pacific Partnership for the United States," testimony before the House Small Business Committee, May 16, 2012, http://www.brookings.edu/research/testimony/2012/05/16-us-trade-strategy-meltzer#ftnte3; "Government: TPP Offers Lackluster Benefits in Near-Term," *The Asahi Shimbun*, March 16, 2015, http://ajw.asahi.com/article/economy/business/AJ201303160046.

55. Tuong Lai, "What Vietnam Must Now Do," *New York Times*, April 6, 2015, http://www.nytimes.com/2015/04/07/opinion/what-vietnam-must-now-do.html.

56. Murray Hiebert and Liam Hanlon, "ASEAN and Partners Launch Regional Comprehensive Economic Partnership," Center for Strategic and International Studies, December 7, 2012, http://csis.org/publication/asean-and-partners-launch-regional-comprehensive-economic-partnership.

57. "EU-Asia Security Factsheet," European External Action Service, http://eeas.europa.eu/asia/docs/eu_in_asia_factsheet_en.pdf, accessed July 10, 2015.

58. "European Union, Trade in goods with China," European Commission, http://trade.ec.europa.eu/doclib/docs/2006/september/tradoc_113366.pdf, accessed April 26, 2016; and "European Union, Trade in goods with Japan," European Commission, http://trade.ec.europa.eu/doclib/docs/2006/september/tradoc_113403.pdf, accessed April 26, 2016.

59. "Countries and Regions: South Korea," European Commission, http://ec.europa.eu/trade/policy/countries-and-regions/countries/south-korea/, accessed April 26, 2016.

60. "The EU-ASEAN Relationship in Twenty Facts and Figures," European Commission, 2013, http://eeas.europa.eu/asean/docs/key_facts_figures_eu_asean_en.pdf.

61. "China Overtakes US for Foreign Direct Investment," *BBC News*, January 30, 2015, http://www.bbc.com/news/business 31052566.

62. "Foreign Direct Investment in the United States, 2014 Report," Organization for International Investment Appendix A, http://www.ofii.org/sites/default/files/FDIUS2014.pdf.

63. "Increasing FDI in Japan," *Japan Times*, July 23, 2014, http://www.japantimes.co.jp/opinion/2014/07/23/editorials/increasing-fdi-japan/#.VTpc8DvF-UB.

64. "Fact Sheet on Foreign Investment," Department of Industrial Policy and Promotion, http://dipp.nic.in/English/Publications/FDI_Statistics/2014/india_FDI_December2014.pdf.

65. Miriam Jordan, "Skilled-Worker Visa Applications by U.S. Companies Reach High," *Wall Street Journal*, April 14, 2015, http://www.wsj.com/articles/skilled-worker-visa-applications-by-u-s-companies-reach-high-1429056123.

66. For a historical study, see Ardath W. Burks, ed., *The Modernizers, Overseas Students, Foreign Employees, and Meiji Japan* (Boulder, CO: Westview Press, 1985); see also Michael R. Auslin, *Pacific Cosmopolitans: A Cultural History of U.S.-Japan Relations* (Cambridge, MA: Harvard University Press, 2011), ch. 3.

67. Lisa Twaronite, "Japan Household Helper Plan Shows Wider Immigration Dilemma," *Chicago Tribune*, December 10, 2013, http://articles.chicagotribune.com /2013-12-10/news/sns-rt-us-japan-economy-immigration-20131210_1_broader -immigration-reform-prime-minister-shinzo-abe-more-foreign-workers.

68. See Robert Kagan, "Is Democracy in Decline? The Weight of Geopolitics," *Journal of Democracy*, January 2015, http://www.brookings.edu/research/articles /2015/01/democracy-in-decline-weight-of-geopolitics-kagan. See also Bret Stephens, *America in Retreat: The New Isolationism and the Coming Global Disorder* (New York: Sentinel Books, 2014).

69. "Trends in U.S. Study Abroad," NAFSA, https://www.nafsa.org/Explore _International_Education/Advocacy_And_Public_Policy/Study_Abroad /Trends_in_U_S__Study_Abroad/. See also "U.S. Study Abroad: Leading Destinations," Institute of International Education, http://www.iie.org/Research -and-Publications/Open-Doors/Data/US-Study-Abroad/Leading-Destinations /2009-11.

70. J. William Fulbright Foreign Scholarship Board, "Annual Report, 2011– 12," U.S. Department of State, http://eca.state.gov/files/bureau/2011-2012_ffsb _annual_report.pdf.

71. "Who's Afraid of the Activists?" *The Economist*, May 9, 2015, http://www .economist.com/news/asia/21650548-democratic-asian-governments-well -authoritarian-ones-crack-down-ngos-whos-afraid.

72. A slightly dated yet thorough study of Japan's NGOs is *Understanding Japanese NGOs from Facts and Practices* (Tokyo: Japan International Cooperation Agency, 2008), http://www.jica.go.jp/english/publications/jica_archive/brochures/2008 /pdf/ngo_dis.pdf.

73. "How Americans View China," Pew Research Center, September 18, 2012, http://www.pewglobal.org/2012/09/18/chapter-1-how-americans-view-china/.

74. Ben Blanchard, "China to 'Regulate' Foreign NGOs with New Law," Reuters, December 22, 2014, http://www.reuters.com/article/2014/12/22/us-china-politics -ngos-idUSKBN0K00NX20141222; William Wan, "China Raids NGO Offices in Latest Sign of Crackdown on Dissent," *Washington Post*, March 26, 2015, http:// www.washingtonpost.com/world/china-raids-ngo-offices-in-latest-sign-of -crackdown-on-dissent/2015/03/26/4badeaac-d3b0-11e4-ab77-9646eea6a4c7 _story.html.

75. See, for example, a report from a World Economic Forum private dinner, Henry Blodget, "Someone Just Said Something about the Japan-China Conflict That Scared the Crap out of Everyone," *Business Insider*, January 22, 2014, http:// www.businessinsider.com/china-japan-conflict-could-lead-to-war-2014-1; and the

comments of America's then-chairman of the Joint Chiefs of Staff in Camille Diola, "US General: Conventional Conflict Threat Highest in Asia Pacific," *Philippine Star*, July 4, 2014, http://www.philstar.com/headlines/2014/07/04/1342405/us -general-conventional-conflict-threat-highest-asia-pacific.

INDEX